DEMOCRACY AND TIME IN CUBAN THOUGHT

Democracy and Time in Cuban Thought

The Elusive Present

María de los Ángeles Torres

UNIVERSITY OF FLORIDA PRESS

Gainesville

Publication of this work made possible by a Sustaining the Humanities through the American Rescue Plan grant from the National Endowment for the Humanities.

Copyright 2024 by María de los Ángeles Torres
All rights reserved
Published in the United States of America

29 28 27 26 25 24   6 5 4 3 2 1

Library of Congress Cataloging-in-Publication Data
Names: Torres, María de los Ángeles, author.
Title: Democracy and time in Cuban thought : the elusive present / by María de los Ángeles Torres.
Description: 1. | Gainesville : University of Florida Press, 2024. | Includes bibliographical references and index.
Identifiers: LCCN 2023019311 (print) | LCCN 2023019312 (ebook) | ISBN 9781683404026 (hardback) | ISBN 9781683404262 (paperback) | ISBN 9781683404101 (pdf) | ISBN 9781683404217 (ebook)
Subjects: LCSH: Democracy—Cuba—History. | Political participation—Cuba. | Democratization—Cuba. | Time pressure. | Time—Sociological aspects. | Cuba—Politics and government. | BISAC: POLITICAL SCIENCE / World / Caribbean & Latin American | POLITICAL SCIENCE / History & Theory
Classification: LCC JL1016 .T67 2024 (print) | LCC JL1016 (ebook) | DDC 320.47291—dc23/eng/20230517
LC record available at https://lccn.loc.gov/2023019311
LC ebook record available at https://lccn.loc.gov/2023019312

University of Florida Press
2046 NE Waldo Road
Suite 2100
Gainesville, FL 32609
http://upress.ufl.edu

In memory of Cecilia Vaisman,
who left us the preciousness of the present.

Contents

List of Figures   ix

Preface   xi

Acknowledgments   xxiii

Introduction: Temporalities and Politics   1

1. The Past   23

2. The Future   52

3. The Present   78

4. Democratizing the Past   110

5. Temporalities and Democracy   133

Notes   157

Bibliography   177

Index   193

Figures

0.1 *La bandera es de todos*   xvii

1.1. "Nuestro Che," José A. Sarol, 1978 postcard   32

1.2. Fidel Castro, Moncada, 1953   41

2.1. *La Edad de Oro*, original magazine covers   61

2.2. May Day parade in Revolution Square   71

3.1. *La Espera*, from the series *Gerundios*, Rolando Estévez   93

3.2. Eliseo Diego   108

4.1. *Havana/Miami*, Nereida García-Ferraz   122

4.2. *Havana/Miami*, Nereida García-Ferraz   122

4.3. *Havana/Miami*, Nereida García-Ferraz   123

4.4. *Tracings* series, *Untitled, (Ferris Wheel)*, María Martínez-Cañas   126

4.5. From the series *Vestigios, Untitled012, Diptych*, 2007, María Martínez-Cañas   126

4.6. From the series *Vestigios, Untitled017*, 2015, María Martínez-Cañas   127

4.7. From the series *Rebus + Diversions, Untitled 010*, 2016, María Martínez-Cañas   129

5.1. Tania Bruguera, 100 horas de lectura de *Los orígenes del totalitarismo de Hannah Arendt*, 2015   141

5.2. *Infinite Ocean, Cárdenas*, 2021, Claudia Padrón   146

Preface

I was born in Cuba a few years before the triumph of the revolution led by Fidel Castro. I remember feeling as a child the permeating enthusiasm with the prospect of change. I also remember how disgust and fear seeped into our lives as the new regime turned its back on its basic promises and began using violence to establish itself. Thus began our journey to leave the island that held my family's past and future dreams.

Cuban history and politics were alive in my family. My great-grandfather Aurelio Vigil was born in Cuba in 1883, shortly after the arrival of his parents from Asturias, Spain. They had crossed the Atlantic, she pregnant with my great-grandfather, in search of a better life in Cuba, only to find the same oppressive Spanish Empire they were fleeing. As a teenager, Aurelio joined the independence movement and helped liberate Santa Clara, then just a village in the center of the island. A small plaque honoring Aurelio Vigil can still be found clinging to an ornate metal fence in the central square of the city. His son, José Manuel, my grandfather, who became a doctor, fought against the dictatorship of President Gerardo Machado in the 1930s.

Decades later, my parents, like so many other Cubans at the time, were ardent supporters of the 1959 Revolution and deeply believed in the need to restore the Constitution of 1940. My mother, María Isabel Vigil Delgado, had been born in Meneses, a small town in central Cuba, surrounded by the region's abundant tropical flora. Her mother's family, the Delgados, descendants of immigrants from the Canary Islands, had prospered and owned cattle ranches and sugar plantations. While it was not talked about, some of them had been slave-owners, their lives were intimately entangled with Black Cubans, as many fathered numerous children with Black women. Indeed, I found out late in life that my real great-great-grandmother was a woman of mixed race. My great-great-grandfather's wife could not bear children, so Micaela had his children for her. We don't know much about her. Was she the daughter of an enslaved woman? We do know that her children and grandchildren made annual pilgrimages to visit her. My mother's grandmother and mother instilled a sense of racial justice in María Isabel that was not just political but was also personal, as we were to learn many years later.

My mother was an avid photographer and loved to take photos of family and friends in the outdoors. She loved science and eventually graduated from the University of Havana with a doctorate in physical sciences. When she left Cuba, she filled her suitcase with photos.

My father, Alberto Torres Domínguez, was born and raised in Matanzas by his mother, who became a nurse after her husband died when my father was three years old. He received what was called a *beca de viudas*—a widow's scholarship—that paid for his education. He became an ophthalmologist, although his real passion was music. He had a wonderful tenor voice and filled our home with operas, *boleros,* and other popular Cuban songs. I was raised reciting poems by José Martí and singing *La Bayamesa,* the Cuban national anthem.

They were both on their ways to successful careers when the Revolution began. They became ardent supporters, which included hiding rebels in our home. My mother was moved by the Revolution's claims of legitimacy based on the rich intellectual heritage of the Cuban War of Independence, and they both dreamt of a Cuba with a clean, democratic government where all Cubans were included, a promise for the future that guided the revolutionary uprising.

But the fact that the democratic elections promised after the triumph of the Revolution never materialized, and particularly, the institution of summary trials and firing squads to eliminate opponents of the Castro regime, led my family, like many who had supported change, to look for a way out. A friend of my parents, working in the underground movement that soon developed to fight the new government, secured a U.S. visa waiver for me. Years later, I would come to understand that this had been part of what became known as Operation Pedro Pan. My family would join me in the United States months after my departure. From Miami, we were relocated to Cleveland, and we later made our way to Dallas, then Midland, Texas, where we would become painfully aware of U.S. racism and I would join a group supporting conscientious objectors to the Vietnam War.

For years, Cuba was our irretrievable past. Occasionally, letters and telegrams would disrupt this sense of time. Or sometimes it was the arrival of family members who, still smelling of the tropics and dark tobacco, began their exile journey in our new home. Yet contemporary Cuba seeped in slowly. I met Chicano activists who had traveled to Cuba. I listened to songs and records of the *Nueva Trova*. Little by little, Cuba solidified in my consciousness as I became more politically engaged. A few more years would pass until I met other Cubans who, like myself, longed to return home. I became part of the leadership of the Antonio Maceo Brigade, a group that organized trips to the island for young Cuban Americans. These were journeys to our memories and a future possibility of return. At the time, I was in graduate school, and Lourdes Casal, a Cuban exile academic and founder of the group behind *Areíto*, a magazine that brought together young Cuban exiles interested in engaging with their homeland, urged me to make Cuba a part of my academic research.

The Antonio Maceo Brigade also organized cultural exchanges with the island. By that time, I was living in Chicago, and our group hosted musicians, writers, and poets. On one trip, Sara González, one of the members of the Nueva Trova, was traveling with the poet Eliseo Diego. He stayed at my home, and we became lifelong friends. Later, in Havana, his family hosted us on those rare nights when we were given time to visit friends and relatives. I also became friends with his children Rapi, Lichy, and Fefé.

My assessment of the Cuban Revolution has evolved since then, and the evolution has influenced my own work on Cuba and Cuban exiles. As a young woman, I had yearned to return "home." Cuba had the allure of my childhood memories. When I returned in 1978, I was filled with hopeful expectations of finding alternative politics. In the early 1980s, there was a certain promise of change in the Cuban government toward a more democratic system, and small private businesses were authorized. So-called *mercados campesinos y artesanos*—farmers and artisans' markets—popped up throughout the island. Extended visits to Cuba—as well as deepening relationships there with Cubans of my generation who were becoming profoundly disillusioned—unraveled the tightly woven narrative of the Revolution as an instrument of progress toward social justice.

A definitive breaking point for me came in the summer of 1989, when I was in Havana during the trial of Arnaldo T. Ochoa, the general who had led the Cuban intervention in Angola. Accused of illegal dealings in drugs, diamonds, and elephant tusks, he and his assistant, along with several other high-level security officers, were tried on national television and sentenced to death by a firing squad. Many believed Ochoa could not have acted without Fidel Castro's knowledge, particularly since Castro had insisted on commanding every detail of Operación Carlota, the name given to Cuba's military operations in Angola in support of one of the many factions that emerged after its independence from Portugal. Angola had become Cuba's Vietnam. This resonated deeply in me, since the Vietnam War had been one of the catalysts that had led me back to my homeland.

Cuba at a Crossroads

Decades later, the Cuban government found itself bankrupt, desperately trying to bring in cash, and cutting costs even at the expense of its legacy. Exiles who had been maligned by the regime became a lifeline for Cubans on the island. In 2021, the dollars and goods exiles sent to relatives constituted a third of Cuba's Gross Domestic Product. Another third was acquired by selling professional services abroad, and to island tourists, including medical care. A stark economic divide could be seen across racial and ideological lines. Foreign investors in Cuba were being wooed while Cubans were prohibited from investing in their own businesses. But even foreign investors became vulnerable to the arbitrary use of power, and some who were owed money by the government were jailed and deported. Medical doctors were internationally bartered for oil. Sex work became common, particularly in government-run venues. Basic infrastructure—water, gas, electricity—began to fail. Many streets and roads in cities and towns became unpassable. Crime against both Cubans and tourists increased. And medical care—a jewel of the Revolution—began to falter. Even before the COVID-19 epidemic of 2020 forced a shutdown of the island, there had been deadly cholera outbreaks.

Aggravating the economic situation was a tremendous power struggle among the ruling elite—described by some before Castro's death in 2016 as infighting between his brother Raúl Castro's people, basically the military, and Fidel Castro's own—spread through various security departments and the Communist Party. There were bold takeovers of economic domains that throughout the decades had been carefully distributed among the elite. Hopes that economic changes would usher in political reforms were dashed. Rising expectations, coupled with the lack of political vehicles for dissent, sparked random outbursts of protests.

In 2014, I returned to Cuba at a moment where the present was, for an instant, once again filled with expectations of change for a better future. That moment had been fomented by the reestablishment of U.S.-Cuba diplomatic relations after more than fifty years of their absence. Incidentally, President Barack Obama structured his new policy in a framework of temporality—a turning point between the past and the future. He stated, "I believed that our nations had to break free from the old arguments, the old grievances that had too often trapped us in the past; that we had a shared responsibility to look to the future and to think and act in fresh ways."[1] His own visit to Cuba in 2016, the first of a sitting U.S. president since Calvin Coolidge's in 1928, rekindled hope of a better future as he dismissed the failed past and urged a better tomorrow for both countries. But hopes were dashed even before the visit took place, as hundreds of Cuban human rights activists were jailed days before Obama arrived in Havana. Nine months later, the U.S. president closed the immigration door to Cubans, a safety valve that had remained automatically on intake for most of six decades. And in Cuba, repression increased.

Since Raúl Castro stepped down in 2019, there has been a new leadership on the island, with the designation of Miguel Díaz-Canel, a trusted military official, as president. The government expanded the kinds of small businesses it would authorize. Yet, as Raúl Castro retained control of the Communist Party and the Armed Forces, dissidents were met with continued repression. It was during that time that the regime again deployed the future to get out of an untenable present. The 2019 Constitution, billed as *El futuro que aún puede ser* (The future that can still be), was ratified even though there was minimal debate around several provisions, including the sanctification of the island's one-party system. It also legitimized foreign investments yet prohibited Cuban nationals from investing in their own economy.

But the focus on *el futuro* has not brought improvements to Cubans' lives. The economic situation has continued to deteriorate, as Venezuela, a major source of oil for Cuba, saw its own economy disintegrate, and in the United States, Donald Trump came to power vowing to reverse Obama's Cuba rapprochement. Then, in the midst of the global COVID-19 pandemic, Cuba shut its doors to tourism, which unleashed further economic chaos—and the populace once again began suffering from food shortages and electrical blackouts. Another failed promised future.

The regime billed the 2021 Party Congress as a process of continuity. Raúl Castro formally stepped down and Díaz-Canel was officially named secretary of the Communist Party. But despite alarming economic and health crises, the Party instead focused on its propaganda machine—on how to better message and recruit members. Modest proposals to license professionals and slightly increase the private sector were initially turned down even though the COVID-19 pandemic forced a liberalization of regulation that limited the kinds of businesses allowed to operate on the island.

With all doors shut, pressure built, and even Party loyalists took to social media networks to denounce the lack of minimal reforms. A group of artists, some residing in the San Isidro neighborhood of Havana, had already begun to organize protests in the fall of 2018 after the enactment of Decree 349, an order that stipulated that all artistic projects had to be submitted for approval by the government. Ten members of the group had staged a hunger strike in one of their homes. Security forces illegally broke in and arrested them. A video tape of one of the arrests circulated widely on social media. The group called for a social media campaign asking people to drape themselves in the Cuban flag and take and post a selfie to the hashtag "*La bandera es de todos*"—the flag belongs to all. Protests increased, and in an unprecedented act, a group of artists now joined by other organized groups, including one headed by performance artist Tania Bruguera and playwright Yunior García, showed up at the Ministry of Culture, demanding to speak with officials. Fernando Rojas, the culture minister, eventually met with them and promised that he would work to soften the restrictions. This short-lived moment was dashed by President Díaz-Canel, who publicly criticized Rojas and called the artists mercenaries and foreign agents.

Still, support for the artists increased. A hip-hop song praised the movement and called for a new slogan, *Patria y vida*—homeland and life. Reclaiming a voice in the present, the song grounds the movement in the defense of the nation. It hearkens back to the Cuban national anthem's dramatic ending, "*que morir por la patria es vivir*" (to die for the homeland is to live), which glorifies dying and which Fidel Castro rewrote and used as an ending to his speeches, *Patria o Muerte* (homeland or death). *Patria y vida* is a liberatory call for life and nation. On July 11, 2021, when spontaneous protests erupted all over the island, the song became the soundtrack of the protests. Young people from marginal neighborhoods, mainly Black, took over the streets with calls for *libertad*—freedom. But as soon as the protests began, the government struck back, violently attacking the protesters and jailing over a thousand of them. Ironically, when young people and artists met in Cuba's jails, conversations across distinct sectors grew.

The social discontent had been building. Fidel Castro's death had made it clear that the heady days of the 1960s and 1970s were long in the past. Indeed, his demise provoked a crisis for the present and a questioning of the island's future. What happens *now?* Does the present have to be only a moment of catharsis, or worse, of violent confrontations? Can there be political options beyond exile? Can there be another form of the present that can be more conducive to an equitable and democratic political system?

Figure 0.1. *La bandera es de todos*. Courtesy of Luis Manuel Otero Alcántara.

Could a distinctive conception of time entertain different political options for Cuba? These are the questions that drive this project.

Why Temporalities and Democracy?

I became intrigued by time and its impact on political projects as I studied Operation Pedro Pan, an early 1960s project through which 14,000 unaccompanied Cuban minors ages six to eighteen were brought to the United States.[2] I was one of those children. At the time, it was the largest unaccompanied children's exodus and movement in the world. Children, and specifically the control of their intellectual and political formation, became the arena through which two dominant versions of the rational project—that is, democracy and communism—waged an ideological battle in Cuba. Renaissance-era rational projects placed the human mind at the center of social constructions, and children were the vehicles through which they would be realized. Unlike adults, children could be easily molded into future and "model" citizens of a nation. On the one hand, the Cuban revolutionary government sought to create a new society by molding the minds of children—creating a "New Man," a socially reengineered human being who would build a new society. Those opposed to this project sought to rescue the children from this plan and through them bring forth a more democratic future for Cuba. Underpinning the struggles over who would control the minds of children was the notion that children were the keys to the future, and the effort to control them a way to control the future of the nation.

Every version of the rational project—including communism, fascism, and democracy—has sought to mold its society through this future temporality. Yet the temporality expressed through the need to control children's intellectual formation stripped society of even its most fundamental institution—the nuclear family as the basic social unit—and placed children in an unchartered territory of an unknowable future constructed through other institutions. The ways of understanding what Operation Pedro Pan was, and what experiences it generated for those involved, also became an arena in which official renditions of the past were codified in a memory zone that only permitted a two-dimensional view of the past, with everyone touched by the exodus expected to conform their experience to a tale of redemption or victimization.

In an earlier project, I explored notions of temporalities and their relationships to politics by studying civically engaged youth in various locales. In the wake of what can be called a crisis of late modernity—that is, the inability of modern societies to fulfill their utopian projects and promises— the question of time became central to those seeking a voice in politics. If children had become pawns in a struggle to control the future, how did civically engaged youth see themselves in relationship to time? This ethnographic project documented the trajectories of civically engaged youth in three global cities in the Americas: Rio de Janeiro, Mexico City, and Chicago.[3] Invariably, almost all the young participants were suspicious of narratives that placed them in the future. Instead, they wanted to be recognized in the present. Rights, after all, are not promises to be met; rather they are conditions that allow the individual to have a voice and be safe in the present.

Much of my work has consisted of finding a way to have an effective public voice. Growing up in the United States during the civil rights movement, I learned that democracy not only needs elections and separation of powers, but it also requires an inclusive society. Working in the trenches of

Latino studies, I have dedicated much of my life to projects that have sought such an inclusive society. While I sometimes focused on the structures of power and on the policies that guided political programs, I have always been interested in the ideas that anchor political action. I am convinced that ideas matter, and that the ways in which we frame concepts have political consequences. Time, and more specifically, the temporalities deployed politically and rhetorically, influence political projects and the political culture in which they reside.

The central focus of this book—a search for Democracy's Time, a temporality that is conducive to individual agency—is also very personal. There are many ways of thinking about why the Cuban Revolution—which was once a massively popular movement—led to such deep ruptures. In my particular family, as I have shared, it was the unfulfilled promise of democracy—the lack of elections and the indiscriminate and arbitrary use of power that made my parents leave the country they so loved. In this book, I turn my attention again to Cuba and its diaspora, and to the ongoing search for democracy in the country of my birth, and also in the United States, the country I now also call home. I am inspired by the calls for democracy heard throughout the streets of Cuba and the lucid articulation by many of the protesters on the island, as well as by second-and third-generation Cuban Americans, of the need for a society and a community that is socially just *and* democratic.

Method and Scope of Inquiry

The method I am using in this book is a conversation between theories of temporalities and the Cuban experience. The theories of temporalities guide the ways I will be "reading" political and cultural expressions as I seek to understand how temporalities impact political possibilities. Theories of temporalities evolve and are conceived in multiple disciplines. There is no one overarching theory, but rather there are multiple ideas about time, human experience, and temporalities that shed light on the complex intersection between politics and the "time" in which they exist. The list of scholars I have consulted is eclectic, but their ideas helped me work through new ways of thinking about time and politics. As such, this manuscript will make references to multiple theorists, although the work of Hannah Arendt is one of the central conceptual scaffoldings of this inquiry.

While I was trained as a political scientist, I also bring psychology to my work. In my studies in both of those fields, I learned quantitative methods, but early in my career I moved to qualitative methods, which have included archival work, textual and narrative analysis, and ethnographic studies. The intersection of Latin American and Latino Studies has been my intellectual home. There, I have had the space to use interdisciplinary methods and ask questions at the crossroads of multiple fields and disciplines, and I have been able to study Cuba and its diaspora through a transnational lens and have come to understand that what is "Cuban" resides in multiple geographic locations.

I bring to this study an appreciation that ideas about our world and our societies are worked out in multiple locations of human creativity. In the Latin American and Caribbean tradition, artists, poets, and scholars are all intellectuals who through their media—the image, word, and text—critique existing ideas and in the process develop new ones. I will be making references to multiple expressions of Cuban thought and political culture, and in each chapter I will provide a more in-depth discussion of two or three cases.

This book will also explore a variety of examples of Cuban cultural expressions reflected in political essays, literary works, and artistic projects. Cuba and its exiles are part of my personal history. I have been involved in some of the movements in which this cultural and artistic production took place, and as such, I will also explore some of my own experiences throughout the book. My generation shared a deep rupture in our lives; we shared a journey into exile as well as returns to the island. Some of the writers and artists I will discuss have been an important part of these journeys. I have had a close relationship with some of the people whose work I explore in this book.

Nereida García-Ferraz and I frequently travelled to Cuba and have shared decades of conversations about the complicated relationship we pursue with the place of our birth; I have closely followed the work of my friend María Martínez-Cañas. Indeed, as I began my readings of Hannah Arendt—someone who understood the condition of displacement as deeply as she understood the dangers of totalitarianism—the artist Tania Bruguera, also a friend, had started exploring Arendt's work as well. Eventually, Bruguera staged a marathon performance based on Arendt's *The Origins of Totalitarianism,* in which people were asked to read portions of the book, and she founded the Instituto de Artivismo Hannah Arendt (The Hannah Arendt Artivism Institute), dedicated to fomenting grassroots organizing with the hope of energizing democracy in Cuba.

Central to my understanding of how temporalities can influence political projects is the work of Eliseo Diego. Eliseo Diego opened the door to his home on the island and became a very close friend, as did his daughter Josefina (Fefé) de Diego. He accepted those of us returning as part of his family even when the official policies toward those abroad changed and we were shunned. His poetry became a way for me to understand Cuban philosophical sensibilities. In his poem *Testamento* (Testament), Eliseo Diego leaves us time. Time imbued with memories and desires. Time in which to live and dream. Time in which personal and social relationships evolve and create what we experience as life. His appreciation of time will be central to the exploration in this book of how temporalities create and limit political possibilities.

Acknowledgments

For years, Cuban Studies was stuck in the binaries of the Cold War. However, it is an evolving field, and I am thankful to my colleagues who are contributing to broadening its scope and who have supported this project. I am grateful to José Quiroga for his support and for his pathbreaking work that informs both subject(s) and the method(s) of study in this book; Jorge Duany, whose own work has helped solidify a transnational perspective on Cuban Studies; Louis Pérez's work on Cuban history provides an important scaffolding for my understanding of the role of the past; and Lillian Guerra's work on the prerevolutionary period documents the richness of organizations that emerged against President Fulgencio Batista in the 1950s. I am also thankful to Alan West-Durán for his comments on earlier essays about Cuban thought and temporalities. As always Ruth Behar's work forms part of our transnational appreciation of Cuban art and culture.

Cuban Studies has continued to evolve by the scholarship dedicated to understanding how race has played out historically and in contemporary politics. Alejandro de la Fuente's work has helped create a new dimension for Cuban Studies. Enrique Patterson's work, as well as Carlos Moore's, became critical for understanding the role of racism in Cuban history, including the revolutionary period. I remain deeply indebted to Charles Mills, a colleague whose work critically reviewed both the liberal project and Marxism and concluded that both had left out Blacks. On the balance, he believed that the liberal project had a better chance of providing social justice because it did not obliterate the individual. I am infinitely thankful to the peer reviewers for their thoughtful comments.

I am grateful to my friends Tania Bruguera, Nereida García-Ferraz, and María Martínez-Cañas for sharing their artwork with me, and to Rolando Estévez for the endless conversations about aesthetics and politics.

I am convinced that angels shepherd manuscripts. This one has had the support of many including Olga Herrera, Stephanye Hunter, and Ileana Oroza, whose close readings and editorial suggestions have made the writing clearer and the substance deeper. Fefé Diego led me through a thorough reading of Eliseo Diego's work, helping me identify his thoughts on temporalities. Her work made this book possible.

As always, I am deeply indebted to the academic and creative work of Lourdes Casal. She was one of the instigators of our returns to Cuba and opened doors that made those journeys possible. She captured our diasporic dilemma in her beautiful poem to Ana Veldford, in which she wrote, "too Habanera to be Newyorkina / too Newyorkina to be . . . anything else."

I dedicate this book to the memory of my dear friend Cecilia Vaisman, for she was the one who taught me to appreciate the *present*.

Introduction

Temporalities and Politics

Each new generation, indeed, every new human being as he inserts himself between an infinite past and an infinite future must discover and ploddingly pave it anew.
Hannah Arendt, *Between Past and Future*

Democracy and Time in Cuban Thought explores the relationship between temporalities and politics. Guiding this book is an appreciation that, at the core of politics, is human action, which as Hannah Arendt suggests, occurs not in the past or in the future, but rather in the present. It can be influenced by the past, but not determined. It can also have its sights set on the future, but it occurs in the present. Still, political discourses and grand designs are usually situated either in the past or in the future, thus denying the potential impact of human agency and oftentimes leading to authoritarian forms of government. This has certainly been the case in Cuban history, even though Cubans have engaged in a long search for democratic alternatives.

This chapter will outline the conceptual underpinnings to the book—democracy and temporalities. I begin by tracing political movements in Cuba that have sought to find democratic alternatives, thus grounding an understanding of democracy not only in theory but also in political experiences. The middle section presents an overview of temporalities in the Cuban experience. I conclude with a broader discussion about the concepts of democracy, time, and temporalities and their relationship.

Search for Democracy in Cuban History

There has been, throughout Cuban history, a search for a democratic republic. After 400 years of colonial rule, Cuban independence fighters and thinkers sought not only to free themselves from Spain, but also to establish a form of government that allowed for broader public participation and was structured in such a way as to limit the power of any one branch.[1] There was a deep current of thought that recognized that a democratic country had to make deep commitments to diversity.[2] Into the twentieth century, this democratic experiment was repeatedly interrupted by internal power grabs as well as U.S. interventions. As in many other countries with a legacy of slavery, power and social goods were unequally distributed along racial lines.[3] Yet clearly, without the inclusion of Blacks in the national project, democracy could not be attained. Women, too, were marginalized within these imperfect efforts at democracy. Still, there was an impulse, a search, and an expressed political desire to create a democratic republic. This is particularly evident in the Constitution of 1940, which despite its extreme nationalism, limited the powers of the president, created an independent judiciary, re-edified voting rights, and protected rights along class, gender, racial, and religious lines. So sacred were these aspirations that the violation of this Constitution became the *raison d'être* for the 1959 Revolution.

The 1959 insurrection had been pluralistic.[4] Several key groups had participated including the Havana-based Directorio Revolucionario Estudiantil (Student Revolutionary Directorate). Key leaders from some labor unions, like Frank País, a teacher from Santiago de Cuba, were also instrumental in leading the insurrection to victory, as were leading figures from the Partido Ortodoxo (Orthodox Party). A consensus document signed on July 20, 1958, in Caracas, outlined the path toward democratizing the island. It called for a brief transitional government with broad representation that would be responsible for ushering in a constitutional and democratic government. But from early on, Fidel Castro's 26th of July Movement took control of the process.[5] Eventually, an authoritarian form of government with a strong security and military apparatus and with a single political party emerged that has ruled the island with repression, incarceration, firing squads, and banishment for more than six decades.

The impulse toward democracy that had coalesced the insurrection would continue to be present in the opposition to the Castro regime for decades, even though at times anti-communism would justify support of right-wing authoritarian regimes. Still democracy was an aspirational goal.

Among the first to be removed from power in the young revolutionary government were the liberal democrats. Their representative, José Miró Cardona, had been appointed by President Manuel Urrutia to serve as prime minister. He was replaced by Fidel Castro only six weeks after his appointment. He would later go on to become the head of the Revolutionary Council, the political arm of the movement that led to the Bay of Pigs invasion in April 1961. Insiders were not exempt from purges and summary trials. Pedro Luis Díaz Lanz, who had been named head of the Revolutionary Air Force, became concerned about the move toward communism and was quickly dismissed from his post.[6] Huber Matos, who had been a commander of the July 26th Movement, Fidel Castro's group, also fell out of grace for criticizing the early pivoting toward socialism and the new alliance with Cuba's Partido Socialista Popular (Popular Socialist Party, PSP), which was aligned with the Soviet Union. Matos was tried and found guilty of treason and sedition and spent twenty years in jail until his release in 1979.

The Revolution's leadership, which was almost exclusively white, argued that they would bring racial equality to Cuba. Despite these claims, questions of race did not become central to the Revolution. Carlos Moore, a Black Cuban who had left the country in the 1950s and had become involved in the U.S. civil rights movement, met with Fidel Castro during his highly publicized visit to Harlem in 1960. Castro invited him to return to Cuba and join the revolutionary government. Moore was originally excited about the possibilities of joining a movement that could bring a more open society to Cuba, yet he too, fell under suspicion as he began to advocate for the rights of Blacks (ironically, much as Castro had done during his visit to the United States). After two detentions, Moore sought asylum in the Guyanese Embassy. He would end up in Egypt and join Jonas Savimbi, the leader of one of the many groups fighting against Portuguese colonization in Angola. (Savimbi, with the support of South Africa and the United States, would eventually battle the Soviet and Cuban-backed People's Movement for the Liberation of Angola [MPLA, for its Portuguese name].) Moore's book *Castro, the Blacks and Africa*[7] has become one of the definitive accounts of the profound failure of the Revolution to democratize along color lines. Suppression of manifestations of Blackness would become ingrained in the Revolution's culture of political repression.

Skin color was not the only human characteristic that was criminalized by the Revolution. The 1960s also saw an increase in control over other aspects of individuals' personal behavior and even their bodies. Mannerisms, fashion choices, and sexuality became arenas of suspicion and repression.[8]

In 1965, the government set up forced labor camps under the rubrics of Unidades Militares de Ayuda de Producción (Military Units to Aid Labor, UMAP). These were meant for those who, for a variety of reasons, could not fulfill their military duty or were not allowed to do so. This category included conscientious objectors, political dissidents, practicing Jehovah Witnesses, and gays and lesbians.

Repression was not just geared toward groups who were "outsiders." Even though the PSP was aligned with the Soviet Union and its members were supporters of communism, they were concerned with the lack of internal debate within the Communist Party, or what was called centralized democracy. In addition, they felt that Castro's impulsive and arbitrary style of governance was creating a messiah-like style of leadership that undermined the rule of the proletariat. Institutionally, they were threatened by Castro's gutting of the unions' power. Before the Revolution, the PSP had been a critical force in the union movement, especially among sugar workers, cultural workers, and other urban syndicates. Finally, they felt that Castro was not really a communist, and were suspicious that his alliance with the Soviet Union was more a political move than a coincidence of ideological commitment. In 1966, Castro ordered the surveillance of a group of PSP militants, and their leader, Aníbal Escalante, was arrested. In the following two years, another thirty-five of the *micro-fracción* (micro-splinter group), as they came to be called, were arrested as well.

On January 24, 1968, in a meeting of the Cuban Communist Party, Raúl Castro presented what he claimed to be evidence the *micro-fracción* had been conspiring against Fidel Castro, and within months, they were sentenced to twenty years in jail. In the following years, Communist parties throughout Latin America protested these arrests, and international pressure eventually led to their release. Many of these leaders would continue to play a role in the formation of human rights groups in the 1980s and have an influence on a second generation of Cuban human rights activists.

And indeed, in the late 1970s and early 80s, as human rights became an arena of international debate, groups calling for human rights proliferated in Cuba. One of these, the Cuban Committee for Human Rights, was founded by Elizardo Sánchez and Ricardo Bofill, who had been part of the *micro-fracción* and had spent time in jail after the purge. The new human rights group served as the institutional basis for the Democratic Socialist Current, founded by philosopher Enrique Patterson, who had been the first Black professor in the University of Havana's Philosophy Department and had fallen out of favor for his choice of books, which included exiled authors like Guillermo Cabrera Infante, along with the classic Greek philosophy texts and European Marxists like Antonio Gramsci. He also faced off with one of the ruling families, which demanded preferential treatment for a relative who was failing his course. The Democratic Socialist Current called for the restoration of the 1940s commitment to social democracy and insisted on racial equality as well.

Other writers and intellectuals also organized. A small political study group was initiated by Roberto Luque Escalona, a former member of the 26th of July Movement. He brought several others, including Fernando Velázquez Medina, Manuel Díaz Martínez, and María Elena Cruz Varela. Concerned with the government's extreme response to the economic crisis that resulted from the collapse of the Soviet Union in 1991, they began to meet with the purpose of influencing the erratic nature of the Cuban leadership. Inspired by the changes in Eastern Europe, especially in Poland, they published a letter, which became known as La Carta de los Diez (The Letter from the Ten), demanding democratic changes in Cuba as well the liberation of what they defined as prisoners of conscience. Even though Cruz Varela had received a prestigious Cuban literary prize, *Granma,* the official newspaper of the Cuban Communist Party, described her as an unknown and semi-literate poet, of doubtful morality, and mentally ill with hysteria. She was further accused of being an agent of the CIA. She was eventually arrested and sentenced to two years in prison. The other members of the group were also sent to jail and eventually forced out of the country.[9]

A generation of Cuban scholars was also inspired by the Velvet Revolution, as the transition away from communism was known in Czechoslovakia. In what became loosely known as La tercera opción (the third option), meaning their allegiances were neither to the government in Havana nor to the exiles in Miami, Madeline Cámara, Rafael Rojas, Osvaldo Sánchez, Iván de la Nuez, and others sought to find a political space beyond the hyperpolarized binaries of communism and capitalism. They were initially encouraged by the proliferation of artistic projects that included painting, performance, and photography during a very short-lived moment of political opening on the island in the late 80s and early 90s. But they, too, were marginalized and eventually forced out of the country, a process that Madeline Cámara describes as the "moment in which the nation abandons you."[10] Many ended up in Mexico and Spain, a few in the United States.

During this time, independent journalism grew as well. But in the spring of 2003, a government crackdown against dissidents resulted in the imprisonment of seventy-five journalists and human- and democracy-rights activists. Some were members of the Movimiento Cristiano de Liberación (Christian Liberation Movement) headed by Oswaldo Payá. They had initiated Proyecto Varela, named after Félix Varela, a priest who had fought for Cuba's independence from Spain and for the establishment of a democratic government. The Varela Project called for a law that would establish basic rights in Cuba and was signed by 11,020 Cubans on the island. The rights outlined included freedom of association, speech, and press. The Cuban Constitution of 1976 had a provision that permitted citizens to propose new laws. As one lawyer pointed out, the Varela Project did not ask for a change *of* government, but rather a change *in* government.[11] Those arrested received harsh sentences that ranged from eight to twenty-two years. Five were sent across the island to a prison in Guantanamo. One was Jorge Olivera, a journalist whose father had been part of the *micro-fracción*.[12] In 2012, Oswaldo Payá and Harold Cepero, chairman of the movement's youth league, would die in a car crash that many, including Payá's daughter Rosa María Payá, have argued was an intentional murder.[13]

Some of the female family members of those imprisoned, including Olivera's wife, Nancy Alfaya, quickly organized a group of women to advocate for their husbands, brothers, and sons. The organization met at a Catholic church in Miramar—named for St. Rita of Cascia, the patroness of impossible causes—and for years held weekly peaceful marches down Havana's prestigious Quinta Avenida (Fifth Avenue). They faced personal retaliation by the security forces, which periodically would sweep in and conduct mass arrests. Many of the founders and members were Black women.

Groups continued to proliferate during the 2000s, and some expected that Fidel Castro's transition from power would encourage a political opening. But instead, repression went on, particularly after the Obama visit to Cuba. Yet the democratic impulse continued to find political expression, and in the summer of 2021, it emerged yet again as thousands of Cubans, mainly young, many Black, occupied the streets of cities and towns throughout the island demanding *libertad* (freedom).

Temporalities and Politics in the Cuban Experience

Political action and political projects are temporalized. For instance, temporalities create a sense of collective identity that binds the nation and locates politics in distinct historical periods. In Cuba, legends from a distant past, as well as a promised future, have created boundaries for political projects. In fact, historian Louis A. Pérez Jr. has argued that history and the nation are symbiotically tied.[14] History informs the national project. The nation is constituted as its history is being contemplated. And the force of the past in contemporary events is undeniable. For the Cuban Revolution, the past has been a roadmap as well as a recurring theme. Heroes of past wars like José Martí are continuously venerated. At one singular moment, the past, history in specific, was also elevated to the role of judge, as a young Fidel Castro, defending himself against the charges brought against him by the Batista regime for his role in the insurrection, taunted his jury: "Condemn me, it does not matter, history will absolve me."[15]

The Cuban regime has also deployed temporalities in the service of the state and its economy. Nostalgia became a way of creating political unity. The Revolution's triumph was enshrined in the past, and its leader, Fidel Castro, was made into a legend through photographs and songs. Pictures and film clips of Castro's triumphal arrival in Havana were constantly published and replayed until they became pseudo-biblical images, and his feats were celebrated in popular songs. Nostalgia was also commercialized as tourists were lured into Havana's Plaza de Armas, where relics of the Revolution were sold from rickety stalls, and albums of *La Nueva Trova* music and books of collectible images of Fidel Castro's *rebeldes* (rebels) were displayed and sold. For American tourists who were obsessed with situating Cuba in a specific temporality, the past, sloppy joes were served in a replica of a 1950s restaurant with the same name. The tourist-perfect Caribbean island has been described as a place where time has stopped. Visitors often comment that when they land in Cuba, they feel as if they had traveled back to 1959. The island and its people seem frozen in a black-and-white photograph. It is, "Out of time, on a time of its own, stuck in time."[16] But the regime does not reserve the appeal of the past for tourists alone: The spring 2021 Communist Party Congress was billed as the "Congress of Continuity," as new leadership used the past to claim authority in the present.

The future, such an essential part of the revolutionary project, is also central to political narratives. The last sixty years are littered with historic moments that are always embedded with a promise of a sunnier tomorrow—a promise that better days would replace present hardships.

In literature, islands have been the setting for utopias—isolated communities of kindred folks.[17] Cuba has been called the land of lost utopias as, in turn, conquistadors, independence fighters, North American businessmen and politicians, revolutionaries, and even those waiting for the collapse of one of the last standing socialist countries, imagined futures that never arrived.

Throughout the world, socialism promises a future shining with possibilities, yet that future is constantly postponed. In the case of the Cuban Revolution, this is embalmed in the figure of Ernesto "Che" Guevara and his echoing call to arms, *¡Hasta la victoria, siempre!* (Until victory, always!). His open-ended proclamation contained a definite direction, if not a resolution, toward an infinite future: *¡El futuro es nuestro!* (The future is ours!)—a socialist tomorrow. This future orientation has its own long history in Cuba. It could be said that the sixteenth-century conquistadors were in search of better places, better tomorrows, when they sailed from Spain for adventures in the New World. The articulation of a future political sensibility is elaborated in the promised nation conceived by José Martí, who bestowed on children the sacred task of creating the future.[18] Martí's children were, like Rousseau's, close to nature and endowed with innocence. These essential traits, and their evocation of a happy nation, also found fertile ground in Catholicism, the predominant religion in Cuba, which holds, for the faithful, the promise of eternal happiness. Cubans living abroad, exiled from the Revolution, still cling to the vision of a better future when they invariably offer, as a year-end toast, "Next Year in Havana!" Yet the future, an integral part of the building of an independent nation, even as it demands passivity in the waiting, never arrives. Notably, after Fidel Castro's death in 2016, the discussion about a new constitution was framed by the slogan *El futuro que aún puede ser* (The future that can still be).

Human engagement occurs in the present, not in time that has elapsed or that has not yet arrived. But where is this present? Is it the now of the *Granma* headlines in the 1980s proclaiming, "*¡Ahora sí vamos a construir el socialismo!*" (Now we are really going to construct Socialism!)[19] Or is it the frozen present of Abilio Estévez, who anticipates a promised paradise in his novel *Tuyo es el reino?*[20] There is also the nihilistic present unleashed by uncertainty, repression, and even hunger, so vividly portrayed in Pedro Juan Gutiérrez's *Dirty Havana Trilogy,*[21] and the purgatory present in Zoé Valdés's *La nada cotidiana.*[22] This present is experienced in the moment, in the activities that Cubans call *resolviendo*—taking care of life's basic needs—and in finding safe haven in carnal pleasures. There is also the present to be managed, as José Quiroga so deftly describes the *periodo especial en tiempo de paz* (the special period in times of peace),[23] which saw new levels of scarcity and misery in the island in the 1990s. Does the present need to be dictated by the government from above? Perhaps the present is more like *La Espera* (The Wait), a series of sketches by artist Rolando Estévez Jordán, in which the same character reappears trying to accomplish impossible tasks and is left hanging passively, like a gerund, witnessing the passage of time.[24] It recalls the present captured by what Walter Benjamin calls homogeneous time, which he described as an unproductive waiting period: The inability of workers to exert influence over the conditions they faced rendered them voiceless and passive, creating an unproductive present. While Benjamin was referring to capitalism, the same can be said about workers in socialist Cuba.[25]

While time is often portrayed as linear, temporalities are not evenly sequenced. Cuba's sense of nationhood, for example, evolved across a four-hundred-year Spanish Empire whose remnants still survive in the crumbling architecture of Old Havana, in the islanders' rhythmic romance language, and in its national culinary dish of *puerco asado* (roast pork). Yet, time is also compressed as, for example, the much shorter U.S. presence in Cuba is captured in the ubiquitous American antique cars that ferry tourists around Havana. On occasion, time seems to be erased, as in the effort to dismiss the intimate, forty-year relationship between the island and the Soviet Union as insignificant due to cultural incompatibility.

Temporalities coexist and Cuba is a place where past and future are omnipresent. Secular and religious notions of the past and future coincide and, at times, become mutually exclusive. In Alejo Carpentier's *Los pasos perdidos,* European temporalities of the past cannot reconcile with the fabulous future as imagined in the Caribbean.[26] Meanwhile, in José Lezama Lima's *Paradiso,*[27] the past is a place from which to explore the future. This understanding of the fluidity across temporalities perhaps can be a paradigm that allows for coexistence among differing generational and political perspectives.

Since the late 1950s, multiple temporalities have been deployed by the island government. Despite the fact that the original leadership of the Cuban Revolution hung on to power for more than half a century, the Revolution itself was a process that could be said to have commenced on July 26, 1953, with the parallel attacks on the Moncada Military Barracks in Santiago de Cuba and the Carlos Manuel de Céspedes Military Barracks in Bayamo, and lasted just a few years, until after the collapse of the Batista regime on January 1, 1959. Yet the Cuban regime often presents the Revolution as an ongoing process that reaches back to the wars of independence and marches forward to some indeterminate future. Indeed, they have frozen the Revolution, a socially forward movement, into an eternal, permanent one. Some have noted that Cuba is like Paul Klee's *Angelus Novus,* the Angel of History, which Walter Benjamin describes as being caught between the past and an unpredictable future as it looks back on ruins.[28] Ruins became a way of describing the island.[29]

What remains *elusive* is the *present*—a place in which the past can be democratized and the future imagined, and most importantly, where the clashes between these temporalities can have "time" in which to be in civil conversation and not in violent contradictions with each other. Could there be a present that encourages connections across differences? The present, as envisioned by Hannah Arendt, gives room to contemplate and act upon the political, to view others' differences without derision and perhaps appreciate their sameness. Without such an expansive present, can the political even exist? I am referring to a political that is deliberated upon by an engaged community, in which individuals can recognize the other despite their differences. Can there be a present temporality where a more democratic society can be imagined? Can there be a "still time," a pause in which we can view the moment and each other as we are—as comforting and as disturbing as this may be?[30] Perhaps this could be a present that encourages a revision of the past to make it more inclusive, and a future grounded in possibilities that are real and not just rhetorical.

Democracy Defined

Democracy itself is a contested and an evolving term. Formally, it can be described as "a government in which the supreme power is vested in the people and exercised by them directly or indirectly through a system of representation usually involving periodically held free elections."[31] Some key institutions have proven vital to democracy, including a robust public education system, free press, and fair elections. This procedural and institutional democracy guarantees that citizens can have a voice in public affairs and that independent institutions can hold government accountable.

With rare exceptions, procedural democracies have not led to equality, especially in countries where there are great inequalities in the private realm. Oftentimes, these inequalities are visible across racial and ethnic lines, as is the case in the United States and many Latin American countries. Power is therefore unequally distributed, and those with greater means exert greater influence in the public realm. Structural democracy is an alternative conceptualization of the classic definition of democracy. It poses that only with a more equitable distribution of resources can there be a functioning democratic society. Structural democracy combines equality in the economic realm with respect for individual rights. It could be said that the promises of the Cuban Revolution were grounded in this perspective—social justice and democracy. And indeed, young, island-based Cuban activists have once again eloquently called for both economic justice and a voice in the public realm.[32]

Beyond laws and institutions, democracy requires a political culture that contains ideas and values about the sense of community and the ways people relate to each other, particularly when there are differences. A more democratic politics also requires a degree of tolerance to differences, as distinct identities structure the ways we see each other, and consequently, how we relate to each other. Politics is a social process, and as such, needs to include notions of community and how the individual is defined within the larger body. Political culture also influences the ways in which we communicate with each other and how people are expected to comport themselves. In sum, we can call these "shared political sensibilities," and they are attributes that cannot just be legislated—they need to be sustained by ideas and cultural practices.

Temporalities deeply influence politics, and particularly our ideas about politics and our political culture.[33] For instance, is authority garnered through deliberation and action rather than from tradition or some mandate from the past? Can all individuals see themselves in national narratives of the past, or are some excluded from the nation's memory because their experiences contradict or contest official renditions? Can individuals expect to have rights and protections today, or must they wait for promised rights and benefits in some undefined future? In effect, political projects lodged in the past or in the future that do not guarantee rights in the present make democracy difficult because human action, the workings of politics, occurs in the present. If political projects are conceived in the past or in the future, individual advocacy will have limited contemporaneous influence and effect. Democracy requires the temporality of the present, and this temporality is key to sustaining political sensibilities that value the individual, respect differences, foment an inclusive society, and create a space for civil deliberations. A sense of community can flourish under these circumstances.

Ways of Thinking about Time

Underpinning the conversation between Cuban thought and temporalities is an evolving understanding of these concepts. David Couzens Hoy distinguishes between time and temporality. He argues that temporalities are

12 · Democracy and Time in Cuban Thought

what we experience and can be understood broadly as past, present, and future.[34] He assumes that temporalities are social constructions, embedded with multiple dimensions of experienced time, natural time, recorded time, and promised time. Distinct temporalities can coexist in the now, for example, as we sit and contemplate memories of yesterday or dream of times to come. Still, we generally understand time in distinct categories of the past, present, and future. This book will be organized around these temporalities with the understanding that at any given moment multiple temporalities are at play even as one may dominate over others.

In effect, I will be developing an understanding of the social and political work done through temporalities, keeping in mind the question of which ones are more conducive to democratic possibilities.[35] Each temporality has a complex set of concepts and processes through which it operates. There are political consequences to this.[36] For instance, social memory is an important component of constructions and contestations of the past. Destiny, hope, and desire are intimately intertwined with the future. Politics in the present finds multiple expressions, which can be passive—an inability to exert influence or become engaged when there is a possibility to interact with others to organize. Throughout the book, all three temporalities will be further developed in each chapter. This organization does not assume that these temporalities exist independently of each other. But rather that at distinct moments one may dominate others.

As described above, the notions of time and temporalities are distinct yet related, and as such, a brief discussion about the evolution of our notions of time can clarify how temporalities will be defined in this manuscript. Time has long been studied and indeed debated from various disciplinary perspectives. There is the physical time studied by scientists, most notably physicists, who have posited time as relative or as absolute: chronostatic or chronometric. In physics, time serves to create context, order, and even chaos. Whether time is continuous is a source of intense debate that raises the question of where it begins and where it will end, in other words, its past or its future.[37] And there is also the debate about absolute versus relative time, Isaac Newton developing the theory of absolute time in the seventeenth century and Albert Einstein the theory of relativity in the twentieth. The relationship between past, present, and future is also explored in physics, even as for some physicists the distinction between them is a persistent, stubborn illusion. For scientists, time at the end is difficult to quantify and define.[38]

For human science, the questions of time have also included the nature and the experience of time. For philosophers, the debate about time initially centered on whether it existed outside of human experiences. Aristotle, for instance, defined time as an accumulation of "nows."[39]

Early Christian philosophers such as St. Augustine who wrote in the 300s, distinguished between human time that ended with death, and God's eternal time—mortality and salvation.[40] Whether or not time exists outside of human experience led to questions about the nature of time as linear or circular, biological or social. Does time flow? In what direction? And can we control it?

Even if scientists and philosophers cannot settle on a definition of time, it is nonetheless experienced. For example, it is common to think about how fast or slowly time passes. Phenomenologists were interested in how time is experienced; particularly how human consciousness is experienced through time. In the 1700s, Immanuel Kant postulated that the source of time was the mind; therefore, time was rooted in human experience. For Edmund Husserl, time was like a melody that was linked to what was heard and what is anticipated.[41] Martin Heidegger's 1927 book, *Being and Time,* was especially influential as he defined time as the condition of possible experiences: Time, for him, did not exist, rather it provided a standpoint.[42]

Time also creates a dilemma for anthropologists, who oftentimes are observing "the other" from a distinctly constructed temporality of the now and perhaps a romanticized notion of the past.[43] Sociologists describe how measured time, particularly after industrialization, has deeply influenced the organization of society itself. Culture can also influence our experience of time as societies place differing values on the past, present, or future. This can also influence the ways in which time is constructed.[44] Psychologists have studied a possible life-cycle effect on our notions of time. Children, for instance, experience the passage of time differently than adults.[45] Adults have a lived past through which they can measure the passage of time. They have also developed a sense of waiting, which children do not have. And of course, the past is the work of historians, a field that evolved from literary studies, and their views and methods are constantly debated.

Often, those who study "time" are working with notions that do not include the coexistence of multiple "times." In contrast, contemporary French philosopher Jacques Derrida recognized an idea of multiple times as he stated that the present is hardly present, since it is imbued with traces of the past and desires for the future. The idea of simultaneous times is not necessarily new. Psychoanalysts understand that the past is always with us, and that it often influences the way we experience the world in the present—indeed how we construct our future.[46] Human experiences are felt through time, even if our unconscious is timeless. Of particular interest is the work of Haitian philosopher Michel-Rolph Trouillot, who explores the presence of the past in the present and how established processes to produce history can exclude the experiences of those who do not fit into official renditions of the past. His observations will be the bases for exploring different ways of narrating the past.

Conflicting temporalities may be one of the sources of social and political discord, indeed of political struggles. One manifestation of this can be the clashes among generations, each with conflicting visions about society that indicate temporalized expectations of politics. The notion of multiple times and what it means for political civility will be discussed in this book's concluding chapter.

Temporalities and Politics

As debated as the concept of time has been for human experiences, few political philosophers have considered the relationship of temporalities to political projects. Hannah Arendt is, of course, an exception. It is her work that provides a point of departure for this journey through Cuban temporalities. Her groundbreaking studies of totalitarian regimes, including communist ones, consider questions of temporalities[47] and are uniquely situated to provide a broader framework from which to ask questions about the Cuban experience. Her work on tradition, the nature of history, and its relationship to authority were central to her study of totalitarian regimes. She grappled with questions such as: From where is authority garnered? Is it from tradition or from consensus? Is there a temporal place in which individuals can effectively have a say in political decisions? Is there a time in which we can contemplate and ready ourselves for political engagement? And her notion of time itself as a gap,[48] a moment that can contain multiple temporalities, can be a key to constructing more inclusive and democratic political spaces.

The driving goal for Arendt was understanding how totalitarianism is rooted in the modernist project, a project that elevated life at the same time that it "massified" it, creating a void that could be filled by messianic movements. In Arendt's analysis, the present had been swiftly unmoored from its past and left with few tools with which to imagine a future, which then lent itself to messianic visions. Modernity also deeply affects the anchors of society; the concept of place today, for example, does not play the same role as it did in feudal societies.[49] In all, when individuals are not rooted and the present becomes a precarious experience filled with wars, they become homeless, both from themselves and from their social environment.

How can the present be my home, how can I feel belonging and contentment, if my age is plagued by wars over territory and resources, mutual disrespect and intolerance of difference, poverty and class conflict, ethnic cleansing and holocaust? How can I make sense of my life—and of history as a whole—if no moral-political progress is evident and if, arguably, just the opposite is occurring? History cannot be merely an accumulation of events, and my estrangement from the social world (and my own rational character) cannot be the permanent predicament of the world. My life may be but a brick, a fragment in the totality called human history; no one will remember my story, no community or polis will grant me immortality.[50]

This lack of betterment contributes to a sense of worthlessness. The unmooring destroys the possibility of an engagement with others. In turn, this contributes to conditions that can foment the rise of authoritarian movements.

It could be that Arendt, in focusing on the horrors of the twentieth century, overlooked the massive movement of enslaved labor in the nineteenth century that presents yet another moment of dehumanization at a massive scale. Still, there may be something to the unique temporality of modernity that bears a second glance, particularly as it relates to politics. For Arendt, modernity unmoored individuals, who then had the desire to belong, but she adds that the overall conditions created by modernity are influenced by the temporality in which they occur. Modernity's unhinged time creates a need to control the narrative of time. Institutions and political systems become heavily invested in dictating an interpretation of the past that gives them authority to rule. Furthermore, it is from that official narrative of the past that modern regimes derive authority to exercise power. She reaches that conclusion by documenting how political projects that relied on the past created modes of authority over the present.[51]

At the core of totalitarianism, both as a form of government and as a type of ideology, Arendt argued, lies the idea that all human action is subordinated to laws of nature or laws of history. In retrospect, one such line leads from Darwin to Nazi racism, another from Marx to Stalinism. The laws of nature and history as used by Arendt assume a predictable evolutionary path for societies. That is, that human evolution occurs in a linear fashion, passing through various defined stages, each creating improvements over the previous one. The laws of nature and history are distinct in that the laws of nature are based on a presumptive biological evolution of humans. For instance, the Nazis posited that certain peoples were *biologically* superior to others and as such defined evolution as a progressive movement that either eliminated the "undesirables" or "watered down" their group by intermarriage. Incidentally this concept also guided nation-building projects in such diverse places as Australia, Argentina, and in the United States, whose history includes the massive orphan train project in the early 1900s that shipped mainly poor, Catholic and Italian children to the Midwest to have them intermingle with white Protestants.

The laws of history basically follow the same argument of a linear evolution, but instead posit that history would bring forth new stages of development, each better than the previous one, and that human character would change and become more enlightened. But for this change to occur, there had to be an implicit political plan of reeducation. So it calls for social reengineering, which leads to social structures that will bring out purportedly the best in human beings as it progressively eliminates the worst. What both have in common is the idea, Arendt noted, "that a superior process of movement has seized both nature and history."[52] Therefore only a totalitarian government, headed by a charismatic leader, can shepherd the march of history or progress.

Totalitarianism, according to Arendt, is largely about executing the laws of nature or history, for these cannot "happen" on their own. What does this mean? It essentially implies "a disastrously distorted, preposterous relation between continuity and change, intransience and transience, timelessness and time."[53] In essence, it posits that human beings can change the course of history by developing master future plans that control the genetics or the socialization of human beings.

Temporalities also function to determine not only the direction of history but to unhinge history from individual human action as it privileges "movement"—one could say a constant unmooring from the present—over structures and individual agency. Kathrin Braun explains it as follows:

> At first glance, the laws of nature or history, in contrast to positive, man-made law, seem to be characterized by their unchanging, permanent quality, their "timeless presence," as Arendt puts it. Laws of

nature or history form laws of movement: first, they allegedly determine the course and movement of history, much as natural laws determine the course of the planets. Second, totalitarian movements make them their highest-ranking source of authority, so they become the laws of these movements. Third, the totalitarian movement as such can only proceed if it avoids the establishment of any stable institutional order.[54]

Modernity did usher in a distinct temporality that promised a future utopian society on earth as the result of a sequenced development model. In fact, the ides of an earthly utopia, one that can be created through politics, may be the legacy of modernity. Law of historical progress models included that of W. W. Rostow, who studied Latin American countries and predicted that societies evolved through distinct stages and that the most developed stage were societies like the United States, which had constitutions.[55] There were other models, like Karl Marx and Friedrich Engels's, that claimed, with a high degree of certainty, that communism would be the end result of history's long march toward progress.[56] In these models, both the past and the future pave the road for progress. These predictions, or utopic prophecies, never came to be. An open-ended, undeliverable future is also problematized in the work of Arendt, as she noted "that the goal of a totalitarian movement is not simply to retain power within the territorial boundaries of a state but to conquer the world and to create a new mankind."[57] Depending on which version of the modernist project, that new mankind would be created through biological or social reengineering.

Yet Arendt does allow for a positive function of the future, in that it could provide a home. She notes, "By identifying with the future ideal of history, however, I come as close as humanly possible to transcending my contingent circumstances, my fleeting existence—perhaps even my homelessness."[58] Imagination, which is a future-oriented impulse, is an important aspect of changing the present, and it can have a positive impact on politics if it is grounded in the present.

But the future also plays a disempowering role as it becomes central to the organization and rhetoric of political systems. It is important to appreciate that it was in the Christian notions of eternity that modernity's utopia found fertile ground, since they share a similar promise of a better future, one in heaven the other on earth. In either case, "modernity casts a disparaging look on the past as it rushes toward the future."[59] It created a definitive rupture with the past and ignored the present.

But still, political projects lodged in the future can deny the individual's agency in the present. The role of utopian thought in modernity is central to my discussion of nation-building in Cuba, as well as the revolutionary process itself, which—much like the Catholic Church it initially fought—promised to create a "New Man" through the transformation of economic structures.

There may be more tempered ways of thinking about the future, a premise that will be developed in later chapters. Consider Theodor W. Adorno, one of the leadings figures of the Frankfurt School, who appreciated that future aspirations could be a form of criticism of the present, a concept he called "utopia of the whole truth."[60] And there is John Rawls' realistic utopias, a dilemma he summarizes thus, "Our hope for the future rests on the belief that the possibilities of our social world allow a reasonably just constitutional democratic society living as a member of a reasonably just Society of Peoples. An essential step to being reconciled to our social world is to see that such a Society of Peoples is indeed possible."[61] Others have underscored the importance of hope in envisioning alternatives.[62]

What is at stake between the past and the future for democracy is the possibility of the individual to have a meaningful voice. In the movement toward the future, the individual is lost, and what is ultimately compromised is the ability to act politically, an act that, to Arendt, is at the essence of human existence and human freedom:

Again, we find that a general feature of modernity culminates in totalitarianism. Under totalitarian rule, there is no room for politics in the sense of expressing and debating different viewpoints and opinions and for acting in concert as opposed to exercising command and obedience. In short, there is no space for political action as an end in itself.[63]

Political action as an end was, for Arendt, a human necessity, and totalitarianism was the antithesis to a society based on human rights. After all, she argued, human beings have the right to have rights.

In this book, what I am most interested in is how temporalities influence political possibilities, particularly in how the "time" they are lodged in either creates or limits human agency, including our capacity to relate to others, as a prerequisite for democracy. I will be looking at how these ideas have evolved in Cuban thought by examining how distinct temporalities have created limitations to democratic practices in particular moments in Cuba, and how they have contributed to the rise of authoritarian government. I take into consideration Arendt's appreciation of the limits of past and future temporalities, and argue that meaningful political action can only happen in the present, not in some nostalgic past or in an undetermined, even hopeful, future. The present, however, has to be open and able to accommodate past and future, and act as a place from which a more democratic past and future can be constructed.

But where is this present? And can the present be productively linked to the past and the future, particularly one that encourages democracy? It is in conversations with Walter Benjamin's writings that we get glimpses of how this present may be constituted. For him, the present was problematic in that it needed to be escaped from since it was oppressive. He also thought of several kinds of present: the idle, the messianic, and the "now-time," which he called the perilous critical moment. In this present, decisions are made with little relationship to the past or the future.[64] Benjamin gives a nod to the past by stating that it needs to be recuperated in order to be dismantled: "A completely remembered world must be set up even faster to oppose it."[65] The recovery of this remembered world occurs in the "now-time."[66]

For Benjamin, in capitalism, time passes through us taking away agency from individuals. But he conceives of another present, which he calls messianic time. Unlike the problematized messianic visions captured by Arendt's analysis of future temporality, Benjamin instead sees messianic time—one lodged in the present—as a moment of revolution and rupture with the disempowering present that merely passes us by.[67]

In Latin America, scholars studying the demise of the future and the rise of the present as a driving temporality have engaged with the idea that we are living the end of utopias. Modernity marched toward the future with grand claims about human behavior and progress. Revolutionary movements promised prosperous, happy, and equitable societies. But in postmodernity, many have questioned the claims of these grand temporalities and unified societies and offered instead a description of time that does not necessarily march into a better future. There was simply no evidence of a rhythmic and inevitable march of history toward that better future.[68] The failure of utopian projects brought what the social scientist Javier Santiso has called the fall into the present.[69] Here, the present is more delineated, which can lead to societies that are automatized. In contrast, American pragmatists suggested a form of the present that was also pragmatic but less rigid.[70] For them, a productive present could reconstruct and give meaning to the past and structure for the future, thus creating a community.[71] There are still other conceptions of the present born out of the disillusionment with the future. Of particular interest will be the work of Octavio Paz, who elaborates the notion of a poetic present that follows the twilight of utopian thinking and calls for an awareness of the moment that allows for individual and communal action.[72] As we will see in upcoming chapters, this elaboration of the poetic present is found in the work of the poet Eliseo Diego, which shares some of the same philosophical and political understandings as Hannah Arendt.

Book Outline

Democracy and Time in Cuban Thought: The Elusive Present seeks to understand how distinct temporal constructions affect political possibilities. I will trace how the Cuban experiences of nation-building and revolution have relied on constructions of politics lodged in the past and projected into the future—both temporal spaces that engender authoritarian regimes. In contrast, democracy—that is, a system that aspires to create decision-making processes that are inclusive and respectful of differing opinions—requires a temporality of the present in order to function properly.

In the past 125 years, Cuba has gone through an intense period of nation-building as well as a revolutionary period, both of which provide windows into how the temporalities of the past and the future influence political projects and how the present may be a temporality more conducive to democracy. The appreciation of time organized as past, present, and future could be misleading, as its linearity may obfuscate the porous nature of time itself. Yet it can give us a readable way to organize our thinking about temporalities and politics. As such, the beginning of this book is organized by these temporal categories. This does not preclude the idea of multiple temporalities, but rather I explore moments in which one temporality *dominates* over the others.

Chapter 1 is dedicated to the "past," as it discusses notions of history and their impact on how the present unfolds. Of particular interest is how the past was deployed during the Cuban Revolution of 1959. We see how the philosophical underpinnings of political projects that claim legitimacy in the past reveal much about the ways politics were conceived. A central document in that chapter is Fidel Castro's *History Will Absolve Me*. This text contains not only the platform of the Cuban Revolution, but also reveals a particular way of thinking about time and politics. Another aspect of the past I explore is the construction and the rendition of historical memory about events of the Revolution and the exile community that have also constituted an arena in which legitimacy and authority are contested.

Chapter 2 focuses on future temporalities, particularly utopian modernist ones that include the building of the nation and the utopic socialist revolution. Central to the building of the nation is the political and literary work of José Martí. For him, children were not only consumers of his stories, but they were also the future—keys to constructing new nations. Embedded in the Cuban Constitution of 1940 are ideas about the preparation of children for the sake of building the nation; these too are explored in this chapter. The rational projects of the mid-twentieth century sought to create "new men." For the Nazis, it was through **genetic** reengineering, and for socialists, it was through **social** reengineering. In Cuba, the proposition that a "New Man" could be created was initially advocated in the early 1960s by the Franciscans, a Catholic teaching order heavily involved in Operation Pedro Pan, but was later redefined in the works of Ernesto "Che" Guevara, particularly in his essay *Man and Socialism.*

The third chapter looks at various constructions of the present, tracing conceptions of the present that emerged after the collapse of the Soviet Union. An alternative to these forms of the present is found in the literary works of some of the members of the literary group Orígenes, particularly Eliseo Diego, who through his poetry and essays, written when he was the director of the Children's Bureau at the National Library in Havana, elaborated a unique temporality.[73] His appreciation of the present makes possible a future grounded in real possibilities. It is what Octavio Paz has named the poetic present.

The fourth chapter backtracks and examines the ways in which the past can become more inclusive. This includes examining memoirs about the Revolution and the exile community that narrate a more inclusive past than the ones promoted in official versions, both in Cuba and in the Cuban exile community. Some artistic projects, like the visual work of Nereida García Ferraz, are reconstructing a past with personal memories that defy official renditions, and others, like the work of María Martínez-Cañas, go further by exploring boundaries between public and private memories and challenging the very notion of who owns the past.

The fifth and concluding chapter explores broader questions about time and democracy. Notions of hope grounded in a more inclusive present are also discussed. I also introduce contemporary deliberations from the island that hint of distinct temporalities that may be more amenable to democracy and explore some of the limits to these discussions and ways in which the present can be more inclusive. A special focus will be on Tania Bruguera's work as an example of a perspective that proposes a future vision grounded in a critical assessment of the present. I end with an appreciation of the work that a poetic, engaged, and inclusive present can do for democratizing societies and communities. What lies at the heart of this book is a search in Cuban thought for a present temporality that can encourage a more democratic political culture.

1

The Past

En Cuba estamos cansados de vivir tanto tiempo en la Historia y queremos vivir en la normalidad.
In Cuba, we are tired of living so much time in History and we want to
live normally.

Leonardo Padura[1]

Revolutions are abrupt breaks with the past thrusting toward a future-oriented political project. But revolutions also rely on the past to justify their
claims to legitimacy. The past justifies and legitimizes present political action, just as renditions of the past often become arenas of contention.[2] This
chapter will explore both of these intersections of the past and politics.

In studying the first, how the past was deployed during Cuba's revolutionary period to ascertain authority, I will focus on a key document, *History
Will Absolve Me* (*La historia me absolverá*), Fidel Castro's famous October
16, 1953, four-hour courtroom speech in his own defense, and the version
he subsequently wrote-up in prison and published in 1954, which was presented to the Cuban people as the platform for Castro's organization, the
26th of July Movement.[3] This text provides a window into how history itself
was constructed by the Revolution and what political implications flowed
and were collectively absorbed from it. History, the past, became a roadmap
for the justification of the Revolution itself and even came to give a young
Fidel Castro the power to judge its outcomes. Castro's notions of history
foreshadowed the philosophical underpinnings to the form of government
he would eventually establish.

The second case study will focus on the aftermath of the Revolution, as
hundreds of thousands of Cubans fled the island. Dueling perspectives on
who belonged within the Revolution came to define nation versus exile. In
the process of consolidating power, the revolutionary leadership relied on

unique official narratives of past events, as did its opposition. In both the island of Cuba and the exile community elsewhere, memories of the past became a militarized zone in which alternative renditions have been difficult to entertain. For the exile community, the loss of our past and imagined futures became the themes of the narrations of our experiences—particularly the sending of 14,000 unaccompanied minors to the United States to save them from communism, in what became known as Operation Pedro Pan—creating tightly woven origin myths. By looking at the debates surrounding the origins of the exile community, the case study will critically examine the consequences of disputing official narratives.

The Past: History and Memory

I begin by noting the intimate relationship between history and the building of the nation, a backdrop that served as the broader stage in which the Cuban Revolution unfolded.

While the past may encompass everything that has ever happened, history and our individual memories become ways of interpreting it. Both history and memories are intimately connected to creating a sense of a temporality that functions in a variety of ways in the political world. It is through the past that we begin to understand our present.

There are numerous debates about what exactly defines or constitutes history. History, unlike memories, is a discipline through which facts about the past are gathered using certain protocols, criteria, and agendas, and then are assembled from various perspectives to narrate stories, biographies, and events. What is contested is what version of the past is counted, what elements are included, how they are investigated and gathered, and most importantly, who has the authority to articulate these historical narratives. As Michel-Rolph Trouillot reminds us, scholarly history has also worked to silence the past, since the production of it is neither a neutral process nor objective.[4]

There is also a question about the nature of history itself: Is it a series of random events or can patterns be discerned? Is there one history—as Georg Friedrich Hegel and Karl Marx, and as we will see, Fidel Castro, claimed—that unfolds through either the search for freedom or the laws of history? Or are there multiple and fragmented narratives in which individuals as well as groups compose an ever-changing past?[5] Does history have a direction? These are crucial questions in understanding the relationship between constructions of the past and present-day politics, particularly taking into consideration Hannah Arendt's observations about the role that the past plays in legitimizing totalitarian regimes, as I noted in the Introduction.[6]

Nation-building is a process that relies on a future temporality as a collective is brought together through an imagined community.[7] However, the past plays a critical role in staging the future nation. In part, this process entails the building of what philosopher Maurice Halbwachs has called the collective frameworks of memory as instruments "to reconstruct an image of the past, which is in accord, in each epoch, with the predominant thoughts of the society."[8] What results is a collective memory that can be distinguished from individual recollections, as he notes, since there are as many memories as there are social groups. This collective memory provides a social framework for individual memories.[9] Memories are located in particular geographies that further define a sense of a collective past. Thus, space and time combine in memory to create a tightly bound idea of nation.

There is a sensory dimension to the processes of bringing together the collective cultural and political memory in various elements of production.[10] For example, while literature in particular plays a critical role in the unleashing of national narratives in the nineteenth and twentieth centuries, music creates a soundtrack for these narratives,[11] and cuisines create olfactory memories. The collective memory can also be transmitted through traditions and corporal performance rituals.[12] Significantly, all these can also be used to reconstruct or erase the past.

There is a distinct political aspect to these processes—which can encompass a set of collective memories about battles, struggles, heroes, events, documents, and symbols—that together further weaves a factual and sensory construction of the nation. This collective political memory enshrines actors and events in the process of creating nation; in turn, this memory is deployed in the present to justify the existing order or dismiss its challengers. The efforts to construct a past political narrative in the present, and indeed to change it radically, is often a reflection of power struggles that have already been waged in the past between competing political factions and power groups. Past struggles can play out in the present and indeed be taken up by future generations.

The effects of an imposed singular rendition of the past can be devastating to individuals who have their own distinct stories of that past. These political narratives can in fact make individuals question their own renditions of their experiences, as the differences create dissonance between personal memories and official ones.[13] In modernity, as time speeds, the bonds between memory and lived experience can easily be ruptured by rap-

26 · Democracy and Time in Cuban Thought

id change. The present swiftly slips into the past and what is dictated from above easily becomes "history" itself.

The Past (as History) and The Building of the Cuban Nation

In the book *The Structure of Cuban History: Meanings and Purpose of the Past*, Louis A. Pérez Jr. examines the political function of the Cuban past.[14] He traces how the development of Cuban history and the Cuban nation have gone hand in hand. History is nation-building. Without a history, the nation could not exist. The past becomes a means to form a collective identity that simultaneously develops a way to create a nation with morals, values, and customs. Most importantly nation-building was tied to the search for sovereignty, a theme that would be repeated time and time again.[15] This, coupled with the struggle to claim a unique geographic place, forms a powerful bond in which memories reside in a place, and that place becomes an intrinsic part of memory. Place and past are fused into the remembrance of homeland, not as an abstraction but as a real space: one to return to, to reclaim, and to redeem a nostalgia for the past. The place becomes the principal sentiment by which attachments to *patria* (homeland) are sustained.[16] In the case of an island nation, the aquatic boundaries form a distinct geography that paradoxically is less porous and open to contestations than landed borders. While space may lose its power under what Zygmunt Bauman calls the austerity of time in modernity,[17] in the origins of a nation, space plays a critical and almost sacred role in establishing national territories and their borders, which become sites to be guarded through bureaucratic and cultural processes and even by force.

Nationalism and history become a secular cult. But as secular as nation-building pretends to be, the religiosity of the process is unmistakable. Pérez says, "*Patria* [homeland] becomes an altar and history its church, with the past a way to justify the aspirations of a nation."[18] Moreover, in the Cuban case, the notion of *patria* provides the specifics to a moral character and what it means to be a citizen, creating codes of behavior that have been strictly policed.[19]

The March of History

The backdrop to the Cuban Revolution contained a deeply politicized notion of history that claimed that the Cuban nation had been marching toward independence and sovereignty from its inception yet had been chronically interrupted by interventions from the United States. I will now focus on what is considered the first armed action of the Revolution.[20] I will analyze the narrative provided by Fidel Castro to look at the ways in which he deployed the past to understand the philosophical and political underpinnings of his personal notions of history and governance.

On July 26, 1953, 170 men and women led by Fidel Castro stormed the Moncada Army Barracks in Santiago de Cuba. Simultaneous actions took place in Santiago's Military Hospital and courthouse and in the Céspedes Barracks in Bayamo de Cuba, symbolic places, two of them named after heroes of the late nineteenth-century Cuban War of Independence from Spain. The year was also an emblematic one in that it was the centennial of the birth of José Martí, the political organizer and leading thinker of the Independence era. By every military calculation, these actions were all failures. Six men died in the fighting and fifty-five others were killed when they were captured. The rest were imprisoned and charged with armed insurrection against the state. Many, like Abel Santamaría, were tortured. In his case, his eyes were removed and presented to his sister Haydee, who was also imprisoned, to try to get her to reveal where other revolutionaries might be hiding. Despite the losses, the actions marked a historic shift in tactics, from electoral politics to armed struggle to oust President Fulgencio Batista. Moncada would go on to be portrayed as one of the most important heroic acts in Cuban history.[21]

The previous year, 1952, Batista, a populist sergeant who in 1933 had shepherded an insurrection against President Gerardo Machado, had staged his own military coup against the democratically elected government of Carlos Prío Socarrás. Batista then suspended the 1940 Constitution and substituted a series of new decrees that gave him the power to revoke civil and political rights. Those who had sought relief through democratic elections were left with little hope of reforming the system through peaceful means.

The trial of those participating in the July 1953 armed uprising became a national stage in which Fidel Castro seized the moment to condemn the Batista regime and present his political platform to the people of Cuba. In his speech, he detailed his actions, justified his right to rebel, and outlined his vision for Cuba. This legendary document was published and circulated in 1954 under the title of *History Will Absolve Me*.[22] In it, Fidel Castro deploys history to justify his actions, and in effect, to be his ultimate judge.

During the first part of the public trial, in September 1953, Castro questioned a government witness about the mistreatment and torture of prisoners, thus deftly turning the accuser into the accused. He was subsequently removed from the courtroom. Castro begins the four-hour speech with an explanation of why he is acting as his own defense lawyer. He relates how he was deprived of adequate legal counsel—he was not permitted to meet with his lawyer in private and denied access to legal documents and books. He adds, "Only one who has been so deeply wounded, who has seen his country so forsaken, and its justice so trampled, can speak at a moment like this with words that spring from the blood of his heart and the truth of his very gut."[23]

He provides details of the plans of the insurrection—how many arms were used, how the rebels trained as a group, and what support they had. In part these details were elaborated as a defense against accusations that he had been financed by the ousted President Prío Socarrás. But perhaps most importantly, Castro boasted that he had wide support from various sectors of the Cuban population.

He then addresses why he believed that an armed struggle would succeed. He summons the past to defend his actions. His first and principal argument is that there were multiple examples in human history that showed that when a struggle was noble and justified, even poorly armed and ill-prepared men could be victorious against powerful armies and enemies. Castro is claiming for himself a place in international history in his invocation of Article 40 of the Cuban Constitution—The Right of Rebellion Against Tyranny—and in his analysis of governmental power throughout the centuries. He mentions rebellions in China, India, Greece, Rome, and Salisbury. He also points to the thoughts and actions of scholars and activists—Aquinas, Luther, Calvin, Mariana, Knox, Poynet, and lastly, Martí—to situate himself in a long line of rebels and to argue for the right of rebellion. Specifically, he suggests rebellion is part of Cuba's DNA. All of this, he says, entitles him to rebel against the oppressive Batista regime, as it has violated national law, making Batista an extralegal tyrant.

History becomes a backdrop to justify present action for the sake of the future. Castro references specific examples in Cuban history, thus situating himself as the heir-apparent who can carry the torch of Cuba's independence movements. He summons past national heroes like Antonio Maceo, a Black general from Cuba's War of Independence from Spain, and especially Martí, in his attempt to take the historical mantle to lead the struggle for an independent Cuba. Notably, he mentions the inalienable rights and principles enshrined in the U.S. Declaration of Independence and the French Declaration of the Rights of Man to fight for freedom and happiness, all part of the philosophical scaffolding that Martí used in his pursuit of Cuban independence.

According to Castro, the revolutionary struggle would undoubtedly succeed because Cubans were living in intolerable conditions: Unemployment, housing shortages, lack of health care, and educational opportunities—particularly for the rural poor—would persuade people that an alternative model of government was necessary. There would be widespread support for his revolutionary laws, with programs that would include land redistribution, worker profit-sharing, and the return to the public of properties and resources stolen by Batista. Agrarian and educational reforms would be the cornerstone of his revolutionary platform. Social justice would indeed be a guide to future policies and one of the rhetorical pillars of the Revolution. Furthermore, he said, Cubans yearned for a country free of foreign control. Foreign holdings, particularly those from U.S. firms and citizens, would be nationalized and expropriated, as would the electricity and telephone companies Compañía Cubana de Electricidad and Compañía Cubana de Teléfonos. Castro's revolution would be the culmination of Cuba's long march toward independence. A few years later, he would baptize his fight as the culmination of 100 Years of Struggle from the first blood shed for independence in 1868 to 1968.[24]

Another source of legitimacy from the past was the 1940 Cuban Constitution, which becomes a leading character in Castro's speech and in his vision for his revolutionary movement. It was the violation of the Constitution that provided the basis for his claim that the Batista government was illegitimate, and its restoration became one of the promises made by Castro to the Cuban people as a rectification of history. It should be noted here that, by most legal standards, the 1940 Constitution was one of the most progressive documents in the Americas, as it included individual rights as well as economic and social ones. It guaranteed equality to everyone regardless of race, gender, religion, and class. It stated that every citizen had the right to a job as well as to fair compensation for work done. It framed an unprecedented educational nationalist agenda that even prescribed that every class on any Cuban subject had to be taught by teachers born in Cuba using textbooks also written by island-born authors. It declared that culture, in all its manifestations, is of primary interest to the state and should be protected. It was a document that called for a democratic state, one in which there would be a separation of powers and where people were guaranteed individual liberties as well as the right to vote. It outlawed the death penalty except in military courts.[25]

About mid-point in the courtroom speech, Castro switches from detailing historical events and social indicators to telling a story to make a point. "Once upon a time," he says, "there was a Republic. It had a constitution, its laws, its freedoms, a president, a congress and courts of law. Everyone could assemble, associate, speak, and write with complete freedom. The people were not satisfied with the government officials at that time, but they had the power to elect new officials . . . public opinion was respected and heeded, and all problems of common interest were freely discussed. There were political parties, radio and television debates and forums, and public meetings . . ." He continues, "One morning the citizens woke up dismayed . . . a man named Fulgencio Batista had just perpetrated the appalling crime that no one expected . . . the crime was of dispensing with the Constitution."[26] In this passage, the immediate past of a short-lived republican experience is used as justification for rebellion. Eventually, his battle cry of restoring the Constitution resonated throughout the island and found support among middle- and upper-class Cubans who would become the backbone of the insurrection.

History as Judge

Beyond his philosophical views about social justice, democracy, and freedom, Fidel Castro's understanding of the past in *History Will Absolve Me* is important to examine.[27] He assigns history the power to judge. In this role, the past is ascribed the role of judging the verity or correctness of present action at some future date. It is a temporal move that straddles the past and jumps into the future, thus avoiding any accountability in the present.

By ascribing this role to history, Castro reveals an authoritarian, not a democratic view of social processes. Classical history evolves from literary genre to "judge" as it begins to expect proofs, not just rhetoric, to develop its narratives. In 1769, the Jesuit Henri Griffet was one of the first to articulate this evolution when he compared history to a judge, thus moving history from storytelling to a discipline that had rules and procedures on how to obtain and accept renditions of the past. Hegel further developed this concept when he declared history to be the world's court of justice. Human actions would eventually be evaluated from the present and looking back, he said. The court of history would render a final judgment. But in contrast to Griffet, Hegel was more interested in the judge's sentence, not necessarily the process of carefully evaluating evidence.[28]

Castro, who studied with the Jesuits at Colegio de Belén in Havana, summoned history to be the judge as well, even though he confined its jurisdiction to the nation, not the world, as Hegel did. He stated that he was compelled to do so because his actual judges—the military ones—were representing an illegitimate government. It would be up to history to judge his actions and to absolve him. And he was sure he would be absolved. Note that he did not say that history would weigh the evidence and then render a decision; rather it would simply absolve him. In this aspect, his conception of history was closer to Hegel's than it was to the historiography that had evolved from evidentiary practices, namely a history that searched and verified factual knowledge. Castro emphasized its movement toward judgment, which brought him closer to the "final judgment" view of history, one with roots in Christianity's idea that God would issue the final verdict on whether a person's life has been worthy or not. Missing in Castro's conception of history was Hegel's proposition that history moves toward the goal of individual freedom, underscoring the influence of theology and Christianity in Castro's thoughts.

Hannah Arendt noted that the move from religious to secular history in the eighteenth century became a search for meaning and recognition. But, she warned, history was not a process but rather an accumulation of experiences. When history did not reflect the totality of experiences and instead was told with tales of heroic deeds as a way of giving them eternal life,[29] myths were created. Secular heroic deeds in the Cuban Revolution were given a religious connotation. Like Jesus and the twelve disciples, so it was twelve comrades and brothers who survived out of the eighty-two men who sailed the yacht *Granma* from Tuxpan, Mexico, to Playa Las Coloradas in Cuba to liberate the island. A postcard with a painting by José A. Sarol entitled "Nuestro Che" showed the Argentine-born revolutionary in a jungle setting with tropical vines circling his head, giving the impression that he was wearing a crown of thorns.

Secular heroes were transformed into quasi-religious figures, thus further separating them from earthly accountability.

History from this perspective is an unmediated force that holds the power to absolve human behavior and actions. There is one history, and it stands above human action. It has the power to judge and to decide what is right or wrong, and from Castro's point of view, this meant the power to decide which deeds had been done for the good of others and which for the self-interest of a few. While history has been summoned to judge on many

Figure 1.1. "Nuestro Che," José A. Sarol, 1978 postcard. Courtesy of the author.

occasions,[30] for Castro, it also had the power to absolve. Indeed, it would absolve him.

This history does not have a participatory process that contributes to setting up an ethical code through which personal behavior could be socially mediated. There is no process to decide the rules with which to gather proof or debate its meanings. Moral behavior is implicit and expected. This conception of history is difficult to reconcile with the democratic tradition reflected in the Cuban Constitution of 1940. A more egalitarian understanding of history would not give history the role of "judge," but rather that of "facilitator"—one that creates a space in which contested memories can be debated and reinterpreted; a space in which multiple individuals can "re-member" the past. In this role, there is not an assumption that there will only be one conclusion; instead, a more open history leaves itself open to multiple interpretations that can accommodate individual experiences and memories.

Without this more open understanding of history, a more open governing process is difficult to envision and achieve. The alternative is an authoritarian form of government, which according to the main rhetorical argument in *History Will Absolve Me* is precisely what had betrayed the course of Cuban history to begin with.

The Past as a Legitimizing Force for State Building

History plays a critical role in justifying the present, particularly in legitimizing the authority of leaders and in building a state. This is done in a variety of ways. One is by telling stories that highlight past struggles toward a common goal. In the case of Cuba, it was about its sovereignty. The nation was forged in an anti-colonial struggle against Spain at the end of the nineteenth century, culminating in the war of 1898, an episode that is still alive, not only in a collective historical memory, but in a lived memory as well. In my own individual case, my great-grandfather Aurelio Vigil fought against the Spaniards and was tortured for his participation in the War for Independence. The story of how his fingers were broken and deformed, making it impossible for him to continue his trade as a tailor, was part of our family's lived experience. In Cuba, the past is recounted as one continuous struggle where the heroes are those who fight for independence and sovereignty, and martyrs become revered legends. Other participants are written out of history.[31] A nation's official history is told as a story of wars and conflicts, heroes, victors, and losers, a process that homogenizes the past to create only one inevitable conclusion.[32] Indeed, Castro carefully crafted his actions within a narrative of past heroes. Political memory becomes a war zone, as will be discussed later in this chapter. History itself becomes an arm in this battle.[33]

Another critically important component to the ways that history is used to legitimize the present is by emphasizing a unitary process with one goal. History has a beginning, one goal, and an inevitable end. In the case of Cuba, it was the one hundred years of struggle for independence, interrupted by U.S. military interventions that began with the incursion of Teddy Roosevelt and his legendary Rough Riders. The Spanish left in 1898, and independence from the United States was finally achieved with the triumph of the Revolution in 1959. Cuba's one-hundred-year-old struggle would culminate in the revolution led by Fidel Castro. As Arendt has noted, history, as a legitimizing force for totalitarian governments, comes from the interpretation that it has one direction and it has a purpose dictated by the

34 · Democracy and Time in Cuban Thought

laws of history. In some ways, while this is supposedly a secular process, the laws of nature simply substitute for metaphysical explanations.[34]

With the victory over Batista, the Cuban Revolution's history had to be written as a tale of heroes and enemies, a civil war.[35] Opponents were homogenized despite their great diversity. Those who opposed the Revolution went from being called counterrevolutionaries, to anti-Castro, and ultimately to anti-Cuban, as the Revolution, the figure of Fidel Castro, and the nation itself were bundled into an inseparable entity called *La Revolución*. Those in favor of the regime became its heroes; Frank País, who was killed in 1957, and Camilo Cienfuegos, who was killed in the first year after the triumph of the Revolution, were sanctified by the regime. A few years later, Ernesto "Che" Guevara left the country to launch international insurrections, first in what was then known as the Congo, and later in Latin America. In 1967, he was killed in the lowlands of Bolivia. He, too, would become an embalmed hero of the Revolution, while his diary from the failed expedition in the Congo, which began with the phrase, "This has been a failure . . ." was repressed for decades. Heroes, after all, cannot admit failures.

But the history constructed about the revolutionary insurrection became unidimensional and did not accommodate the multiplicity and diversity of men and women, groups, and events that contributed to the social and political momentum that led to it. Prior to the Revolution, there had been many movements that sought to bring social justice and democracy to the island. Curiously, although Castro claimed to be the heir to the mantle of a century-long war, the details of that history are blurred and somehow leap from Martí and Maceo to Fidel Castro. Omitted were the struggles of Black Cubans, who fought against the segregation imposed by the United States during its military occupation in the early 1900s[36] and who continued to organize in professional and political groups until shortly after the Revolution, when independent organizing was criminalized.

The thirties had been marked as well with struggles for democracy that the Revolution only selectively recognized. President Gerardo Machado, a general of the Cuban War of Independence, had been elected by wide margins in 1924. Despite a presidency marked by rampant corruption and a vocal opposition that came mainly from students and unions, he was reelected in 1928. A popular uprising supported by many organizations, most under the umbrella of what became known as ABC—for the letters that had been assigned to underground cells—succeeded in ousting him from power. The army supported this movement, and Fulgencio Batista, then a young sergeant, helped shepherd their support.

The next two decades would witness the rise of nationalist populism, which in part resulted in the forward-looking Constitution of 1940. There were multiple attempts to establish democratically elected governments. In fact, in 1940, Batista ran successfully for president with the backing of unions and the Democratic Socialist Coalition, which included the Partido Socialista Popular (Popular Socialist Party, PSP), Cuba's communist party. After his hand-picked candidate lost the following presidential election, Batista left for the United States. In the subsequent years, new political leaders equally critical of the country's major party, the Partido Auténtico (Authentic Party), and of Batista, emerged. One movement that captured the imagination of the country was headed by Eduardo Chibás, who organized the Partido Ortodoxo (Orthodox Party). Through his radio programs, Chibás sought to instill a nationalist pride in the citizenry as well as outrage over the corruption of politicians.[37] The death of Chibás—a suicide by some accounts, a stunt gone wrong by others—left a vacuum in the national leadership. Batista returned to Cuba to run for the presidency in 1952, but as he was losing in the polls, he staged a military coup.

Yet Chibás's activism, along with the work of other movements, laid the groundwork for a popular insurrection against Batista. The following seven years would witness an explosion of civic and labor mobilization as well as armed insurrection. A noteworthy book is Lillian Guerra's *Heroes, Martyrs, and Political Messiahs in Revolutionary Cuba, 1946–1958*. She describes this period as a time when Cuba was "on the verge of a truly dramatic, democratic change."[38] In her study, Guerra brings to life the massive nature of the insurrection against Batista and the political culture of resistance that developed along with it. And she highlights the formation of the Partido Ortodoxo and the regrouping of intellectuals who had lived the disillusionment of the Machado regime, as well as the Federación de Estudiantes Universitarios (Federation of University Students), another critical democratizing social movement.

The official story of the insurrection de-emphasizes the role of the young members of Directorio Revolucionario Estudiantil (Student Revolutionary Directorate) under the leadership of José Antonio Echeverría. While Echeverría is acknowledged, the impact that the group had had is minimized. Many in the group had close ties to Acción Católica (Catholic Action) and other Catholic youth groups; were affiliated with Villanueva, Havana's Catholic University; and were inspired by their faith in social justice. The Directorio's most visible act was the attempted assassination of Batista at the Presidential Palace in 1957. Yet the operation, which included the taking over of Havana's premier radio station to announce Batista's death (prematurely, it turned out) backfired. Batista had stepped out of his office and his guards were able to stave off the attack. Over forty rebels, including Echeverría, were killed.

Today, many recognize that the Directorio's urban arena was a far more dangerous battleground than the second front Castro established in the Escambray Mountains in central Cuba, but the Directorio is barely recognized in the official story of the Revolution.[39] The Revolution's version of history did not have room for competing groups, especially groups that ended up opposing the authoritarian nature of the post-insurrection regime. Despite the multiplicity of organizations and individuals active in the insurrection against Batista, the history of the Revolution emphasizes one, Castro's 26th of July Movement. Indeed, years later, the filmmaker and novelist Jesús Díaz would write a novel about the urban insurrection, *Iniciales sobre la Tierra* (Initials over the Earth), which would be suppressed for twelve years until it was finally published in Spain.

If groups critical of the victorious Revolution needed to be obliterated from history, so did any emerging opposition to Castro's move to centralize power. Those challenging the direction of the new Castro regime were delegitimized and stigmatized as enemies. Such was the case of dissidents like Huber Matos, one of the commanders of the Revolution who voiced concern about Castro's embrace of socialism. He was tried for treason and sedition and sentenced to twenty years in jail. Some Cuban historians of the Revolution openly declared that the only valuable history was the one forged by the faithful revolutionaries. Indeed, the history of Fidel Castro. It is significant that, in 1989, during an acute economic crisis, one of the few institutes that continued to be handsomely funded by the Cuban Government was the Communist Party's Instituto de Historia (History Institute), which had been tasked with writing the history of Fidel Castro and the Revolution. History had become the pyramids of the Cuban Revolution.

Philosophical Underpinnings of Authoritarianism

The view of history as a unidimensional moving force is usually accompanied by the idea that it moves through predictable stages toward a predetermined goal. For Hegel, despite all its ambiguities, history's sequence of events represents an intrinsically rational process of the unfolding of the absolute spirit—roughly translated to culture—that seeks through humanity to reach complete freedom. Each attempt is superseded by a new development that builds and expands on the previous one. Thus, history is the place in which the human search for freedom is worked out.

After Hegel, the next major philosophical revision of notions of history came from Marx, who viewed history as a march toward progress in his conception of Historical Materialism. In early Marx, the propelling force of historical change was class struggle. Later he would come to emphasize tensions in property relations and material conditions. For Hegel and Marx, the direction of history is toward the future. Both sought to find universal perspectives, not just a nationalist one. History has an independent course as well as an end. For Hegel, it was free society; for Marx, it was advanced communism. They both thought that outcome would be first reached in Europe.

Few would deny that social forces shape events. What is questionable, however, is the predictive outcome of the future from the past. And the uncritical acceptance that history supersedes human agency.

The Cuban Revolution operated with two historical temporalities: a break from the past and a construction of a future society.[40] History served as a backdrop both to justify tragedy and to claim progress.[41] Ironically, the past became the roadmap for a political struggle and would continue to be an arena for claiming legitimacy. But there was a temporal leap from 1898 to the 1950s. The nation's past, which was rich with organizations, plurality, and men and women of action, was selectively narrated. Indeed, the deep connections between Batista's nationalist populism and Castro's radical nationalism were erased by presenting the recent past as an aberration, a pseudo-republic that interrupted that noble march toward independence. Also de-emphasized were the struggles of Afro-Cubans for equality after the War of Independence, the students' mobilization in the 1930s, and the labor movements in the 1940s and 50s organized by the Partido Socialista Popular. There were certain figures from the past that were elevated and celebrated, like Julio Antonio Mella. But the official history re-edifies only one main living hero, and that was Fidel Castro, who accepts the torch of history to fulfill the historic destiny of creating an independent nation.

Despite the consolidation of the Communist Party in Cuba in 1965 and Castro's vow to adhere to Marxism-Leninism, the rendition of the past as the story of one hero and one revolution mimics not Marx's but rather modernity's crude way of thinking about human history itself. For Arendt, a flattened rendition of history was exactly what allowed totalitarianism to emerge.[42] It paved the way for the declaration of a sole authority and sustained claims for a singular party with a singular ideology. It also became the basis for claiming exceptionalism.[43]

The tendency toward claiming exceptionalism was part of early modernity's ethos. The age of invention and discovery in the nineteenth century was not concerned with finding a way of connecting the world, but rather of declaring superiority over the past. The era was unconcerned with the past as time marched forward. Monumentalist-constructed renditions of history, that is, history that emphasizes and enlarges certain events, encouraged autocratic and antidemocratic political formations. Unlike liberal regimes that lay claim to their legitimacy by speaking for the majority, communist regimes lay claim to their legitimacy by citing a state of war.[44] In Cuba, this war finds its culmination in the victory of the revolutionary upheaval of the 1950s. It could be said that this then would have been the end of Cuban history, since the march of history was toward this victory and once it was achieved, national destiny ceased to exist as well: the nation had been accomplished. But during the next decades, the United States was made to be a constant enemy and threat to the island. Cuban society was in permanent war mode.[45]

The promise of the restoration of the 1940 Constitution had played a dominant role in the Cuban Revolution's efforts to recapture the recent past, yet its democratic articles were never reinstated. Immediately after the triumph of the Revolution, Castro declared that elections would be held within a year. Shortly thereafter, he promised that elections would be held after illiteracy and poverty were eradicated. But within months, Castro offered that it was unnecessary to hold elections since the majority of the people, as evidenced by the frequent mass rallies he conducted, supported his revolutionary government. In order to have elections, there would have to be opposition, which he argued did not exist. Those who opposed him were dismissed and stripped of their "Cubanness" since they were siding with the historic enemy, the U.S. In fact, his discourse went, why hold elections since the first task of the Revolution had now become restoring social justice and political morality. On May 1, 1960, in front of a crowd of thousands of cheering Cubans, he asked, *Elecciones, para qué?* (Elections, for what?) Eliminating the past and instituting a new regime was paramount, not establishing democracy.

Two months later, in celebrating the seventh anniversary of the assault on Moncada, Castro addressed the crowds again. This time, he challenged those who claimed he had betrayed his own platform as elaborated in the manifesto *History Will Absolve Me*. Castro declared that Cuba was a true democracy. He said, "Those who speak of communist infiltration are enemies of the Revolution and defending class interests. The crowds that assemble publicly are true expressions of democracy." He added, "Those who want to find out what the real word democracy means should come to Cuba. Our democracy is so pure that we can compare it to the first that existed in the world, such as the Greek democracy, where the people discussed and decided their fate in the public square."[46]

As opposition mounted, the Castro government tightened the reins of control. The right to rebel, which had been so eloquently defended by Castro as he declared that revolution was the right of those who were attempting to restore the Constitution, was denied to those who rebelled against him. He had argued this right was established in Article 40 of the 1940 Constitution, as well as rooted in Western thought. That it came from Montesquieu's *The Spirits of Laws,* which posited that power lay in the sovereignty of people, not in one person's interpretation of the law. Back in 1953, Castro had reminded the judges of his military tribunal that even philosophers in ancient China and India had upheld the principle to resist arbitrary authority. It was a principle that could be found in the political writings of the Greeks and the Romans, and throughout the Middle Ages, including in the writings of St. Thomas Aquinas. He had made references to the writings of John Milton, Jean-Jacques Rousseau, and John Locke, and to their legacies in the narratives of the French and American Revolutions, all of which justified uprisings with the right to rebel against despotic governments. In post-revolutionary Cuba, however, rebellion was not only outlawed and quelled, but those who opposed the Castro regime were subjected to summary trials and sentenced to death by a firing squad, imprisoned, or exiled.

A major point of contention with the new Castro regime became the protection of freedom of expression, a right that had been guaranteed by the 1940 Constitution. The first major clash between intellectuals and the revolutionary government came shortly after the 1961 Bay of Pigs invasion, the U.S.-backed operation aimed at toppling the Castro regime. The object of contention was *PM,* a short documentary by Orlando Jiménez Leal and Sabá Cabrera Infante about Havana nightlife.[47] The black-and-white documentary follows a group of men getting off *el barquito de Regla,* the ferry that connects Regla, a municipality on the Havana Bay, to the mainland, and arriving at a small bar where people, mainly Afro-Cubans, are dancing and drinking. In colonial times, Regla was known as a center for piracy, and during the 1900s as an important place for Santería, one of the Afro-Cuban

40 · Democracy and Time in Cuban Thought

religions. It is hard to imagine why *PM* was so offensive to some of Castro's close allies, but they objected.

Cuba's top intellectuals were called to an emergency meeting at the Biblioteca de la Habana (Havana library). It would become the last time that many would dare to challenge Fidel Castro publicly and to defend intellectual freedom. During the meeting, Castro admitted that he had not seen *PM*, but added that he had been assured it did not represent the appropriate mood the country needed at the time. Perhaps it was indulgent to think about pleasure, particularly racialized pleasure, at a time of war; regardless, what happened next would set the tone for decades to come. When pressed about artistic freedom, Castro responded, "Within the Revolution, everything. Against the Revolution, nothing."[48] The cultural supplement *Lunes de Revolución*, the official newspaper of the 26th of July Movement, which had positively reviewed the documentary, was shut down. The revolutionary government was beginning to rewrite its own history to suit its needs and destroying its own tools of propaganda in the process.

A form of selective memory operates in times of rapid change, particularly when a new political regime is trying to consolidate power.[49] A form of mythic memory, as opposed to history, helps simplify often conflicting central themes. This in turn makes it easier for the state to enforce its version of memory on the populace. When this fails, repression and banishment become arms with which to silence the present and to create a particular view of history.[50]

Whether or not the promises made by Fidel Castro in *History Will Absolve Me* were fulfilled or ignored still frames the debate over whether or not he betrayed the Revolution. The failure to call for elections in 1959 and the subsequent repression of individual freedoms led many to say that the Revolution had been betrayed. But the notions of history implicit in Castro's 1953 manifesto foreshadowed his authoritarian government, since he conceived history as a singular force moving in one predetermined direction, led by one man who had inherited its mantle.

Exile and Return: The Making of an Official Past

The Cuban Revolution was initially a radical nationalist movement against the Batista government and inclusive of broad sectors of the Cuban population. Yet the regime it engendered was not. Beginning in 1959, Castro consolidated his power through mass mobilization, fear, and repression of the opposition. Emigration surged. Over the next six decades, more than one

Figure 1.2. Fidel Castro, Moncada, 1953. Photo 12 / Alamy Stock Photo.

million Cubans would leave the island. This massive exodus questioned the very premise of a nationalist revolution, and as such, the government has been very careful in crafting its explanations for it. After all, if a government could not contain its citizens, could it claim to represent the nation? Controlling the historical narrative of emigration as well as the history of exile became crucial for the competing power elites on both sides of the Florida Straits. Their historical renditions justified their geographic and political positions.

Stories born of wars easily lend themselves to being told through heroes and villains. From the early days after the Revolution, staying in or leaving Cuba became a litmus test of loyalty or betrayal—heroism or cowardice. In this terrain, dichotomous renditions of events were spun to constitute narratives that justified over sixty years of hostilities between those who stayed and those who left. Depending on the vantage point, island or exile, people were not merely leaving, they either were abandoning their homeland or escaping persecution and political repression. The earliest film to treat the subject of contradictory feelings about family divisions was 1968's *Memories of Underdevelopment,* directed by Tomás Gutiérrez Alea. Based on an eponymous novel[51] by Edmundo Desnoes, the film follows the internal thoughts of a wealthy writer who decides to stay in Cuba despite the departure of his family members, who are depicted as traitors to the Revolution.

Contacts between family members were discouraged and some aspects were criminalized by the regime. Until 1978, both the Cuban and U.S. governments had legal prohibitions that impeded family contacts.[52] Travel between the two countries was forbidden. Cubans leaving the island were not allowed to return, while U.S. residents were not allowed to travel to Cuba. On the island, maintaining contact with relatives and friends abroad was a sign of ideological weakness to the point that those who did were denied certain jobs and educational opportunities. Mail service was slow, and in Cuba, letters were systematically opened. Deteriorating underwater telephone cables made long-distance calling difficult, and it was common knowledge that calls were under surveillance by state security.

Exiles became the political "others," a process reinforced by derogatory terms, images, and narratives constructed in political speeches and cultural products. Those who left were called *gusanos* (worms) and *escoria* (scum) and ultimately branded as anti-Cuban. Conversely, those who stayed were seen by exiled Cubans as lackeys of the regime and opportunists. Advocating for contact on either side was seen as suspicious.

However, in the mid-1970s, young Cuban exiles in the United States initiated a movement to return to the island of their childhood. Under the auspices of *Joven Cuba* and *Areíto,* magazines published by progressive Cuban Americans, two groups came together and started lobbying the Cuban government to allow them to travel back to their homeland. Initial suspicions from the Cuban government eventually dissolved and formalized exchanges began. Out of these early visits, the Brigada Antonio Maceo was formed. I was part of this movement. Our return to Cuba challenged the political dichotomy that had been erected between the island and the exile community, even though in some ways they re-edified the dichotomy since many of us at the time were sympathetic to the Revolution. Our trips were met with hostility and even acts of terrorism in Miami, and also fueled political propaganda on the island. Carlos Muñiz, a twenty-six-year-old Brigade member from Puerto Rico, who had helped establish a travel agency to facilitate travel to Cuba, was killed in April 1979.[53] Omega 7, an anti-Castro terrorist group, took credit for his killing. No one to date has been detained or tried for his murder but it has been noted that many of these groups were infiltrated by Cuban security agents. On the island, we were symbols of the bankruptcy of exile, the sons and daughters of traitors seeing the light their parents had failed to appreciate.

The story of our exodus and our return home with the Brigada Antonio Maceo became the stuff of documentaries, films, and plays. In the movie *55 Hermanos,* Jesús Díaz, at the time an official filmmaker, follows the first group of fifty-five *Brigadistas* (Brigade members) as they travel the island, meet relatives, party, and share their stories of exile and return. Theatergoers would often leave the screenings crying. Several of the *Brigadistas* were Pedro Pan children, and their stories began to create a level of sympathy on the island for the children who had been taken out of the country. Books like *Contra Viento y Marea* narrated these stories, while some of the island's artists wove this material into their cultural production.[54] Leading actress and theater director Flora Lauten's play *Principito,* for example, takes a scene from *55 Hermanos* in which a young woman climbs the stair up to the terrace of her childhood home and remembers how she used to fly kites. When the *Brigadistas* finally meet with Castro, and they ask him about the possibility of returning to the island to live, he responds that it had come to his attention that there was a strong sentiment to return, but that it needed to be studied, and that perhaps the group would be more useful for the Revolution returning to the United States.[55]

For me, returning to Cuba became a way of discovering a past—my family's and my own childhood.[56] It was also a search for political alternatives. We had rituals: visiting the house in which we were raised, connecting with island relatives, developing friendships, and constructing a collective memory. I had left Cuba, unaccompanied, at the age of six; my cousins had as well, some ending up in foster homes and others temporarily living with relatives until their parents could join them. Being in Cuba with others who had left under similar circumstances gave us a context and indeed a narrative of our journeys as unaccompanied minors. It was while in Cuba that I learned our departure had been part of something called Operation Pedro Pan.

If there is a singular chapter of Cuban immigration that has become an arena of mythmaking for both the Cuban government and its opposition, it is Operation Pedro Pan. "Definitive" narratives of the exodus of children were forged both on the island and in the exile community in the United States. For the exiles, sending the unaccompanied children to the United States became the myth of origin for the community: the story of a child who

44 · Democracy and Time in Cuban Thought

led others to safety—a myth that has been repeated in multiple iterations in religious and secular narratives. There was no more poignant example of the horrors of communism than that of parents' desperate attempts to save their children from indoctrination. The ultimate sacrifice was separating from one's children. The Pedro Pan children became heroes. And indeed, some grew up to become accomplished businesspersons, politicians, artists, performers, and writers who have contributed to the myth of the success of the Pedro Pans. These include Mel Martínez, the first Cuban American ever elected to the U.S. Senate; Eduardo Aguirre, a businessperson and former U.S. Ambassador to Spain; Ana Mendieta, a noted visual artist; and Willy Chirino, the popular music performer, among others.

Conversely, on the island, Pedro Pan became a tale of how the nation had been robbed of its future. In this narrative, we were victims of one of the most infamous crimes against Cuban children ever perpetrated.[57] Cuban renditions of Pedro Pan stories in films emphasize the cruelty of family separations. Even Fidel Castro wrote about Operation Pedro Pan in *Granma's Reflexiones* column, using part of my own research to show that the United States had shut the door to parents who were still in Cuba, unable to reunite with their Pedro Pan children. Conveniently, he never mentioned that I also documented how the Cuban government would not allow the children to return to the island. Cuba too, not just the United States, had shut the door to family reunification.

Contesting Official Narratives

Debates about the nature and history of Operation Pedro Pan have erupted throughout the last twenty years. Getting to the facts has been difficult, because technically this was a secret operation run at the margins of U.S. congressional oversight. Indeed, during congressional hearings about Cuban immigration in general, when a representative asked about the unaccompanied minors, the hearing was moved to a closed session, as the program was classified. Only fragments of Operation Pedro Pan are known, and what is still kept secret contributes to the mythmaking.[58]

In the early nineties, an article in *The Miami Herald* suggested that there were more complicated motives to the operation than simply saving children.[59] Around this time, I had begun a book project that eventually became *The Lost Apple: Operation Pedro Pan, Children in the U.S., and the Promise of a Better Future*. The research process took ten years and included interviews with parents, members of the Cuban dissident underground, governmental officials in the U.S. and in Cuba, and participating children, now adults. I also made extensive use of Freedom of Information Act requests, and when the CIA balked and denied them, I successfully sued, but only received some of the documents. I was working with a colleague from the University of Havana who was given access to some of the Cuban records. Cuba, too, has many more documents in secret storage.

Still, I was able to piece together a more complex picture of the operation, and the book was met with mixed reactions. Some Pedro Pans have reduced the book to my findings on the CIA's involvement in the operation, as if being critical of the U.S. government somehow translated to support for the Cuban government. Even more curious was their defense of the CIA's role in the Pedro Pan exodus, given the agency's reputation of betraying Cuba's dissident underground. Many others, however, including members of the anti-Castro underground, praised the book, among them many who had stories to tell about how their own children had fared poorly under the care of the U.S. government and the Catholic Church. Albertico Campanería, whose brother, Virgilio, was one of the many young men killed by a firing squad at La Cabaña prison days before the Bay of Pigs invasion, sent me a message through my mother, thanking me for telling a story that resonated with his experiences. He had sent his daughter to the United States while he was fighting in the underground and felt she had not been well cared for. He felt doubly betrayed by the CIA, first for their failure to support the invading forces during the Bay of Pigs, and then by the neglect of his daughter.

Other Pedro Pans wanted to understand their plight and were eager to hear a more complex version of their own history. One was Elly Chovel, who, at the time I met her, was organizing a group of Pedro Pans in Miami and was serving as its president. She had persuaded Monsignor Bryan Walsh, the person in charge of Pedro Pan in Miami in the 1960s, that the now-grown children needed to explore their stories, including aspects that did not fit neatly into the official, heroic narratives. Chovel invited me to join the group at their yearly gatherings. Both joyful and painful memories were shared, and difficult questions explored. In 2001, in one of these annual gatherings, seventy-five Pedro Pans met at Barry College in Miami. Someone asked if anyone knew how many Pedro Pans had been separated from their parents for a long time. There are no official numbers, but Monsignor Walsh responded, "Not many." I asked the group how many of those present had been separated for long periods of time from their parents;

46 · Democracy and Time in Cuban Thought

almost thirty of the participants raised their hands. We now know there were 8,000 children still unaccompanied in the United States when the U.S. shut the door to flights from Cuba.

The challenge to the organizer's version of the history of Pedro Pan was done respectfully. No one tried to impose a single memory for all Pedro Pans or tried to claim that the group in attendance represented the views of the 14,000 Pedro Pans who had arrived in the U.S. in the early 1960s. This process, taking place in Miami, for a moment in time, encouraged democratic practices of listening and debating. A community was forming, made up of diverse members, from many walks of life and holding different political points of views, including views about relations with Cuba, which at the time was a polarizing issue. The occasion also allowed for personal stories of loneliness, isolation, abuse, and family separations to emerge and be told, contradicting U.S. official renditions and histories.

The debate about Pedro Pan erupted anew in 1999, when a six-year-old boy named Elián González survived a shipwreck in the Florida Straits in which his mother died. Elián was placed with distant relatives in Miami, and almost immediately a major international custody battle ensued, as the Cuban father tried to reclaim his child while anti-Castro Miami relatives refused to turn him over. The boy became the symbol of salvation for the exile community in Miami, and in Cuba, a symbol for its stolen children. Cintio Vitier, one of Cuba's national poets, compared the child to Moses, declaring that a boy would save the nation once again, and in the process imbued Cuban politics with religious references. Thousands of Cubans on the island were rallied by Fidel Castro to demand that the boy be returned. A book marker promoting the book *Operación Pedro Pan,* written by two retired Cuban military officials and released during this time, referred to Pedro Pans as the 14,000 *Eliancitos* (little Eliáns).

At the height of the saga, Chovel organized a birthday party for Msgr. Walsh at her home in Miami. The crew of the PBS documentary series *Frontline* was in town filming a documentary on the Elián controversy and were invited to interview Pedro Pans. Publicly, only a very few of us, including Chovel, offered the opinion that the boy should be returned to his father in Cuba. This position had been met with wrath by many Cubans in Miami. Yet as many Pedro Pans were interviewed, they privately admitted to the filmmakers that they, too, felt ambivalent about not letting the boy go back to his father. After all, many of them believed that they had been sent to the United States so that their parents could decide what kind of education they should receive. Shouldn't all parents have the same right, whether in Cuba or Miami? In 2000, Elián González was returned to Cuba, where he was welcomed back as a national hero.

The power of the myth of salvation was again displayed after the massive 2009 earthquake in Haiti, as the Catholic Charities of the Archdiocese of Miami launched a campaign to airlift and relocate to the United States Haitian children believed to have been orphaned by the disaster. They dubbed their efforts "Operation Pierre Pan." This time Msgr. Walsh, the priest who had facilitated the exodus of Cuban children, co-signed a letter advocating that the Haitian children should not be separated from their families. UNICEF also urged that the program be discontinued. Many of the "orphans" initially airlifted to the United States, it turned out, had parents in Haiti.

A few years later, CNBC produced a documentary about the original 1961 Pedro Pan Operation.[60] I was one of the many interviewed. By this time, Chovel had died, and the group she had founded had new leadership, one that believed in a more reductionist rendition of the program. In an open letter to CNBC, members of the organization objected to the critical views I expressed in the film, as well as to the views of other Pedro Pans who said the U.S. should normalize relations with Cuba.[61] In an email letter circulated among members of the group, someone contended that I was not a Pedro Pan. They based this on the idea that no "real" Pedro Pan would want to normalize relations with Cuba. Somehow, my views, which contradicted the official exile narrative of the redemption story, made me ineligible to claim my very own experience and place in its history. Ironically writers on the island who criticized the government met similar fates. In a poignant poem by Antón Arrufat titled "They" he laments how:

. . . One day they will come for me I can assure it . . .
They will call me, they know my name
Then they will expel me from classes
And from History . . .[62]

The myth of origin of the exile community, which manifests itself politically in the immigration debate today, continues to be anchored in the past. In the spring of 2022, debates in Florida about providing shelter for immigrant children and adolescents fleeing violence and uncertain futures in their homelands have divided Cubans, including, perhaps predictably, Pedro Pans. Some affiliated with Operation Pedro Pan—an organization that initially sought to unite all Pedro Pans, but that in recent years has taken a sharp ideological and political turn—were supporting Florida Governor Ron DeSantis, who had launched an ultraconservative campaign to bol-

48 · Democracy and Time in Cuban Thought

ster his national standing. He espoused a sweeping anti-immigrant agenda that included shutting down the Florida shelters that had been established for undocumented minors and shipping the young immigrants out of the state. In a press conference at the Cuban Diaspora Museum announcing measures to eliminate these shelters, DeSantis was flanked by several Pedro Pans. DeSantis said: "The organized effort to rescue the children of communist Cuba 50 years ago is a far cry from the Biden administration's disgraceful border disaster. Operation Pedro Pan was an organized, pre-planned program administered with visas and flight manifests to specifically rescue children from an oppressive communist regime."[63] In other words, it did not break any laws. The governor went on to say: "There's a lot of bad analogies that get made in modern political discourse, but to equate what's going on with the southern border . . . with Operation Pedro Pan, quite frankly is disgusting."[64]

To further distance the Pedro Pans' experience from that of today's unaccompanied minors and make a case for Cuban exceptionalism, Carmen Valdivia, the museum's executive director at the time and the head of the Operation Pedro Pan group, added, "We came into the hands of the Church, we had documents. None of us got lost; anything that had to do with us, our parents would be consulted." Valdivia also claimed that the Pedro Pan children were middle class, had come vaccinated, and under the authority of the government.

The backlash was immediate. Miami Archbishop Thomas Wenski weighed in, as did other Pedro Pans who felt that all children deserved safe haven. They pointed to the similarities between the two groups. In both cases, children and their families were fleeing from violence, and their parents, just like those of the Pedro Pans, were making the heart-wrenching decision to send them abroad. Contrary to the claims by the Florida governor that Operation Pedro Pan was a legal project, they said, there had been no established legal channels in the early 1960s by which the United States could process would-be Cuban exiles. The U.S. Embassy in Havana had been shut down. Nonetheless, federal agencies involved in the war against Castro created and operated classified visa-waiver programs on—and perhaps over—the margins of legal channels. One of these, and there were multiple such programs, was aimed at minors who, unlike adults, were not seen as a potential security risk. Through this program, Operation Pedro Pan, anyone under the age of sixteen could come into the United States with a mimeographed letter signed by a Catholic priest granting a visa waiver. It became one of the quickest ways to leave Cuba for those who did not have visas. Once in the United States, papers would be filed on the children's behalf to claim their parents, and if the parents passed a security check, they too received waivers. In a period of eighteen months, more than 14,000 unaccompanied Cuban children made it to the United States. More than half of the children had relatives here. Others were placed under the care of the Catholic Welfare Bureau, a predecessor of Catholic Charities. When the United States shut the immigration doors for Cubans in 1962, Cuba had already closed its doors to returnees, and more than 8,000 minors were left in the United States, unable to reunite with their parents for years.

Despite heightened national sentiment against communism at the time of the Pedro Pan program, popular opinion about the children's arrival in the U.S. was mixed. As news of the secret immigration program leaked out, Congress received hundreds of letters from irate Americans complaining bitterly about spending taxpayer dollars on foreigners; a particularly sore point was that the money was going through the Catholic Church. "It is a bold scheme by the Catholic Church to assure its future political power," one unhappy citizen wrote. Others worried that the children could be "communist spies sent to infiltrate the U.S." Miami politicians complained that the children would "change the complexion of the city."

Despite this pressure, three U.S. presidents, Eisenhower, Kennedy, and Johnson, continued to give Cubans safe haven and perhaps most importantly, continued to allow the children to "claim" their parents so they could come to the United States. It was a well-funded, welcoming program. By the turn of the century, there was no comparable national or state leadership speaking out for a humane welcoming of the children arriving at U.S. borders. Instead, immigration had become a wedge issue, one that corrupted the very essence of the American experience.

In 1965, flights between Cuba and the United States resumed, and most families were reunited. The same year, Congress passed an immigration reform act that made family reunification the cornerstone of U.S. immigration policy. A year later came the Cuban Adjustment Act, which legalized the immigration status for Cubans.

The tactics of writing someone out of history were at play when Carmen Valdivia went as far as to claim, falsely, that the Pedro Pans who wanted to keep the shelters open for the new immigrant children were not from Florida and therefore did not understand the situation. She was giving geography the power to legitimize her political views. She also lashed out at Sylvia Figueroa, a Pedro Pan who had opposed DeSantis's proposal and had been interviewed by a local reporter. Valdivia claimed that Figueroa was an imposter, since her name did not appear on then airport log that Msgr. Walsh had kept of the children as they arrived in the United States. In fact, the log, which has many errors, did include Sylvia's name—her maiden name; she had since acquired her husband's last name.

For some Pedro Pans, the idea that theirs was not an exceptional journey of salvation was threatening. There was comfort in a simplified view of the operation that glorified it as a rescue mission.[65] Somehow, this could assuage the cultural dislocation and other possible personal experiences that might have resulted from Operation Pedro Pan. Unfortunately, some believe that critiquing U.S. actions related to Operation Pedro Pan or comparing the exodus of Cuban children to that of contemporary immigrants minimizes the role that political repression had played in the decision by Cuban parents to send their children abroad. Instead, they want Operation Pedro Pan appreciated as a solely humanitarian gesture. However, viewing the Pedro Pan exodus exclusively through the salvation narrative leads to a story of heroes and villains, the stuff myths and Hollywood movies are made of, oversimplifying complex political and personal histories. Most telling of the process of imposing an official narrative have been the attempts by some in the leadership of the group to strip others of the right to their experiences when they do not like the views expressed by them.

The Limits of the Past

The mythmaking around Operation Pedro Pan can be seen and considered as an instance in which official narratives trump historical facts while attempting to obliterate individual memories that do not comport with them. Recollections of the official story become a ritual that works to shape a group identity. But many individual memories do not comport with collective memories. When there is a gap between individual and public memory, individuals can become alienated and be silenced.[66] Creating more inclusive accounts of the past is a complicated task. Those who dared raise questions about the suffering of some of the Pedro Pan children or perhaps questioned the program itself were cast aside. Those who draw parallels between their experiences and that of recent immigrants are also chastised, since they are seen as questioning the exceptionality of a "chosen people." Contradicting the official narrative can lead to being banished from the official history.

Conceptions of the past played multiple roles in the Cuban Revolution and its aftermath. During the insurrection against Batista, the past was a point to return to, exemplified by the proposal to restore the Constitution of 1940. It was a form of evoking heroic stories to mobilize public sentiment. The past also provided a platform for a revolutionary leader who claimed he was the undisputable heir to the mantle of his nation's history. The past, in the form of history, was given the authority to judge. But the reliance on the past as the temporal place in which human action is justified closes the possibilities of questioning in the present. The past bequeaths those in the present with a fixed roadmap and anoints heirs to the inevitable future as it moves in linear fashion though human action to a predetermined goal. This appreciation of history includes a vision of politics that privileges authoritarianism since it collapses complex experiences into a unidimensional space and with it obliterates the multiplicity of voices and re-edifies a sole authority.

The past can also become a place in which certain stories are enshrined. In the case of the Cuban Revolution and its aftermath, the past became militarized as tightly woven narratives were jealously guarded and counternarratives punished. The government promoted the narrative of a fearless leader who inherited the mantle of history and who now was charged with fulfilling his country's destiny. On the island, the past was used to claim authority in the present. In the exile community, there was a narrative of a lost past that drove a nostalgic politics.

Both on the island and in the exile community, simple myths about the origins of the Revolution and exile became arenas in which to engage in battles about contemporary political issues. Self-appointed guardians of "the truth," bidding for political power, guard official narratives that in turn are used to claim legitimacy in the present. They rely on repression and exclusion as a means to protect their versions of the past. Reliance on the past as a temporal point of reference for political projects has led to authoritarian forms of government on the island and a political culture of intolerance in the exile community.

2

The Future

> Along with the image of the multitudes marching toward the future comes the concept of institutionalization as a harmonious set of channels, steps, restraints, and well-oiled mechanisms which facilitate the advance, which facilitate the natural selection of those destined to march in the vanguard, and which bestow rewards on those who fulfill their duties and punishments on those who commit a crime against the society that is being built.
>
> Ernesto Che Guevara, *Socialism and Man in Cuba,* 1965

Without a moment to spare, the past rushes through the present and toward the future—a time after the present. If the past is an arena from which to extract legitimacy for contemporary political projects, the future then is the place where political projects mythically reside. The future was not always on the political horizon; it became a political space as modernity ushered in ideas about progress. In the nineteenth century, futuristic projects imagined the nation; in the twentieth, they envisioned the solidification of a nation perfected through revolutions. Latin American history—with prolonged searches for independent nationhood and later radical revolutions to perfect them—was, as Alejo Carpentier wrote in his book *Lo real maravilloso,* a chronicle of utopian impulse.[1]

Future temporalities framed both the Cuban struggle for independence and the 1959 Revolution. The Revolution itself unleashed a political imaginary that captivated an international political left that had become disillusioned by Joseph Stalin's destruction of the socialist utopia. The Cuban Revolution would become the savior of the lost utopic dream and reset its historic course. But the institutionalization of the Fidel Castro regime gave rise to waves of discontent. In fact, scholars have said that the crisis of revolution is indeed the crisis of the future itself. In other words, the future is now a thing of the past.[2] As the Cuban revolutionary project unraveled, the future in crisis has even become fodder for humor in the island—witness Utopito, a comic character created by the visual artist Pedro Pablo Oliva, a fellow who forgets the past, criticizes the present, and expects a better tomorrow.[3] Other artists have turned to the exploration and a literal definition of utopia—a no-place land evoking an empty and meaningless void.[4] Utopic aspirations have also fueled the Cuban diasporic imagination and its sensibility toward a temporal space.[5] "Next Year in Havana" became a mantra for nostalgic exiles longing to return to the motherland. By the new millennium, Miami was touted as the city of the future, transforming nostalgia into a bustling tourism industry and only looking forward.

But unlike the past, where facts and imagination can be contested, the future is open-ended, a blank slate onto which almost anything can be conjured. This is the power of the future in politics. It is also what limits a more democratic politics, since it is illusionary. In this chapter, I trace the emergence of the future as an arena for politics and look at the dynamics that utopianism unleashed. I then examine two instances in which the future shaped the contours of political possibilities: nation-building and revolution in Cuba. In the last segment, I look at how future temporalities limit democratic practices.

From Eternity to the Secular Future

Modernity generated and brought forth new ideas about the ability of human beings to control their destinies and transform previous notions about fate and time.[6] As secular movements somewhat eroded the power of the Church, the ability of human beings to control their own future through new ideas, work, and political organizations emerged. Soon the modern world's time clock began to replace a dominant religious concept of an eternal afterlife—of what comes after death. This transformation brought forth the rational project and with it a metamorphosis of that eternity to a secular future. It was at this very moment that the political future was born.

Modernity disrupts the present and creates something new, including the idea that the imperfect present can be easily transformed into a perfect future.[7] It separates past from present, allowing for a sense of newness to penetrate the future.[8] The rational project is at its core a futuristic one that assumes that, politically, the future can be controlled and the past can be projected onto the future. Modernity also frees the individual, albeit with the anxiety of the unknown and the "uncontrollable."[9] In this freedom lies the possibility of action toward the future, as Georg Friedrich Hegel once proposed. For him, the movement of history was akin to the spirit moving through time to a realizable goal of freedom. The secularization of freedom of action leads to a world not fixed but one defined by constantly changing progress.[10]

However, modernity also incorporates prescriptive laws of change. In modernity, history marches forward through predictable stages. As Hannah Arendt noted, the laws of nature and the laws of history became parallel yet distinct currents of thought that ran through the twentieth century and contributed to creating the momentum toward totalitarianism.[11] The laws of nature culminated in political regimes embracing notions of biological superiority of one group over another. The laws of history, instead, led to totalitarian regimes whose very legitimacy resided in their own appropriation of history. This last variation had multiple versions of the outcome, with stages of development that either predicted that society would move toward capitalism or toward advanced communism. In both cases, the future would be better than the previous stages: History, through its movement to the future, would correct itself.

These proposed laws were based on a central notion of a promise and the inevitability of progress. History and progress often merged to become a perpetual force that propels humanity forward. Technological advances at the dawn of modernity further exalted this momentum, as human beings acquired the power to sail across oceans to discover new lands and peoples. The "discovery" and the European expansion to the New World became intimately tied to the idea of inevitable progress and superiority.

But progress was not always embraced.[12] In fact, in the mid-1900s, philosophers and cultural critics warned that progress could end up taking humanity to a worse, not a better, future. The weight of the progress paradigm on politics has been criticized from various intellectual perspectives. Walter Benjamin pointed out how modernization collapsed human beings into classes, just as the present is bent by a messianic notion of progress that ultimately produces complacency.[13] We will see how this appears in the writings of Ernesto "Che" Guevara. For philosopher and cultural critic Friedrich Nietzsche, progress in the nineteenth century was a mere illusion, the eternal recurrence of the past lending itself to promises that could never be kept.[14] For critics of Marxism's perpetual optimism about the future, such as the twentieth-century Austrian-British social and political philosopher Karl Popper, progress had failed as a scientific theory to explain social phenomenon.[15] Somehow, human beings—their ingenuity, their failures, and their desires—were left out of the equation.

Progress throughout modern history has also been associated with imperialistic universalisms deeply embedded in modern science and Christianity.[16] The American pragmatist, social critic, and historian Lewis Mumford noted in the 1960s: "Today, the notion of progress in a single line without goal or limit seems perhaps the most parochial notion of a very parochial century."[17]

But the link most appropriate to our understanding of the Cuban situation is Arendt, who thought that modernization obliterated the individual into the masses, creating a breeding ground for totalitarian governments.[18] With a unidirectional construction of time and a narrative that emphasized monumental events, Arendt posited, it is almost impossible to have individual voices and agencies. As thus, the political future lent itself to forms of government and politics that were rarely or seldom democratic.

The Nation as Utopia: The Future in the Nineteenth Century

If the Christian notion of eternity held the promise of heaven or hell, the secular future—modernity's quintessential temporality—was imagined through utopias. Utopianism has been defined as social dreaming, a collective way of imagining new societies despite its original meaning in Greek: *there is no such place*.[19] Time-signified utopias came to include ecclesiastical and millennial promises of an inner-world redemption with provisions of happiness for the majority.[20] Religious radicalism, voyages of discovery, scientific progress, aspirations for a better society (inversely, future societies that were worse off) were all influenced by Christianity.[21] In some cases, social utopias were mere prescriptions of how to set up societies that would bring forth the best in humanity and guarantee peace and happiness. The early 1900s were filed with varying versions of these elaborations.

In all these projects, there was an assumption that the lived present was incomplete, and that it would only be completed once the future arrived.[22] As Mumford observed in the mid-1900s, "Utopia has long been another name for the unreal and the impossible. We have set utopia over against the world. As a matter of fact, it is our utopias that make the world tolerable to us: the cities and mansions that make people dream are those in which they finally live."[23] A key element in utopia is that of a "unified people" or one community. Indeed, part of the allure of utopia is precisely the promise of an idealized community to which we all belong. As French philosopher Michel Foucault observed, an ideal world of modernist literature lures all readers into the narrative: "Utopias afford consolation: although they have

56 · Democracy and Time in Cuban Thought

no real locality there is nevertheless a fantastic, untroubled region in which they are able to unfold; they open up cities with vast avenues, superbly planted gardens, countries where life is easy, even though the road to them is chimerical."[24]

The political utopias of the nineteenth century lured people into national narratives. These processes are key to understanding how future temporalities came to define Cuban politics. These utopias promised the building of inclusive communities. Nation-building is precisely based on imagining such communities.[25] The power of this utopic promise led men and women to sacrifice their lives for the nation—*Morir por la patria es vivir* (to die for the homeland is to live) is part of the Cuban national anthem. Death becomes a patriotic act that is glorified; the dead are enshrined as heroes of the nation.

The nation, as has been noted, brings together past and future temporalities, and when geographic space is added to this, a powerful bonding force that touches deep desires is created. In the case of Cuba, this two-step time dance between the past and the future led Louis A. Pérez Jr. to observe that the "aspirations to nation expanded simultaneously as an awareness of the past and a sense of the future, a process of both subversion and conversion, of displacement and replacement of a people at one and the same time engaged in the development of a narrative of nation and absorbed with ways of inserting themselves in it."[26] As early as the mid-1800s, people in Cuba could see themselves reflected in the future of the nation, even those who were new immigrants to the island.

The concept of the nation also unleashes a semantics of inclusion and exclusion. History becomes godlike, as embodied in Hegel's notion of the spirit, which in essence is a conception of freedom whose end it is to create the nation.[27] The nation becomes the Promised Land. And the nation becomes a place in which the past is embodied. As scholar of nation-states Ernest Renan wrote, nation is remembering although it can also be forgetting[28]—and I would add, a place where inconvenient truths are erased. Take for example the mysterious disappearance of the indigenous people of Cuba, who were literally killed out of history—their extinction blamed on the diseases brought to the New World by the conquering Spaniards. The racial "mixing" that occurred during colonization, which invariably included rape, is left out of the national narrative. (In the Cuban mythology, an exception is made for Hatuey, a leader of the Taínos who bravely stood up to those who were about to burn him at the stake, specifically the priest who tried to baptize him. As the priest attempted to administer last rites, Hatuey supposedly asked him if priests like him would go to heaven. When the priest responded yes, Hatuey declared that he would rather burn in hell. Still, the story suggests that indigenous people were exterminated, not raped, exploited, or suppressed.)

For Latin America, the dawn of the nineteenth century brought forth the end of the colonial era, of an old and fast-declining Spanish Empire, and the beginning of the building of national dreams. For some in the region, the United States, having launched the process of independence in 1776, became a model for independence movements. Dreams born of anti-colonial struggles envisioned sovereign nations, although there were multiple competing versions of what these would be like.[29] By the end of the nineteenth century, nation-building was also informed by modernity's notions of progress. As Pérez Jr. has observed, "The narrative of progress and modernity provided Cubans a compelling discursive framework in which to advance the proposition of the sovereign nation as a means of collective fulfillment."[30] Interestingly, even though Cuba's colonial situation lasted much longer than that of other countries in Latin America, the concept of the modern nation was taking root in the island early on, through repeated insurrections against Spanish rule.

All these nation-building projects, under the banner of the future—oftentimes depicted by an idealized image of a young woman wrapped in a flag and breaking free of chains—advocated for unity. They promised an ideal homogeneous nation, one that shared an economy, a political system, a culture, and a language, even though there was a diverse population already cohabiting the same space. This modernist notion of a unified culture and place are the underpinnings of a future nation. The appeal was so strong that it obfuscated the deep political, cultural, and racial differences that, in the long run, would erupt in conflict, as subgroups that did not see themselves reflected in the ideal nation became disenchanted. In some cases, these subgroups were blamed for the lack of progress of the nation itself.

The notion of individual nations was not the only utopic project that emerged in Latin America. The idea of homogeneity expanded to the entire hemisphere. Some independence leaders like Simón Bolívar in the early nineteenth century, and José Martí in that century's second half, advocated for Latin American nations to work together to promote regional unity. Bolívar envisioned a federation of like-minded states in his Letter from Jamaica, written in 1815.[31] Martí elaborated his vision in the essay *Nuestra América (Our America)*, written in 1891 and published in New York and Mexico.[32] While citing unique cultural practices in different parts of the

58 · Democracy and Time in Cuban Thought

region, Martí nonetheless paints a picture of a common Latin American culture. "There is no racial hatred because there are no races . . . Anyone who promotes and disseminates opposition or hatred among races is committing a sin against humanity."[33] This colorblind perspective glossed over the deep ethnic and racial divisions that have characterized Latin American and Caribbean populations, and it would not accommodate the lingering effects of slavery.

Nuestra América was also a call to arms. In the essay, Martí detailed the threat he perceived from the United States, and he set out to defend the sovereignty of Latin American republics, which in his eyes had a unique culture, mainly encased in history and geography. Latin America was distinct from North America. He warned of "The hour of unbridled passion and ambition from which North America may escape by the ascendency of the purest elements in its blood—or into which its vengeful and sordid masses, its tradition of conquest, and the self-interest of a cunning leader could plunge it."[34] In contrast Latin America had a nobler culture, one that was increasingly in tune with the "natural" man as it got rid of outside influences—namely the Spanish Empire. The document reaches a most utopic moment as it elaborates a series of values and traits that can contribute to a unified cultural identity and make Latin American culture superior to that of the United States. *Nuestra América* would go on to inform twentieth-century revolutionary projects and many U.S. Latino movements that called for a Pan-American identity. To an extent, a version of Martí's dream of political and cultural unity has become reality in the United States, as many communities originating from different parts of Latin America have coalesced, albeit with a lot of internal tensions, under what has been defined as an ethno-political category, Latinos.

Children and Future Temporalities

In modernity, children are constructed as the future. New societies require new people and as such, children are seen as the keys to a better future. Educating them is the task of nation-building, as their existential temporality is to be played out at some time to come. Martí's work in the realm of future temporalities conceived of children[35] as special and holding an important place in his imaginary of the nation. They were not only consumers of his stories, but they were also keys to building the new future nation. Indeed, the literature he wrote about and for them are windows into understanding how a future temporality was deployed at a critical moment of Cuban nationhood and politics.

Like Jean-Jacques Rousseau, Martí believed that youth was a special stage in life, one of "growth and development, activity and liveliness, imagination and impetuosity."[36] As children were naturally curious and experimental, educators needed to tailor their teachings to enhance these qualities and not deaden their intellect with rote memorization. Children needed to learn science as well as deepen their natural harmony with nature. For Martí, education should be both universal and secular. Even as his appreciation of girls was obviously still quintessentially of the nineteenth century, he believed girls, like boys, should receive an education. For him, Peter Cooper, the founder of the Cooper Union in New York, a school dedicated to giving boys and girls opportunities they otherwise did not have, was a saint, as he had given children of both sexes the gift of free education. Martí saw education as a right and believed that those who were educated had an obligation to teach others. He tied the destiny of a nation to its individuals, who needed to be educated as children. Happiness, another important concept of early modernity, was central in Martí's writings about education: The happiness of a nation is a direct result of the level of education of its citizenry. He wrote, "Happiness for a nation rests upon the individual independence of its inhabitants." This independence was tied to education.[37] Furthermore, just like the North American philosopher and educator John Dewey posited, Martí believed that democracies could only exist if there was an educated citizenry. "An instructed people will always be strong and free . . . the best way to defend our rights is to know them well; education was the only means of being saved from slavery. When all men know how to read, all men will know how to vote."[38] Education formed the citizen.

While Martí believed that all people had a shared humanity, he acknowledged that they also possessed distinct national characteristics shaped by culture and geography. Like other Latin American thinkers of his time— the Argentinian Domingo Sarmiento, for instance—Martí believed people were a product of their backgrounds and regions, and of the resources available in their immediate environments to satisfy them. Martí elaborated this deterministic view of human character after years of living in the United States, where he experienced racism and gained firsthand knowledge of the demeaning ways in which Latin America and its people were depicted. He was particularly concerned about how these views could distort children's image of themselves. He worried that the children of the nineteenth-century Cuban exile or expatriate community would somehow lose their national character if they were educated in the United States, outside their nation. Even learning a foreign language could estrange them from themselves, he believed.[39] This was not the poetic Martí, but the cultural nationalist author who wrote *Nuestra América,* for whom cultural differences between the United States and Latin America had stark boundaries. Martí went even further, sustaining that *Nuestra América*'s culture was superior.

It is Martí's immigrant experience in New York, where he battled to preserve a cultural identity in the face of discrimination and racism, that led him to understand that children need to be taught in their own native lands. Children need to be protected from discrimination; they are, after all, future citizens of a distinct nation. In the next decades, Martí's ideas about how to teach Cuban children in exile were incorporated into the island's curriculums and even found their way into the 1940 Constitution, which required that all courses on any Cuban topic be taught by teachers born in Cuba and with books written by Cuban authors.[40]

Martí's *La Edad de Oro:* Constructing the Future by Educating Children

In 1889, while living in New York, Martí began publishing a Spanish-language magazine for young readers titled *La Edad de Oro* (The Golden Age). Original stories and poems as well as translations of great literary works were to be included. In the first issue, Martí stated his purpose: "We publish *La Edad de Oro* so that children of the Americas can learn how people lived in the past, and today in America, and in other lands."[41] He was interested in teaching children about science and nature. *La Edad de Oro* would also be a place of magical encounters, pleasure, and rest. "We work with children because they know how to love, because they are the hope of the world."[42]

Only four issues of *La Edad de Oro* were published, but in them are contained beautiful stories and poems that clearly fulfill Martí's wishes for his magazine—to educate the future. Latin American history is told through the story of the three heroes of the wars of independence: The South American generals Simón Bolívar and José de San Martín and the Mexican priest and rebel Miguel Hidalgo. An essay about Bartolomé de las Casas, the priest who defended the indigenous people of the New World and denounced their abuse, details the young friar's struggle to treat indigenous people as human beings. A story about pre-Columbian ruins recounts the legends

Figure 2.1. *La Edad de Oro*, original magazine covers.

and real-life struggles of the indigenous of Latin America. In educating for the future, Martí relied on the past—particularly a version of the heroic past.

In the issues of the magazine, the world of the young reader was geographically broadened, as stories about the Annamese's struggle against the French, whose territory would later be incorporated into Vietnam, are recounted in splendor. Human history is told through an exposition of all the various kinds of dwellings human beings have constructed. This essay in particular shows Martí's egalitarian and humanistic impulse, as there are no grander or lesser dwellings, only a presentation that all human beings need shelter. Another essay details the history of forks and spoons, but does so, not exalting one group of people over another, but simply as a manifestation of human culture. Equality was a uniquely modern political tendency for Martí, as was his awe of technology. Scientific breakthroughs and industrial inventions are presented in an essay about the 1889 Paris Universal Exposition, suggesting his appreciation of human innovation.

Beyond history and science, *La Edad de Oro* also included Spanish versions of the fairy tales and fantastical stories of the French writer Édouard René de Laboulaye, such as *El camarón encantado* (The Enchanted Shrimp) and *Meñique* (Thumbkin), about a Tom Thumb-like hero. There is a poem inspired by Ralph Waldo Emerson about a quarrel between a mountain and a squirrel that exalts individual differences and talents. *Los zapaticos de rosa*, Martí's beloved poem about empathy and generosity, which he dedicated to a Mademoiselle Marie (María Mantilla, Martí's goddaughter in New York City), was also featured in the magazine. Empathy, one of the keys to being able to develop a non-judgmental and more egalitarian way of viewing human history, would become a guiding principle in the education of children in Cuba, where generations of children would learn to recite Martí's *Los zapaticos de rosa*.

The characters in Martí's children's literature are rich. They come from all over the world. There are heroes and ordinary folks as well as enchanted animals. His children's literature includes modernity's awe of inventions and industrial progress; Martí espouses an anti-materialist philosophy and privileges generosity and sharing, values that run contrary to the materialism and competition often associated with the early onset of the Industrial Revolution and a rapacious, capitalist United States.

As focused as his political writings were on the organization of a war of independence and on building an independent nation, his children's stories imagine a much more open world in which human beings are driven by curiosity as well as by a desire for freedom. Martí the universalist is found throughout these stories as he explored various cultures and moments in history to find deep parallels in all human experiences. Through his stories, Martí offered children a special lens through which to view and understand humanity. Steeped in a legacy that combined Romanticism with the expressive innovations of modernism, Martí believed in the idea proposed by Novalis, the eighteenth-century philosopher of early German Romanticism, that wherever there were children, there was a "Golden Age"—a moment in which there was perfect harmony with nature, a paradise on earth. These stories tilt toward the creation of an earthly utopia.

Modern Utopias

Nations that had been imagined as future-perfect societies arrived in the twentieth century marked by social inequalities and imperial ambitions. Utopic political thought reached an apex as rational projects emerged seeking to perfect existing societies. As mentioned earlier, Arendt observes that two currents of thought marked these movements, one focused on the laws of nature and the other on the laws of history. Projects based on the laws of nature aimed to create a new race by exterminating certain groups, particularly Jews and European Roma, Sinti, and Lalleri. Projects based on the laws of history propose that one class destroys the other and thus creates a new society. Both laws require elaborate ideological systems to sustain the movement toward the future, and both tend to end up requiring totalitarian governments to implement their utopic goals.

A radical break from the present was needed to construct new societies by revolutionary means and movements. Utopian revolutions based on the laws of history were particularly influenced by the work of Karl Marx and Friedrich Engels. For them, change toward the future was an inevitable resolution of structural tension created by a hierarchical organization defined by economic classes that divided the productive process into a proletariat (those who produced) and a bourgeoisie (those who controlled the means of production). In their version of the history of human society, people first lived in primitive communism, that is, in communities where there was no division of labor. As technology evolved, new social forms emerged that created class divisions. These divisions, they predicted, would give way to various stages of structural tensions that would inevitably culminate in communism, a more developed form of the original state of men. Ironically, Marx criticized utopian thinkers for not having plans rooted in the material reality.

Twentieth-century utopian thought in Latin America was also influenced by these currents.[43] Many of the nations that emerged from anti-colonial struggles were oligarchical and oppressive. Despite the raceless perspective advocated by Martí and others, deep divisions existed between *criollos* (the children of Europeans born in America), indigenous people, former enslaved Africans, and immigrants. Movements to correct these divisions at the end of the nineteenth century ran the political gamut from positivism to anarchism.

In the first decades of the twentieth century, two major social revolutions, in Russia and in Mexico, "shook" the world, as John Reed, a reporter who covered both, described the events.[44] These revolutions sought to restructure peasant societies; Russia eventually focused on industrialization and Mexico on land distribution. Other movements followed throughout Latin America, as radical thinkers devised ways to reconcile Marx's prescription that communism would come first to industrialized countries with a Latin American economic structure that relied on agriculture. The work of Peruvian José Carlos Mariátegui is particularly notable in this regard, as he went to great lengths to categorize peasants as a rural proletariat poised to lead a revolution.[45] He also advocated for the incorporation of the indigenous and supported movements to study and preserve the indigenous cultures

64 · Democracy and Time in Cuban Thought

of Peru. The failure of these revolutions to usher in egalitarian societies resulted in a proliferation of ideological sects trying to improve on the revolutionary project by searching for the magical formula for a better future.

Still other movements focused on pedagogical projects as a way to "perfect" the future. Some found its expression in save-the-children movements, for instance in Brazil.[46] Others set out to develop elaborate pedagogical projects that would educate a future citizenry. The Chilean Gabriela Mistral, for example, was one of these advocates of education.[47] Her friend and collaborator, the Mexican José Vasconcelos, went further, predicting that Latin America embodied the future of humanity because a new race was being forged by the mixture of various races—indigenous, Black, and European, into what he called *la raza cósmica* (the cosmic race). Unlike Hitler's pure race, the *raza cósmica* would be superior *because* it was mixed.[48] To be sure, both Hitler's and Vasconcelos' projects were deeply influenced by the scientific utopic project of eugenics.

By midcentury, Latin America saw the rise of populist projects influenced by both fascism and communism. In Argentina, *Peronismo* was fueled by a labor movement seeking better living conditions. The formula required a strong leader to lead the masses—in this case Juan Domingo Perón—and convert them into *un pueblo* (a people).[49] In Cuba, Fulgencio Batista oversaw a process that led to the development of the 1940 Constitution, a document that protected labor rights and promoted a narrow nationalist agenda.[50] In both cases, the nation was exalted by nationalist populist movements and ideas. Both projects were also deeply rooted in the multiple labor movements.

But the Latin American militaries insisted on controlling the movement toward the future. Their interests would coincide with U.S. Cold War geopolitics. In the case of Cuba, the promise of the republic was eventually interrupted by a military coup, led by Batista, that in turn was contested by a more radical nationalist movement. These unique circumstances would lead to a new Cuban revolutionary movement deeply steeped in nationalism and its utopic impulses.

Cuban Revolution: *El Futuro Es Nuestro!* (The Future Is Ours!)

The 1959 Revolution was a process that could be said to have commenced on July 26, 1953, with the parallel attacks on the military Moncada Barracks in Santiago de Cuba and the Carlos Manuel de Céspedes Military Barracks in Bayamo, and lasted until a few years after the collapse of the

Batista regime on January 1, 1959. However, the revolutionary government often presents it as an ongoing process that reaches back to the wars of independence and marches forward to some certain future. The earthly future, as we have seen, is a temporality that is a quintessential part of rational projects, which assumed that the future could be controlled. What those mechanisms of control were depended on the philosophical underpinnings of the political projects that arose during this time. Of particular interest are those that promoted socialism with a future constructed by rearranging societies and socially reengineering human beings. Youth were the keys to this new experiment, just as they had been for nation-building.

Initially, the Revolution led by Fidel Castro was not framed as a socialist utopic project, but rather, as explored in the previous chapter, as one that was fulfilling the historic destiny of creating a sovereign nation. Democracy and the restoration of elections and a constitution were paramount to its program. It could be said that the Revolution proffered a social democratic vision of politics and society. Yet the search for an independent nation was propelled by the past, not the future. Shortly after Castro's rise to power, however, the future replaced the past, which Castro recast as a dangerous temporality that could detain the progress of the Revolution.

> And in these two years, while the enemies of the Revolution have advanced from words to deed, the facts have increasingly clearly revealed the conflict between these two criteria, between these two forces: those of the past and those of the future, those who cling to yesterday and those of us who cling to tomorrow, those who did not want change, those who wanted the continuation of a system and an existence in which the most inconceivable injustices were inherent, and those of us who are determined to create a new world for our people.[51]

The emphasis toward the future would appear time and time again over the next six decades. The future had become a key element even as the heroic past would continue to help build legitimacy for the regime. Nostalgia for the Revolution's early years would also be deployed. But the past *before* the Revolution had to be eradicated in order to build a new society.

There was no more enthusiastic exponent of creating the future than Ernesto "Che" Guevara.[52] Che, as he would become known worldwide, was an Argentinian medical student when he set out on a nine-month journey throughout Latin America that, according to his own account, awakened his commitment to social justice. In 1955, while in Mexico, he met Raúl

Castro, who along with a small group was organizing a military expedition to Cuba. Raúl introduced him to his brother Fidel. Guevara enthusiastically joined the effort to topple Batista and quickly became a trusted military advisor to the group. After the Revolution's triumph, he came to hold several key government posts, including directing the dreaded La Cabaña fortress, where summary trials were held and prisoners were executed. He later became head of the national bank and eventually minister of industry. In 1965, he left Cuba to organize armed revolutionary movements in Africa and later in Bolivia, where he was killed.

Guevara was a prolific writer who kept meticulous notes of his military adventures as well as elaborate political reflections of contemporary events. He wrote books about political theory, socialism, and guerrilla tactics. His diaries have become bibles for guerrilla fighters worldwide, and his manuals are carefully studied, even though many of his excursions were military failures. Needless to say, Guevara became a revolutionary icon revered worldwide by those seeking social justice even as he became a symbol of repression for those whose family members were executed under his command.

If Fidel Castro's *History Will Absolve Me* was a call to arms and an effort to claim legitimacy from the past, Guevara's famous essay, *Man and Socialism in Cuba,* became the road map to creating the new society.[53] In it he elaborates an ambitious social reengineering project that would entail eradicating the past, restructuring the economy, and creating a "new man." He wrote, "To build communism it is necessary, simultaneous with the new material foundations, to build the new man."[54] And also, "What we must create is the human being of the twenty-first century, although this is still a subjective aspiration, not yet systematized."[55]

This essay was originally written as a letter to Carlos Quijano, editor of *Marcha,* a weekly published in Montevideo, Uruguay. Guevara finished the letter while traveling in Africa and it was published in March 1965 under the title "From Algiers, for *Marcha.* The Cuban Revolution Today." Essentially, Guevara describes the process of building socialism in Cuba, the obstacles that emerged, and the methods he thinks would eradicate them. In closing, he describes his ideal "new man" and "new society."

He began his letter by detailing the revolutionary process, starting with the attack on the Moncada military barracks—which, curiously, he described as a disaster—and culminating in January 1959. His main concern in this essay was to trace how a society could be transformed from a capitalist to a communist one. At the time, the Revolution had clearly laid a path toward socialism and had cemented its ties with the Soviet Union, and the communist international and the effects of communism versus capitalism were hotly debated worldwide. Guevara jumped into these arguments even as he was trying to educate others on how socialism was being built in Cuba. The main debatable position he refuted was the criticism that socialism fortified the state and stripped the individual of rights. Throughout the essay, he returned to this question as he interlaced his observations about the Cuban revolutionary process with theoretical discussions that relied on classic Marxist thought.

The Masses and the Vanguard

The temporal context to Guevara's essay is the tension between the past and the future. The past is a continual problem in building a new society and needs to be eradicated. The society in formation must compete fiercely with the past, which is now cast, not as the place that legitimizes the struggle, but rather as the temporal enemy of the future.

The first step toward building socialism was a practical one, Guevara wrote: seizing state power. The next step was recognizing how the past in its multiple forms created obstacles toward history's movement toward the future. Immediately, the rebels had to purge the newly formed Cuban government from those who were looking backward and not forward. During the first months, he wrote, they had had to deal with the "treacherous" bourgeoisie. He was referring to the liberals who had supported the Revolution and were now reclaiming that democracy be restored, often objecting to the use of summary trials and executions. A coalition government had been formed immediately following the rebels' triumph. Manuel Urrutia had been named president of the Council of State, with Fidel Castro as premier. But tensions had mounted in the subsequent months as Castro consolidated his power. In a dramatic gesture, Castro accused Urrutia of conspiring to defame the Revolution and threatened to resign. Instead, Urrutia resigned, and the new president refused to accept Castro's resignation. Days before a planned celebration of the 26 of July armed action, Fidel Castro was able to complete what Guevara called the first, heroic phase of the Revolution—the consolidation of power by the Rebel Army.[56] A new past was being written that not only contained heroic deeds, but also villains.

The next step would be a major challenge, for it was not only the bourgeoisie that needed to be eradicated; the citizenry, too, were "haunted" by the past. "The vestiges of the past are brought into the present in one's consciousness, and a continual labor is necessary to eradicate them,"[57] Guevara wrote. Then, in what he described as the next stage of the Revolution, a new "historical character" appeared: the masses, which will have an important role in the building of a new society.

> In the history of the Cuban Revolution there now appeared a character, well defined in its features, which would systematically reappear: the mass. This multifaceted being is not as is claimed, the sum of elements of the same type (reduced, moreover, to that same type by the ruling system), which acts like a flock of sheep. It is true that it follows its leaders, basically Fidel Castro, without hesitation. But the degree to which he won this trust results precisely from having interpreted the full meaning of the people's desires and aspirations, and from the sincere struggle to fulfill the promises he made.[58]

What is important to note about this statement is Guevara's understanding of the *masses*. While he admitted that this could be confused with a lack of individuality, in his view, the masses were an aggregate of individuals that were symbiotically tied to a leader, Fidel Castro, who propelled them forward. Guevara was careful to point out that "the mass" was not homogeneous. Curiously, even as he defined his ideology as Marxist-Leninist, his thoughts about people and their need for a strong leader were identical to those of Evita Perón, who had written that *el pueblo* (the people) needed a strong leader who embodied their aspirations.[59] The people themselves were not capable of understanding their historic destiny to create a new future/nation and therefore could not, on their own, bring the nation forward. Evita Perón and Guevara just differed on who that leader should be. For her, it was Juan Domingo Perón, her husband; for Guevara, it was Fidel Castro.

> In this Fidel is a master. His own special way of fusing himself with the people can be appreciated only by seeing him in action. At the great public mass meetings one can observe something like the dialogue of two tuning forks whose vibrations interact, producing new sounds. Fidel and the mass begin to vibrate together in a dialogue of growing intensity until they reach the climax in an abrupt conclusion crowned by our cry of struggle and victory.[60]

Guevara believed that the need for a strong leader was a transitory situation. What was missing in the masses was consciousness. Capitalism had lulled the masses into complacency and had stripped them of their ability to understand what was good for them. Thus, the need for strong leadership. For Marxists, consciousness was a necessary condition that distinguished revolutionaries from "the masses." Cadres, those chosen to lead, were needed. These were individuals who had reached an almost nirvana state of being in which individualism was replaced by a connection to the higher goals of the Revolution.

Guevara admits that the process of raising the consciousness of the masses (*concientizar*) may give credence to the argument that the state usurps their individuality, but he argued: "Viewed superficially, it might appear that those who speak of the subordination of the individual to the state are right. The masses carry out with matchless enthusiasm and discipline the tasks set by the government, whether in the field of the economy, culture, defense, sports, etc. The initiative generally comes from Fidel, or from the revolutionary leadership, and is explained to the people, who make it their own."[61] The subordination was necessary because the individuals had not yet become a "new man."

There was also a need for an elite to help shepherd the Revolution forward. For Guevara, this new vanguard, forged in the heat of battle, creates heroic individuals who could lead the "sleeping" masses forward.

The vanguard group is ideologically more advanced than the mass; the latter understands the new values, but not sufficiently. While among the former there has been a qualitative change that enables them to make sacrifices in their capacity as an advance guard, the latter see only part of the picture and must be subject to incentives and pressures of a certain intensity. This is the dictatorship of the proletariat operating not only on the defeated class but also on individuals of the victorious class.[62]

The rebels were deemed to be more enlightened than the "masses" because they had the "new man" inside them, the result of their participation in the revolutionary struggle. But even they required special attention. Their socialization, just like that of the masses, required a top-down approach. If Guevara did not admit that individuality was lost in the masses, he did believe that an authoritarian form of government was needed in order to carry out this enormous social engineering project. The vanguard had a vehicle through which it did its work, and that was the Party, which in the early days could not be a mass party even though that was its aspiration. The process of becoming "vanguard" was also thought out. Through a series of rewards and punishments, the vanguard would be forged.

Along with the image of the multitudes marching toward the future comes the concept of institutionalization as a harmonious set of channels, steps, restraints and well-oiled mechanisms which facilitate the advance, which facilitate the natural selection of those destined to march in the vanguard, and which bestow rewards on those who fulfill their duties and punishments on those who commit a crime against the society that is being built.[63]

In this vision, the future is not expansive or inclusive, but rather it is reserved for those who are chosen. It is an echo of the Christian dogma that establishes the afterlife as the reward for those who sacrifice and behave according to Christian rules during their lifetime.

Economic Changes and the New Man

The work to *concientizar* the masses was multilayered. And Guevara's essay elaborates on various philosophical and practical ways to encourage individuals to act on behalf of the collective, not for themselves. Like Marx's early assessment of the human condition under capitalism, Guevara sees that individuals are alienated from their society and from themselves. Human beings were conditioned to act by the economic structures within which they lived. Capitalism encouraged individualism, not social responsibility. As he noted, ". . . the economic foundation that has been laid has done its work of undermining the development of consciousness."[64]

Socialism was the stage after capitalism and before communism in which "we can see the new man being born. The image is not yet completely finished—it never will be, since the process goes forward hand in hand with the development of new economic forms."[65]

This new economy was being achieved by nationalizing private property. Ideally men could simply develop a social consciousness. But because the past was so influential in the present, the creation of the new man, more specifically a new consciousness, required both material and moral incentives.

However, material incentives alone could lead to a distortion of the person. "It is not a matter of how many kilograms of meat one has to eat, or of how many times a year someone can go to the beach, or how many pretty things from abroad you might be able to buy with present-day wages. It is a matter of making the individual feel more complete, with much more inner wealth and much more responsibility."[66]

Figure 2.2. May Day parade in Revolution Square. Julio Etchart / Alamy Stock Photo.

Material incentives should be used wisely, and should encourage the development of a collective consciousness, he argued. In effect, as moral incentives were introduced and material ones minimized, work was redefined. It would acquire a "new status." No longer would human beings be commodities whose labor and its profits could be extracted, but rather they would be owners of the means of production. This collective ownership would give individuals a sense of belonging and of being in control. Their labor would no longer be work but rather a duty to the whole.

Youth and the Future

As in other future-oriented political projects, youth for Guevara was central to the project of building a "new man." As in other modernist, futuristic projects, youth were considered the most impressionable and therefore could still be educated and molded to fit the requirements of the future society. "The basic clay of our work is the youth; we place our hope in it and prepare it to take the banner from our hands."[67]

This particular task would require massive mobilization of young people and an overhauling of educational institutions.[68] To that end, right before the Bay of Pigs invasion, all schools had been closed; subsequently, only public ones reopened. Formal education was to be placed under the direction of the Ministry of Education and the Party's informational (ideological) apparatus. Education was expanded across the island, and by the end of the 1960s there were 30,000 students in technical schools and 40,000 at universities. Before the Revolution these numbers were 6,000 and 2,000, respectively.[69] Emphasis was to be given to technical and ideological instruction. Teachers were trained in Marxism-Leninism. Along with the imposition of a single ideology came the policing of education, which was entrusted to the cadre.[70] The educational restructuring was accompanied by a massive literacy campaign that took young people to rural areas to teach peasants how to read and write. Over a million Cubans participated in the campaign as educators, teachers, literacy workers, and organizers.

The literacy campaign has received much attention throughout the decades. For many scholars, the campaign was the crowning achievement of a socialist Revolution that reflected its humanistic values as it prioritized providing education to the poor and the illiterate. Others have recast this chapter of the Revolution as a countercultural move aimed at stirring the enthusiasm of young people.[71] And in fact, many of those who participated in the literacy campaign speak of their time teaching peasants to read and write as an inspirational experience. But this account incorrectly casts the Cuban Revolution's leadership as countercultural hippies seeking to change the culture of a country. Undoubtedly, the Revolution did aspire to create a new society, but many of its political and cultural values were conservative, not liberal. And missing from this laudatory account are the power dynamics behind the mass mobilization of young people. One ancillary outcome of the campaign was to dismantle the patriarchal family[72] and to set up a conservative, authoritarian, and thus a patriarchal regime with Fidel Castro as the father of the homeland. It is important to note that while the Cuban peasants were taught to read and write, they and others in Cuban society were not given freedom of speech.

Even though Guevara wrote of the youth as the key to this new future, in his vision, young people had no agency. He writes, "In our society, the youth and the Party play a big part. The former is especially important because it is the malleable clay from which the new person can be built with none of the old defects. The youth are treated in accordance with our aspirations."[73] The pay-off is the creation of a new generation that is "free of original sin"—a type of baptism through education. The parallels to Christian thought are unmistakable.

Sacrifice and the Promise of an Idyllic Afterlife

The future orientation in Guevara's writings is an example of secularized Christian thought. The building of a new society required sacrifices that included putting the Revolution over family, delaying material gratification, and thinking of the moral rewards that would be obtained. "The leaders of the Revolution have children just beginning to talk, who are not learning to say 'daddy'; their wives, too, must be part of the general sacrifice of their lives in order to take the Revolution to its destiny. The circle of their friends is limited strictly to the circle of comrades in the Revolution. There is no life outside of it."[74]

The cadre, in particular, had to be ready to lead the masses to complete the task of building the Revolution. They would confront adversity but be rewarded. Being a cadre of the vanguard was both magnificent and agonizing. Guevara warns that the cadres should be prepared for a long journey since they were battling not only their enemies but the past as well. But the cadre, were ready. They had already struggled during the insurrection. Their sacrifice would go on to make Cuba the vanguard of the Americas.

74 · Democracy and Time in Cuban Thought

The most important "pay-off" was the creation of a new society that would be made up of free individuals who "labor," not work, since their efforts were for the good of all. With this freedom would come the possibilities that creativity, and artistic production, would flourish. Of course, these artistic efforts had to be closely monitored and led by the vanguard, since the "masses" could commit excesses and confuse social freedom with individual freedom. They were not yet ready to be given this responsibility.

The essay closes with an appeal to the sentiment of love. "At the risk of seeming ridiculous, let me say that the true revolutionary is guided by great feelings of love. . . . Our vanguard revolutionaries must idealize this love of the people, of the most sacred causes, and make it one and indivisible."[75]

Sacrifice and total dedication to the Revolution will be rewarded in the future, Guevara predicts: "The vanguard has its eyes fixed on the future and its reward, but this is not a vision of reward for the individual. The prize is the new society in which individuals will have different characteristics: the society of communist human beings."[76] Promise of a better life is sustained in the future, he continues, "We will make the human being of the 21st century—we, ourselves. We will forge ourselves in daily action, creating a new man with a new technology. The present is a time of struggle; the future is ours."[77] And thus, the secular future has replaced the afterlife, which is also obtained through sacrifice.

A few years before Guevara wrote *Man and Socialism in Cuba,* a Franciscan priest who was running the camps established in Florida to house Pedro Pan children, addressed his charges. The occasion was a variety show put on by some of the older camp residents, and the speech was captured in a United States Information Agency-sponsored documentary entitled *The Lost Apple,* after the Spanish nursery rhyme. In a rather abrupt departure from the festive mood, the priest told the gathered children, "There is evil in the world. It is communism."[78] He went on to say that it was the children's duty to combat communism by becoming the Men of the 21st century. So on the other side of the Florida Straits, the creation of the new men of the twenty-first century was also a pedagogical project, in this case for those combating the Castro regime. In the end, both were just variants on the rational project aimed at creating a better future. It is an idea with many historical referents, including Martí's idea of the *pinos nuevos,* his romantic prediction that on the tombs of the young rebels who died fighting for Cuba's independence "new pine trees" would grow—that is, a new generation of stronger, more committed fighters for freedom.

The creation of the new man is an idea that became central to the utopic projects in all their variants in the twentieth century; it was also, in some manifestations, a biological project based on eugenics, with Nazism being one of its most virulent examples. Following the laws of nature, a superior human being could be created, and a new future built on this new biologically superior man. But there were related projects based on positive eugenics, and indeed Vasconcelos's *raza cósmica* had elements of this. Guevara's "new man" project was anchored in the idea that through education, rewards, and punishment, a new human being with a different moral compass could be created. It was a social project, not a biological one, even though all three of these projects stand on a similar temporal home—the future.

The Limits of the Future

Early modernity gave us a future temporality in which nations were imagined as places where people with a shared culture, politics, and economy could thrive and equal societies would flourish. Instead, nation-states engendered inequalities. Coming from the disillusionment of unfulfilled nationalist dreams, modernity then unleashed a futuristic imagination that included travel to space as well as earthly political utopias. But by midtwentieth century, it was clear that all the rational socialist projects—and nationalists as well—had engendered authoritarian regimes and unequal societies. Utopia had become synonymous with Stalinism, even though Marx himself criticized utopians for lacking a political program, regardless of the fact that his own prescription included a future temporality. The Cuban Revolution briefly offered a regenerative promise. Alas, this too resulted in a corrupt military regime.[79]

Taking a closer look at how the promise of a better society failed, several premises need to be critically examined to understand the limits of the future as a political temporality. One is the notion of limitless progress, which assumes that human evolution has a predictable course that unfolds without human intervention. This denies human agency. If the past, justified by tradition, obliterated agency in the present, in the creation of a future society, agency is put on hold.

In addition, this progress toward the future has to be shepherded, so consequently, it requires a strong leader. At the end, the only way to guarantee the movement toward the future is by imposing authoritarian dictates that select the vanguard, punish the outliers, and carefully construct a society based on a narcissistic image of the self.

The notion of a one-vanguard party rule through democratic centralism excludes all those who do not comport to the requisites of having the right attitude. A conceptual shortcoming in utopic thought is that the emphasis on herding individuals through temporalities requires a conception of people as a "mass" or a "*pueblo*." Somehow their aspirations would be "felt" and expressed through a strong leader who in turn would be judged on how well he or she expressed these sentiments. Thus, the public square is reduced to one voice that is applauded by the masses.

Another conceptual shortcoming is the idea that a "new man" can indeed be created. Focusing on an ideal, as opposed to a real human being, denies the individual the possibility of being. A tautological argument is presented—despite Guevara's attempt to unravel it through political statements—by the claim that a new society requires a new man and a new man requires a new society.

Despite its ontological flaws, the socialist utopian project held a powerful grip on the international left. But in the mid-1960s, academics, including some ardent supporters of socialism, began to question the limits of the utopian. A special issue of *Daedalus,* the journal of the American Academy of Arts and Sciences, dedicated to utopias and published in 1965, presented works from a diverse group of scholars, many of whom shared concerns about the troubling impact that impossible promises had on social organization, on the well-being of individuals, and on the environment. When projects are hinged to an ephemeral future promise, they noted, the present is often ignored.[80] This encourages a relationship detached from our realities. Further, it assumes that our realities are bad, and that we need to search for a better future. As such, it denies the complexities of reality and encourages us to look away from what is there in front of us.[81]

Unfortunately, those on the left who have been critical of utopias, particularly Hannah Arendt and Karl Popper, important critics of authoritarianism, were tagged as anti-utopians, as if their critiques somehow delegitimized the search for alternative politics. Fredric Jameson, a Marxist theorist, made sweeping statements to the effect that anti-utopians, in the end, are anti-socialists.[82] But Popper was concerned about the anti-rational nature of utopian projects and the implications that this had in building political processes in which ideas and facts can be debated instead of simply believed.[83] Arendt's criticism of future-oriented projects was concerned with what happens to human agency. These concerns are about the limits of future-oriented political projects and their effects on democratic practices.

Time may indeed contain the utopian energies to resolve the difference between promise and fulfillment, as Hegel indicated. But when time does not generate meaning, there is a crisis. The end of the Cold War in 1991 constituted such a crisis, one that put into question many of the utopic projects of the twentieth century. The abrupt end to the future as the place where political projects were headed also halted the notion of history marching forward. With the end of modern history, and the demise of the future, it seemed as if time itself had failed to contain a sustainable promise. Liberalism seemed to have triumphed over utopian thought.[84] At the very least, it was a moment to question mega-narratives and all-encompassing ideologies. This does not necessarily translate into a triumphalist declaration of the end of alternative politics, but rather signals the need to critically examine the temporalities that led to obliterating individuals into the "masses" and dreamed of completely reorganizing human societies and indeed human beings into something "new."

While grand political schemes may have fallen by history's wayside, fervent religious projects that offer paradise in the afterlife again proliferated with the beginning of the twenty-first century. Scholars have expressed concern that, beyond these religious projects, there are no moral counters to unbridled capitalism,[85] and that apathy limits the imagining of political alternatives.[86] Perhaps if socialism had been seen as a normative ideal rather than a historical force propelling societies toward the future, it would still be able to offer a viable alternative.[87] Perhaps the end of socialism is the end of the future itself—at least as a temporality in which to achieve democracy and equality. This development now requires a search for other temporalities.

3

The Present

For a long time, I have firmly believed that the twilight of the future heralds
the advent of the now. Thus, just as we have had philosophies of the past and of the future,
of eternity and of the void, tomorrow we shall have a philosophy of the present.
The poetic experience could be one of its foundations.
   —Octavio Paz, *In Search of the Present,* 1990

The collapse of the future signaled the end of modernity as it had been constructed—a pathway to unending progress and prosperity, and as such, to creating room for a new temporality to emerge. The twilight of utopias, as Octavio Paz called the demise of twentieth-century socialist political projects, ended abruptly as the Soviet Union collapsed and with it the dreams of a worldwide egalitarian society. Capitalism had also failed to create wealth for all. Some have described this moment in the 1990s as the end of history; others saw it as the end of ideas, as various projects that had promised the fulfillment of a historic mission to create better societies disintegrated. Grand narratives became empty promises even as a new mantra of globalization promised to connect the world. At the heart of the matter was a crisis of the Enlightenment's promises of progress.[1]

After the Renaissance, the eternal rewards promised by religion had been replaced by a vision of an earthly paradise where life would be better and humans would be happier. In fact, the right to the pursuit of happiness was embedded in documents such as the U.S. Declaration of Independence, as it was also recognized by José Martí as an aspirational social goal for new nations. But as Carlos Fuentes noted in 1985, "we were living with the consciousness that modernity had not brought happiness."[2] And growing global inequalities dashed hopes of the possibilities of bettering our lot in life. Hope itself as a political sentiment was replaced with deep disaffection in the political process and with the eclipse of a vision of a better future.

The collapse of the futuristic projects also challenged the political vehicles that had propelled them forward. What would happen to the masses or *el pueblo* if history was no longer moving through them? Are they replaced with the individual citizen? How to transition from the "we" to the "I"? In reality, individual agency had also been exhausted and citizens, even in more open political systems, felt alienated from their governments. In describing the Chilean situation in the new millennium, Norbert Lechner observed that without some cognitive maps to lead it forward, "a void is opened which may explain the silent response as it faces the tomorrow."[3] The future was bracketed from the present. As a temporality, it appeared to be at stake, as were the political projects attached to it. Socialism, as a project, was supposed to be an alternative to capitalism. It had an explicit utopic vision, and as such, its fall had more immediate consequences on the temporality of politics in the twenty-first century in those countries that had experimented with the project. For many intellectuals in Eastern Europe, the end of socialism challenged the temporalities that had sustained it. The speed of time also seemed to change in the post-socialist crisis; it felt accelerated as it rushed forward from what Václav Havel, Czech writer, statesman, and human rights activist, referred to as a frozen past.[4]

In Latin America, exhaustion with the hyped and failed revolutionary movements led to referring to utopias as tired old men.[5] By the end of the twentieth century, Jorge Castañeda, Mexican politician and academic, in a book titled *Utopias Unarmed,* concluded that armed movements, many of them supported by Cuba, had only engendered authoritarian regimes.[6] The critique was particularly aimed at the Cuban military leadership and its security apparatus, which had encouraged guerrilla movements around the world in part to diffuse the United States' singular focus on the island. And even though there has been a nostalgic resurgence of socialist projects, like Hugo Chávez in Venezuela, Lula in Brazil, and Bernie Sanders in the United States, there is an unmistakable understanding of the economic and political failure of the socialist projects that had gained power.

In Cuba, that decline can be dated to the late sixties and early seventies, when the Revolution began a slow, painful descent into militarized bureaucracy as well as an unproductive economy. The shining star of socialist states lost its luster as the leadership aged and became entrenched in a rigid and repressive structure that was repurposed to bring in cash to the impoverished island. Hundreds of thousands of Cubans chose to flee. In the

80 · Democracy and Time in Cuban Thought

1980s, encouraged by the Cuban government over 120,000 fled through the port of Mariel and by the 1990s many were overstaying visas or leaving in dangerous, rickety rafts instead of staying and facing a certain metaphorical death. Massive emigration continued, and in 2022 an unprecedented annual number of over 200,000 Cubans left though sea and land, many making their way up through the Darien Gap, a dense jungle in Panama, and then continuing through Central America and Mexico. By the twenty-first century, as the angel of history looked back on sixty years of revolution, s/he saw rubble. Ruins now described Cuba.[7] The struggle to survive in those ruins became a dominant theme in literature, including Achy Obejas's *Ruins*,[8] and Abilio Estévez's *Los palacios distantes*.[9]

A certain disdain for politics unmistakably grew in these ruins. Scholars and writers began to ask, what happens next? Multiple answers were proposed. Iván de la Nuez, who has called for the building of a "new future by the children of the future," proposed a radical reexamination of the revolutionary rhetoric and iconography.[10] Ruth Behar studied the trajectories of island-based writers and artists from the 1990s, children of the Revolution whose faith in the process had faded, and noted that many had started to abandon the island and reset their intellectual coordinates in Europe, Latin America, and the United States.[11] Anke Birkenmaier and Esther Whitfield started mapping Havana after 1989 in *Havana Beyond the Ruins*, a volume that explored the aftermath of the "fall."[12] Multiple writers proposed aesthetic, literary, and even architectural projects that could help society move away from the massifying effects of state-run socialism.

What was certain was that a new temporality was emerging. After the end of the hopeful socialist utopic projects, the future was becoming the past, so there was a double crisis: both history and the vision of political earthly utopias were collapsing. The failure of utopic experiments meant the demise of the future as a political temporality and the ascendance of the present. And multiple forms of the present emerged.

The immediate political present was characterized by disenchantment. The problem was not exclusive to socialist countries. A decline in optimism for the future also characterized Western democracies throughout the 1990s and into the twenty-first century. In Latin America, military regimes of the left and right had promised better societies but had not delivered them. As these were replaced by democratically elected governments, political temporalities were refocused toward the present. Market-driven reforms also created immediate expectations. As Javier Santiso noted in 1998, "What we call the 'fall into the present' refers to the presentist focus of politics and the extra-ordinary re-evaluation of the present in the modern era: the present became omnipresent and overruled both the past and the future as the referential horizon of politics. The changing nature of the perception of time was particularly acute in Latin America, where the future was being replaced by the present as the focal point of politics."[13] Market-driven economies, along with the growing disillusionment over empty political promises lodged in the future, gave rise to the present. The individual was exalted and hyper-individualism replaced the collective.

In this chapter, I will explore the multiple forms of the present that came to be after the collapse of the Soviet Union. And I will explore the work of Cuban poet Eliseo Diego, which suggests an engaged and poetic present akin to the one proposed by Octavio Paz.

Defining the Present

What is the present? How can the present be appreciated? Can there be multiple forms of the present? Aristotle thought of the present as the Now, the connection between the past and the future.[14] For philosophers in the fourth and fifth century, such as St. Augustine, there was no other time but the present. In one of the first elaborations of the relationship between time and space, he argued there can be no existence where there are no beings, and beings exist only in the present.[15] As he visited emerging nation-states in the Western Hemisphere, Alexis de Tocqueville saw the nineteenth-century present as a place that swallowed the future. Others developed the notion of the dynamic present, a temporality with possibilities not that different from the past or the future.[16]

The present has also been conceived as a singular moment unhinged from the past and the future. Without connections to consequences beyond the moment, this temporality encourages hyper-individualism. This form of the present can lead to hedonism, or indeed nihilism, since its detachment does not encourage the development of either meaning or values. Instead, an unsophisticated form of Horace's *carpe diem* encourages enjoyment of the pleasures of the moment without concern for the future or how actions in the present affect others.

American pragmatists like William James developed a philosophy of the present that underscored its importance based on the notion that experience could only occur in the moment, for the present was not a fleeting moment, it did not rush through experiences. James described a specious present that allowed social interaction to occur. For the pragmatists, the present was not so much a space were values disappeared, as one where life was experienced in its entirety. George Mead elaborated on this concept as well as on the way the present can determine and influence our conception of the past. The past, he said, arises through memory and exists in images that form the "backward limit of the present."[17] Yet reality is always in the present, since social interactions occur in the moment. Mead also underscored that a specious present is a place in which to reflect before acting.[18]

For Friedrich Nietzsche, the present was time punctuated by repeating moments. As he faced an approaching era where the meaningless of life would pervade, he perceived the present as a time of stillness. Stillness, or emptiness of time, was a condition of the present that Walter Benjamin also explored. As he argued, this present was a consequence of capitalism, which obliterated humans, turning them into productive machines. All was permissible for the sake of progress: "The idea of progress is inseparable from the idea of homogeneous empty time,"[19] he wrote. "The present is not a transition between moments. Time originates and reaches a standstill in the experience of the present. Instead of an eternal past depicted as linear, we need a rupture in experience of particular moments which stand out."[20] However, Benjamin did not see the present as a linear progression from the past. He thought that the present offered opportunities for change. But change was not necessarily sequential or evolutionary. It could also occur when the present "deviated" from a linear progression as it broke free from its customary predicted linear path from past/present. Benjamin described these moments of disjuncture of time as messianic.[21]

Like Benjamin, Jacques Derrida saw the present as a period of waiting, not with a promise of inevitable change but rather holding the possibility for transformation. But the present required the future in order to accomplish this work, since awareness comes not at the moment in which it is experienced, but rather in retrospect and in anticipation. In other words, the present is constructed in the past and the future.[22] The present, like a moment captured in a photograph, in many ways is only appreciated by a representation that is in the now.[23]

The present has been understood as the place between the past and the future, yet the present can also be home to both the past and the future. For Marcel Proust, the present was a moment in which the past could be remembered.[24] Derrida rejected the idea of the now as exclusively of the present, arguing that the now has traces of experience. Giorgio Agamben, for his part, wrote about the fluidity of the present, where different social projects work though a moment simultaneously.[25] What is clear is that the future as a place where political dreams were to be realized is no longer politically viable. And while tradition—in the form of religion in all its manifestations, including extremism or nostalgic socialist projects—may be used to replace the void created by the failure of future-oriented rational projects, the present is the place to explore alternatives to the authoritarianism that often resulted from these projects.

The Poetic Present

Octavio Paz's work is particularly relevant for this inquiry. Paz focuses on the ascendance of the present as the future disappears. In his acceptance speech for the Nobel Prize in Literature in 1990, Paz recalled his experience with time. As a child, time seemed boundless. But as he matured, that sensation changed. Indeed, he remarked that the passage into adulthood was marked by a fall into the present.[26]

His personal appreciations of time led him to develop an understanding of how temporalities function politically, and specifically, why futuristic temporalities had failed and what could replace them. To begin with, Paz noted that future-oriented projects were based on the problematic notion of unbridled progress. In the first place, he wrote, the concept of a process open to infinity did not consider that natural resources are finite and will run out one day. This attitude, he noted, had already caused damage to the environment and had placed human beings in danger. Furthermore, scientific innovations offered as examples of human progress had not always been used to better humanity; some had been used in wars.

Paz also questioned one of the precepts of the modernist notion that "man" would become more evolved, enlightened, and rational. Rather, he noted, human behavior has revealed that people can be hateful and destructive. This was proof, in his view, that the rational system, the underpinnings of modernity, had failed. History had not facilitated the evolution of better, more humane, and prosperous societies.

Paz was particularly critical of political projects that promised to liberate men, since he thought that instead of bringing freedom, they had given rise to "gigantic prisons." Was this the end of utopias, he asked? His answer: "It is rather the end of the idea of history as a phenomenon the outcome of which can be known in advance. Historical determinism has been a costly

84 · Democracy and Time in Cuban Thought

and bloodstained fantasy. History is unpredictable because its agent, mankind, is the personification of indeterminism."[27]

His battles with both the political right and left led Paz to have an understanding of the limitations of utopic projects, particularly those of the left, which promised better societies that turned out to be as corrupt and authoritarian as the ones they replaced. The end of the twentieth century was characterized by the end of mega-narratives that promised to solve all of mankind's problems. The disillusionment with these political projects led to ascendance of the present. But the focus on the now, he warned, could turn the present into a hedonistic place where the effort was placed on solving smaller problems, perhaps with limited resources. From his perspective, this was not satisfactory. "Yet the present requires much more than attention to its immediate needs: it demands a more rigorous global reflection. For a long time I have firmly believed that the twilight of the future heralds the advent of the now. To think about the now implies first of all to recover the critical vision."[28]

To replace unattainable futures and unproductive presents, Octavio Paz proposed a new temporality, the "poetic present," which could emerge from the ruins of the failed future. Like Hannah Arendt, he questioned the idea that history could predict future outcomes through its laws. "The search for the present is neither the pursuit of an earthly paradise nor that of a timeless eternity: it is the search for a real reality."[29]

Paz noted that "just as we have had philosophies of the past and of the future, of eternity and of the void, tomorrow we shall have a philosophy of the present." The poetic experience could be one of its foundations. "Poetry is in love with the instant and seeks to relive it in the poem, thus separating it from sequential time and turning it into a fixed present."[30] After all, poets understood that the present "is the source of presences." In this poetic present or philosophical presentism, a temporality in which the individual can be situated and in which there is a recognition of differences can emerge. This poetic present is one in which individuals replace categories and where commonalities and differences are recognized. "The doors of perception open slightly, and the other time appears, the real one we were searching for without knowing it: the present, the presence."[31]

Living and thinking in the present, according to Paz, does not imply forgetting the past or ignoring the future. The present is the place in which temporalities coexist. The present, for Paz, is not a linear time, but rather a time that can encompass past and future. In the present, the past exists as a memory of trauma but also of pleasure. Think of Proust's *Remembrances of Things Past,* where past pleasurable events can again be savored in the present.

A qualification is warranted even for the poetic present. For Arendt, as for Paz, the present is the place where thinking and reflection occurs. But for this to happen, there must be a political culture that values ideas and analytical thinking, and individuals need to be trained and socialized to think. In her book *In Between Past and Future,* Arendt noted, "we seem to be neither equipped nor prepared for this activity of thinking, of settling down in the gap between past and future."[32] The insight was particularly important as the present gained political significance. This observation becomes especially relevant in understanding the present in Cuba.

The Fall into the Present: Cuba's Post Utopic Moment

Like other parts of the world, the utopic project that promised egalitarianism and prosperity for all never became reality in Cuba. At the end of the nineteenth century, José Martí had warned Antonio Maceo, one of the generals of the Cuban War of Independence, that a nation could not be governed like a military camp. Midway through the twentieth century, Fidel Castro set up a militarized government that went to war with his opponents, including the young cadre of fellow revolutionaries who had fought for a democratic and egalitarian country. The U.S. administration at the time viewed the world through a Cold War lens. Geopolitically, the Western Hemisphere needed to be guarded from the Soviet Union. When President Eisenhower ordered the overthrow of the Castro regime, the effect was an acceleration of the process of militarization on the island. Eventually, generals became a ruling elite. The alliance between Cuba and the Soviet Union resulted in the establishment of an intensely bureaucratic government supported by subsidies that were not always invested in productive enterprises. The Cuban economy stagnated. Repression of the opposition took on many forms, including summary trials and firing squads. Intellectuals were warned, "Within the Revolution, everything. Against the Revolution, nothing."[33]

Varying temporalities have operated in revolutionary Cuba. Initially the revolutionary movement relied mostly on the past for its legitimacy, but shortly after the triumph of the Revolution, the future was emphasized even as past war heroes were reified. However, the present was also deployed, and "the revolutionary moment" was frozen into a repeating present, particularly through use of photographic images, which had gained ascendancy as a

86 · Democracy and Time in Cuban Thought

propaganda tool. Historic moments, immortalized in images, became omnipresent. The Revolution was captured in black-and-white photographs: the bearded rebels entering Havana with rosaries around their necks; Fidel Castro giving speeches to applauding masses; Castro meeting with Harlem residents in New York; Castro jumping out of a tank to meet the Bay of Pigs invaders. Statues were not needed as the images—both still and moving—became enduring relics.[34] Fidel and Ernesto "Che" Guevara were enshrined in the frozen present. Nostalgia, the yearning for a perfect past, shrouded the iconography of the revolutionary movement and its leaders like a security cordon.

Official temporalities of the present were also summoned in instances where obvious promises were not being fulfilled. For example, twenty-five years after coming to power, the revolutionary government declared, "NOW we are going to build socialism."[35] This of course prompted ordinary Cubans to wonder what they had been doing up to then. Most telling was the attempt to inscribe into the present a way to forget the past. The nearly six decades of the Cuban republic was repackaged as the "pseudo" republic. The fight for labor rights and for racial equality were rhetorically bundled into an unspecified "one hundred years of struggle." It was almost as if the revolutionary present had swallowed the past for the sake of constructing its own image.

Cuba's "fall" into the post-utopic present can be dated to the collapse of the Soviet Union in 1991. Not only did the larger utopic project disappear, but with it the extensive subsidies that had allowed the Cuban commanders to keep the island's economy afloat. Since 1991, multiple and discernible forms of the present have emerged. These have included an immediate present focused on survival, as the daily activities of most Cubans were circumscribed to the search for food and basic living supplies. People did not know where they would get their next meal, and survival became the immediate goal. Opción Cero (Option Zero), the government's emergency survival plan, called for neighborhoods to organize collective cooking cauldrons, and people shared recipes of how to make *picadillo*, the quintessential Cuban ground meat dish, with grapefruit peels.

Many predicted that this crisis would bring about the fall of the regime. But a decision to open the economy to global markets to do business with the government, particularly around tourism, gave the government breathing room. While economic changes and restructuring projects were initiated, political change was shunned and the opposition repressed. Another, less performative, present arose, one that emerged from the economic collapse and was paralyzed by a political inertia. Popularly, people described this moment as *la espera* (the wait), which some interpreted as waiting for the death of the aging Fidel Castro. In all, it was a passive and empty present.

I suggest that still another form of the present began to be noticeable in Cuba in the 1990s, particularly among young Cubans—a temporal space in which action and feelings as well as thinking and contemplation—necessary elements of a temporality that encourages a democratic culture—began to take hold. It requires an attitude toward time and indeed, even toward "waiting," that is productive and respectful of others. During conversations among Cubans, which had been punctuated by unilateral statements and superlatives such as "*la línea recta y derecha*" (the straight and narrow line) or "*no te equivoques*" (Don't get it wrong), the simple phrase of "in my opinion," began to be heard. "In my opinion" may be a mild phrase of dissent, but it is nevertheless a recognition that there may be multiple opinions on a given issue.

To me, this recognition of difference and plurality is a form of the "poetic present"—one that, I believe, is a component of a political culture, and necessary for democracy. This and other elements that constitute this "poetic present" can be found work of the Cuban poet Eliseo Diego, which I will discuss in this chapter. But first, I will explore the various forms of the present that emerged in Cuba in the post-Soviet period.

The Present as Survival

Unlike other Latin American countries that have "fallen into the present" with more open political systems and market-driven economies as part of a new wave of neoliberalism, Cuba's military regime hung on to power despite the disappearance of the Soviet Union and its subsidies. The island's economic viability had depended on the Soviet Union, and the almost overnight disintegration of the Soviet bloc had a profound impact on Cuba, leaving its people hungry and sickly. The government gave a name to the crisis of 1991–1995, *El periodo especial en tiempos de paz* (Special Period in Times of Peace). Official contingency plans called for organizing collective kitchens. For a worrisome number of Cubans, malnourishment led to the onset of temporary blindness and limb paralysis. The lives of Cubans were marked by desperate attempts at survival. Raquel Mendieta, at the time a professor of Cuban culture at the Art Institute in Havana, asked in an essay: "Do you know what is the worst thing about this Special Period? Everything: the tiredness, the blackouts, the boredom, the hunger."[36]

One could wonder, was this the future or the end of the future? The regime was at a crossroads. In an attempt to mobilize cadre, the Cuban Communist Party initiated discussions with Party members throughout the island. They were asked to share their views and offer their criticism. Yet instead of these sessions resulting in reforms, the information gathered in them was used by the security apparatus to quietly but effectively purge the disaffected. Jesús Díaz, a prominent filmmaker who had been a member of the Communist Party, participated in the process and shared critical perspectives of the political and economic situation in Cuba. He called this his last act of faith in the Revolution. Seeing that he had been betrayed, he left the island for Europe.

In a reversal of revolutionary practice and rhetoric, the regime opened its doors to foreign investment while repressing any form of individual entrepreneurship. The military, in what became known as market-Leninism, acted as an economic agent as well as an agent of repression. Massive emigration once again ensued. Those who had the ability to travel abroad simply left, then overstayed their visas; those without means took to the sea.

The Special Period proved to be devastating. Mendieta further described in detail the distressing emotions she experienced: "I've tried to fight against my spiritual deterioration with all my might. I wouldn't let myself be dragged away by hopelessness, desperation, apathy, and depression, but where has it gotten me? It's gotten me nowhere, because there is no escaping this reality. Every road leads to some point, like an infinite labyrinth with no exit."[37]

This anguish indeed led to a deterioration of personal codes of conduct, with many Cubans seeking out carnal pleasures in a last-ditch attempt to connect and as a way of disassociating themselves from the horrific present. Perhaps one of the best written fictional accounts of this Special Period attitude can be found in Pedro Gutiérrez's *Dirty Havana Trilogy*, which has been described as "a steamy, sex-soaked series of short stories about the hell Havana became in the early 1990s, when the Soviet Union ceased all assistance and aid to the Cuban government."[38] It is also representative of the breakdown of social mores and the demise of a future-oriented culture. It is loosely autobiographical, a reflection of a time when both the author's marriage and country were collapsing. In discussing the novel, Esther Whitfield described the main character as ". . . a new hedonist, self-concerned and proudly so. As one might expect, given the duplicities that encase the book, the author does not succumb lightly to the complexly Cuba-phile demands of his foreign readers. Instead, he perceives, from the tourists who flit in and out of his Centro Habana *barrio,* that what visitors to Cuba want is some form of physical contact."[39]

The idyllic image of Cuba as the socialist paradise is displaced in this novel. Francisco Leal writes that the *Havana Trilogy* "exhibits scenes of abjection, such as attraction and repulsion, spectacles of sex linked to the freak show and descriptions of crime scenes: all are manners in which 'dirty' Cuba has become an international object of consumption."[40] The present becomes a temporal site for global tourism, while the puritanical revolutionary morality gives way to producing an exoticized image of Cuba. What is most striking is the insistence on the moment, on instantaneous gratification and hyper-individualism, a sharp contrast to the official rhetoric that called for collective sacrificing to be followed by a redemptive promise of prosperity and happiness.

During this period, sex work, or what Cubans called *jineterismo* (jockeying), became a dominant mode of labor as young women and men cruised new tourist strips in search of money and a way out of the country. The state soon became a kind of official pimp, as it promoted tourism and required that tourists who wished to bring a Cuban guest into their hotel room pay for a special permit issued by the state. Indeed, Fidel Castro announced to the world that "Cuba had the cleanest and most educated prostitutes in the world."[41] And if a tourist wanted to marry a Cuban, another fee was imposed to pay for an exit permit in what could be called a state dowry. Gender and racial divides became more visible in this state-run enterprise. The promotion of tourism included explicit representations of race. It became conventional wisdom that Canadians wintering in Cuba preferred lighter skinned women, Germans darker skinned, and Spaniards *mestizas* (mixed race). Boarding houses were set up in tourist spots like Varadero to give Cuban women temporary housing. Women of various skin tones and from different parts of the island were encouraged to come during different seasons, depending on what country tourists were coming from. The long lines of women waiting outside embassies to receive permits to travel abroad seemed to confirm this.

However, what could have been a descent into total individualism did not quite happen in Cuba during this time. To survive on the island, people needed to rely on each other despite, or perhaps because of, the repressive regime. Black markets that operated informally provided a social network that reinforced personal connections. Over the decades surviving socialism

90 · Democracy and Time in Cuban Thought

had built a certain camaraderie among people as an illegal barter economy helped provide basic goods. This informal market with unwritten rules and regulations created a form of interdependent community that continued through the worst economic moments. The political and the state permeated every aspect of people's lives in Cuba. This resulted in a lack of differentiation between the public and the private, which in turn influence the spaces in which the present emerged. Without democratization or legalized private entrepreneurship, the present arose in people's daily life as it forced them to *resolver*—to find a solution for immediate problems. A certain rearrangement of priorities, along the Maslow's hierarchy of needs, took ordinary Cubans to the most basic physiological needs, food and immediate gratification.

The Idle Present

Walter Benjamin wrote about the idle present—an unproductive time that he argued was the result of a capitalist system in which workers, not having control over their lives, become passive to the forces of history. The lived experiences under socialism would suggest that an idle present also emerged under authoritarian, leftist regimes.

In *El arte de la espera (The Art of the Waiting),* Rafael Rojas writes about the period between the end of communism and the eventual end of the Castro regime. He calls it Cuba's in-between parenthesis, a place where it is clear that the Revolution has failed but where reforms have not yet succeeded in making significant changes.[42] Since the fall of communism, Cuba has tried to reinsert itself in a capitalist world market while refusing to open up internal markets. In 2008 Fidel Castro announced that he would be stepping down and his younger brother, Raúl Castro, would be taking the reins of power. Raúl Castro, the more pragmatic politician of the two, did issue a series of rules that legalized certain entrepreneurial activities, many of them already well-developed in the informal market. There had previously been similar moments, such as the beginning of the '80s, when small restaurants and shops were allowed to open, but those moments did not last. In distinction, this new period was marked by the lack of international partners that could subsidize the island, so there was more flexibility in the internal market. But even the legalization of certain entrepreneurial activities fell short of creating any real domestic market. Tellingly, even the mention of free markets was discouraged from proposals developed by U.S. and Cuban scholars.

While there were modest, if not successful, reforms to the economy, the political realm was another story. Off and on, certain groups had been allowed some forms of expression, such as the human rights advocates of the 1990s, especially before visits by international human rights organizations, but these periods, too, tended to be short lived. Any attempts to organize alternative political movements were met with harsh punishment. The lack of liberties and of the ability to exercise political practices led to a passive population that waited for change to come from above even as groups emerged organizing for change. At that moment, the notion of politics itself was shunned even by critics of the government, as politics was only understood—in fact experienced—as the exercise of power, not its contestation.

For Rojas, the waiting is a product of the de-politization that occurs in totalitarian countries where people lack opportunities for meaningful engagement in public affairs. This is similar to citizens' skepticism brought on by unbridled markets in post-authoritarian capitalist countries. The difference, however, is important to note. In democratic regimes, the state of disengagement occurs because there is a retreat from "the political" arena, which is perceived by citizens as ineffective and corrupt. In contrast, in totalitarian regimes, the disengagement stems from a saturation of the political, which invades every aspect of an individual's life;[43] people are inundated with requests for performative political participations that are empty and ineffective.

This sense of the in-between is poignantly captured in Zoé Valdés's novel *La nada cotidiana*.[44] While the author explores a present of excessive immediate gratification similar to that of Gutiérrez's *Dirty Havana Trilogy*, she also provides a deeper understanding of that idle, unproductive present that lies between a past and a future that never arrives.

Her opening line signals the skeptical view of the utopic project: "Ella viene de una isla que quiso construir el paraíso" (She comes from an island that wanted to construct paradise).[45] The story's leading character was born in 1959, the year of the triumph of the Revolution, and her father named her Patria (Homeland). The first chapter begins in purgatory, where according to Catholic doctrine, those who are not worthy of heaven but not deserving of hell go in the afterlife. Patria, who is later named Yocandra, remembers nothing. At the end of the first chapter, the narrator has been sent back to her island, the island that "queriendo construir el paraíso, ha creado el infierno" (wanting to build paradise, has created hell).[46]

Her present has become mechanical, her daily routine is monotonous and unproductive. "Hace dos años que hago lo mismo todos los días: peda-

92 · Democracy and Time in Cuban Thought

lear de mi casa a la oficina, marcar la tarjeta, sentarme en el buró, leer algunas revistas extranjeras que continúan llegando con dos y tres meses o años de retraso, y pensar en las musarañas."[47] (It has been two years that I do the same thing every day. Pedal from my home to work, clock-in, sit at my desk, read a couple of two-, three-month-old foreign magazines that still find their way here, and daydream.) The same sentiment of a suspended present is found in Mendieta's essay when she says, "We've turned into a country without hope, as we were swimming eternally in some third lap that leads to nowhere."[48]

Yocandra lives her disillusionment with totalizing grand narratives such as the hypernationalism and Marxism-Leninism of the Cuban government in a state of suspended animation. James M. Griesse, a scholar of Cuban literature, has remarked: "Clearly, then, *La nada cotidiana* is the portrayal of the anguish of a subject who counter-identifies with the Revolution. For Yocandra, existence in the Revolution had become hell as the utopia unraveled and the promise by the Revolution has become a dystopia."[49] At the end of the novel, Yocandra returns to purgatory. Here in this in-between space, all you can do is wait for others to make decisions over your destiny.

Rolando Estévez, an artist from the Cuban province of Matanzas, also explored the theme of "waiting." A painter, writer, and editor of the magazine *Vigía*, a handmade literary journal, Estévez remained on the island when his parents emigrated in 1965 and stayed until his death in 2023.[50] At the time of his parents' departure, boys fifteen and older could not leave, since they were about to enter military age. He studied art, and in the 1980s began an artisanal project in his hometown. There was a scarcity of paper and few publishing outlets, so a group of writers and artists decided to launch a series of handmade books. With paper from the butcher shop and very rudimentary printing presses, they began publishing a series of journals. One was dedicated to reclaiming the history of Matanzas and included, for instance, the rich contributions the city's pharmacists has made regarding natural remedies. Another collected children's stories and poems. Yet another was dedicated to writers, poets, and intellectuals. Each number of the limited edition had original ornaments added to it. One, devoted to the work of Eliseo Diego, has a wax candle with a wick carefully placed on each cover.

Estévez also continued his own artistic work. In one series, he explored the frustrations and the futility of the Special Period. The title of the series, *La Espera (The Wait),* suggests an immobile present.[51] Each sketch includes a figure of a man and an appropriate phrase. These phrases all include the

Figure 3.1. *La Espera*, from the series *Gerundios*, 1997, Rolando Estévez. Courtesy of Ruth Behar.

verb *esperar* (to wait) in the first person present, *espero* (I wait), and a second verb, this time in gerund form, expressing a continuous, private action: *pensando* (thinking), *escondiendo* (concealing), *soñando* (dreaming).

The final piece of the series is *Espero tratando* (I wait trying). In this last sketch, a small man is trying to move a boulder that is being pulled in the opposite direction by a hook. Poised at the edge of the cliff, he waits. At the end, nothing happens although there is a sense of precarity in the present.

The Poetic Present: Eliseo Diego's Temporality

Octavio Paz considered Eliseo Diego to be one of Latin America's greatest poets. I would like to suggest that the poetic present that Paz wrote about is found in Diego's work. I will examine his work in depth to show how many of the sensibilities that can encourage a more democratic culture are woven throughout his poems and essays. His work has a very intimate relationship with the past as he reminisces—which is distinct from just remembering— as a way of maintaining the past alive and connected to the present.

94 · Democracy and Time in Cuban Thought

This distinction is palpable in a poem by one of Diego's contemporaries and literary associates, Fina García Marruz, *No, no memoria*. In the poem, García Marruz asks the memory of another day not to darken today. She does not want to return to the past. Yet in the last stanza, she allows a bit of the past into the present.

> . . . Volver a lo pasado no es mi ruego . . .
> ¿Pero y aquel aroma de la vida?
> Retenga su promesa, no su fuego.[52]

> . . . Going back to the past is not my plea . . .
> But what about that scent of life?
> Hold its promise, not its heat.

Both García Marruz's and Diego's work could be thought of as the poetry of the moment. The present, for both, is filled with possibilities and contains other times as well. We can recall Paz's appreciation that poetry is "in love with the instant" and attempts to turn time into a fixed present.

In his work, Diego constructed a nonlinear time that stood in contrast to modernity's unidirectional sense of time. He elaborated a sense of the present in which individuals could recognize each other, an essential component of a democratic sensibility particularly needed in diverse societies. There is in his poetry an insistence on the need for humans to communicate with one another, as well as faith in the role that the arts can play in facilitating this communication. Diego delighted in taking different points of views, even if it privileged the villain's. Lastly, in his ever-expanded present, there was room to daydream and contemplate.

Diego was born in Havana on July 2, 1920, and was raised on the family farm in Arroyo Naranjo. His childhood experiences were beautifully narrated by his daughter, Josefina de Diego, in her book *El reino del abuelo,* which suggests a magical place filled with personal warmth, beautiful physicality, and nature.[53] Diego learned to speak English from his mother, who had lived in New York. He attended university but never graduated, quickly becoming immersed with other writers and poets in Havana.

Diego became part of *Orígenes,* a group of writers and artists led by José Lezama Lima and Pepe Rodríguez, who published a quarterly journal of the same name from 1944 to 1956. Despite its stated mission to establish the essence of *cubanía* (Cubanness), the journal also featured works by Paz, Jean-Paul Sartre, Elizabeth Bishop, and Wallace Stevens, among others. The members of the group were Catholics, and therefore imbued their philosophical musings with allusions to Catholic thought. Concerns about the Incarnate Word and eternity became reference points for much of their aesthetic journeys. At the same time, they were not closed to the world of ideas, as they brought together poets and writers from the Americas and Europe to debate the place of Nietzschean thought in their philosophy of aesthetic production.

At the time, there were other competing literary magazines in Cuba, many of which had become the means through which differing political and aesthetic ideas were projected.[54] For instance, *La Gaceta del Caribe*, a project of the Popular Socialist Party (PSP, Cuba's communist party), sought to reorient Cuban culture toward popular Black culture. *La Gaceta's* project was explicitly political. This coincided with the International Communist Party's strategies around what was referred to as "The Negro Question."

La Gaceta proposed that Afro-Cuban culture was the essence of Cubanness. Slavery had been fundamental to the colonial experience, it asserted, and the emergence of a new nation had the responsibility to rescue a marginalized culture and give it a central role. Their goal was to reorient Cuban culture away from either Europe or the United States and situate it in the Afro-Caribbean world. Locating Cuba in the Caribbean was a way of recognizing Black culture and recasting it as central to the nation.

Like other communist-aligned artistic movements, *La Gaceta* was antiracist and anti-imperialist. Aesthetically, it promoted historicism and social realism. The experiences and language of ordinary people were woven through the literature and poetry. Art and culture were terrains in which to engage in the class struggle, and as such, they advocated a more political cultural production. Its members were involved in politics.

Anchoring this movement was Nicolás Guillén, whose poetry sought to elevate popular musical rhythms clearly associated with Afro-Cuban culture, such as *son*, to the ranks of poetry. *Son* is a popular form of folk music originating in Cuba's eastern provinces and with roots in African culture.[55] The debate over where to situate race in Cuban art included music along with literature and poetry. Guillén recognized and incorporated this into his poetry.

The explicit aesthetic, social, and political intention of the *La Gaceta* stood in direct contrast to *Orígenes* on several aspects. Aesthetically, *Orígenes* sought a more universal language and one more closely allied with Spanish tradition. They did not anchor their project geographically. They did not seek to define Cubanness from a sociological or racial perspective. Lezama was also particularly critical of the claim that Afro-Cuban culture was the most important element of Cubanness,[56] even though he was being inclusive of Afro-Cuban themes and art in the journal.[57]

But even as Blacks appeared in marginal roles in Lezama's work,[58] Gastón Baquero, another member of *Orígenes* who was of mixed race, tackled the tension between "high white culture" and "Black populist culture" in his work. For instance, in his poem, *Piano y tambor*, (Piano and Drum) he counterposed two worlds, "the first refined and cultured, the second the powerful ancestral voice."[59] And while Baquero recognized that there were no "pure races," he understood the existence and the power of racism. Indeed, he explored the origins of racism and concluded that it was born of fear—fear of hunger and fear of the lack of economic opportunities.[60] His understanding of the origins of racism may have placed him philosophically closer to Guillén, as both considered that racism arose from socioeconomic conditions and human reactions fueled by segregation. Baquero eventually would leave the island and go into exile. Interestingly, the majority of the other members of *Orígenes* would stay in Cuba.

While there were deep ideological and political differences between the two groups, the differences were aired through a discussion about aesthetics and the place of art in society. *La Gaceta's* explicit political program promoted the communist PSP. They were involved in real politics, which at the time was rife with corruption. Guided by the principle that communist revolutions could not happen in non-industrialized countries, the communist parties worldwide concentrated on "internal contractions," such as racism, that could heighten mobilization. So working for the inclusion of Blacks in politics and culture became a priority for the PSP.

In contrast, the stated objective of *Orígenes* was to create an alternative to the corrupt political situation in Cuba, which was one that did not reflect the essence of the humanist perspective they believed held the potential for a nation. It was an orientation away from politics to philosophy and aesthetics. Lezama, in particular, called for a nation of letters. He advocated an aesthetic project to develop an alternative to bankrupt politics and to explore essential elements that could regenerate a nation based on ethical poetics.[61] *Orígenes* argued for a profound reflection on the essential elements of the nation.[62] Its members premised their views on an "unsaturated past," that is, a past with little history that made room to create a new historical memory. In contrast, the past for the protagonists of *La Gaceta* was precisely what justified the revision of Cubanness to privilege Afro Cubanness.

For the *Originistas,* poetry became suprahistory as well as a method to know reality.[63] According to María Zambrano, a Spanish member of the group, "poetry united with reality is history."[64] If the nation itself did not have a deep history, then poetry was a way of rewriting history for the future. Poetry, according to Cintio Vitier, was where the past and the future were united.[65] In the *Orígenes* aesthetic, poetic time unified past, present, and future, memory, suspension, and desire.[66]

What happens in that moment of unification? There seems to have been two distinct currents of thought in the *Orígenes* group about what to do in and with the present. One current "understood writing as the testimony about nothingness and the absurd"; the other believed in the "mission to fill the void with memory."[67] These currents brought forth distinct intellectual projects. Eliseo Diego's poetry became a way of filling the void of the moment. As such, it created a new way of rethinking the present and establishing a sensibility that recognized and encouraged respect for "the other." As we will see, this also holds the possibility of a reconciled vision between the various literary and political camps.

The essence of time, the pausing of time, and the possibilities of the moment became central themes for Diego's work. The mystery of time and its relationship to human experiences would dominate his poetic explorations:

Me fascina la insondable realidad, su inmersión en el fluir temporal, su transformación en imagen, recuerdo, sueño, su deshacerse en muerte o en olvido, su transfiguración en palabras, color, formas, música (. . .). Lo que me apasiona es el tiempo, el fluir del río "nuestras vidas son los ríos . . . ." Pero, ¿cómo se aviene esta imagen con el futuro que hasta cierto punto es posible provocar? Quizás la solución sería decir "encauzar." De todas formas, el misterio del tiempo es inseparable del otro mayor que es el hombre.[68]

I am fascinated by the unfathomable reality, its immersion in the temporal flow, its transformation into image, memory, dream, its undoing in death or oblivion, its transfiguration in words, color, forms, music (. . .). What I'm passionate about is time, the flow of the river "our lives are rivers . . ." But how does this image fit with the future that to a certain extent it is possible to provoke? Perhaps the solution would be to say "channel." In any case, the mystery of time is inseparable from the greater other that is man.

Diego's sense of a unique temporality of the present can be seen in his early writings. Diego was not only a poet but also a teacher. At the onset of the Revolution, however, he was removed from his teaching post because of his religious faith and placed in the national library in charge of children's literature. In this new position, he developed a series of essays about childhood, children, and literature that outline some enduring themes about time and the place of individuals Diego would explore in his later poetry.

His views on childhood are imbued with an open sense of endlessness. This special time of life allowed for the coexistence of diverse points of views, a necessary component to a more democratic culture. It was a shared stage of human development in which paradise could exist, even though it would ultimately be lost.[69] He shared Martí's views that childhood should be seen not just as a pedagogical project, but as a special moment. For both men, children's imagination was a sacred place to enter respectfully and tenderly. However, unlike Martí, who placed children in future temporalities, Diego asked teachers to consider them as they were, not as they had been or could be.

Children, he believed, had the capacity to imagine and create their futures. His understanding of the present included room for imagining a future: *Soñar despierto* (dreaming while awake). Diego's sense of the present was integral to the way he viewed children on their own terms. In contrast to religious philosophies that marked children with original sin, he wanted to engage with children as they were—a respectful recognition of the other. Children were not just a vehicle to build the future, as Martí saw them, they were entities in their own right to be recognized. In politics, this recognition creates a more inclusive community.

Sense of Time in Eliseo Diego's Poetry

In conjunction with his appreciation of the place of children in the present, Diego developed a sense of a temporality distinct from modernity's, in which the past gushes toward the future in a unidirectional linear fashion. This unilinear direction tends to obliterate the possibilities for the more intimate and sustainable engagements necessary to a more democratic culture. In Diego's conception, there is a possibility for time to move back and forth, between past and future, as it does in *Único y curioso libro del ajedrez:* ¿Tú sabes si ha llegado o ya se ha ido aquel que nos traía los recuerdos como panes dorados con el alba? (Do you know if he has come or gone, who used to bring us memories like golden bread at dawn?).[70]

Incidentally, Fina García Marruz also had a similar notion that time could be experienced at different paces, as is evidenced in the following poem:

Del tiempo largo

A veces, en raros
instantes, se abre, talud
real y enorme, el tiempo
transcurrido.
Y no es entonces
breve el tiempo. . . .
Sometimes in rare moments
it opens up
real and enormous, slope,
time that has passed.
And then time is not brief . . .[71]

Unlike the modernist conception of time, which can only hold one temporality at a time, Diego's time encompassed multiple temporalities, perhaps creating a space for mutigenerational engagements and even differences of perspectives. In the moment, he could remember a forgotten past, an appreciation of time that runs throughout his poetry.[72] In an almost Proustian-like recall, he recreated a past that had been assumed forgotten. In his poem *Las ropas,* for instance, he recalled with lucid detail every aspect of the suit his grandfather wore to mass on Sundays.[73] Yet his notion of the present can also include the future, underscoring the simultaneous existence of distinct temporalities. In *Imaginemos un tiempo,* he envisioned "un tiempo en que me haya alejado tanto que los hijos de mis hijos y sus hijos no vean en mí sino un extraño" (a time when I have strayed so far that my children's children and their children do not see in me but a stranger).[74]

The poem describes not just an accumulation of endless moments, but rather moments that disappear into a distance with time. Indeed, time can be recreated outside its progressive tempo. Memory and dreams, remembering and forgetting, the past and the future are constituted in the moment, giving the present a sense of broadness and fullness. It is not that time does not pass. It does, and indeed, it can obliterate the moment, as Diego noted in *El domingo (Sunday),* where Monday erased all that had occurred the day before.[75] And while noting the passing of time, Diego recognized its mysterious workings. In *Coplas del Tiempo,* he wrote:

Nadie vio jamás el tiempo
Ni escuchó sus leves pasos
Ni su aliento
Sintió nunca en la mejilla
Con las hojas del otoño
Con el viento
Se proteje a maravilla.
Lunes y martes y pronto
la mañana
vuelve a ser la que antes era?[76]

No one ever saw time
Nor heard its slight steps
Not its breadth
Ever felt on the cheek

With autumn leaves
With the wind
It protects itself wonderfully.

Monday and Tuesday and soon
the morning
Is it back to where it was before?

The passing of time, however, has a distinct rhythm that is suggestive of something more complicated than a straight path. Time's passing is imperceptibly slow, even as life is being created in the moment. In the poem *Tú te inclinas despacio a la tristeza (You bow slowly to sadness)*, Diego observed that in the calm of the moment, as nightfall arrives, he could perceive a life that has been created in time.[77] But the present is not boundless, it cannot contain all lived experiences. In *El día de hoy,* (Today) Diego further mused about how he was reading, at the moment, an essay written by William Butler Yeats in which Yeats had referred to then-young poets who were now either old or dead.[78] In the present, the act of reading can contain the past. Time for Diego was never a neutral force; it could be ravaging, and it could be bountiful. And he was always anxious about the power of time to erase all that had been lived, a recognition of the relationship that the past can have with the present. In *Biografía,* he lamented that he did not understand that he was no longer here, doubting his existence. His fear of the passage of time reflected his fear of death:

Comienza un lunes
La eternidad por fin comienza un lunes
y el día siguiente apenas tiene nombre
y el otro es el oscuro, al abolido.

Y en él se apagan todos los murmullos
y aquel rostro qua amábamos se esfuma
y en vano es ya la espera, nadie viene.

La eternidad ignora las costumbres,
le da lo mismo rojo que azul tierno,
se inclina al gris, al humo, a la ceniza.

Nombre y fecha tú grabas en un mármol,
los roza displicente con el hombro,
ni un montoncillo de amargura deja.

Y sin embargo, ves, me aferro al lunes
y al día siguiente doy el nombre tuyo
y con la punta del cigarro escribo
en plena oscuridad: aquí he vivido.[79]

On a Monday eternity finally begins
and the day that follows is scarcely named,
and the other is the dark, the done.

On that day are extinguished all whispers
and the face we loved dissolves in mist—
hope becomes hopeless: no one is coming.

Eternity knows nothing of our habits,
indifferent to red and the softest blue, it prefers
gray, smoke, ashes. You scratch
a name and a date on a piece of marble
and it rubs them out
with a careless shoulder, not even
a pinch of bitterness left behind. Yet see,

I cling to Mondays
and I give the next your name;
in total darkness I write
with the tip of my cigarette:
here have I lived.[80]

102 · Democracy and Time in Cuban Thought

In this sense, there is a modernist, existentialist sensibility that, nonetheless, Diego did not take as given. In fact, one of his lifelong hopes was to be able to stop, or at least slow down, the passage of time. At this slower pace, contemplation would be possible, and contemplation is something that, as Arendt has noted, is a necessary component of democratic cultures. Diego found that time could be stopped by reading.[81] But most importantly, he came to believe that art might be able to detain time.

In *Quién sabe* he writes:

"El tiempo debe detenerse," reclama un Aldous Huxley anhelante. Sí, pero, ¿cómo?

El tiempo corre o vuela, fluye como los ríos a la mar, ya lo sabemos. "Hoy se está yendo sin parar un punto." Cierto, mi Don Francisco. Junto con Huxley y vuestro humilde lector—¡y qué de tiempo por medio!—, todos quisiéramos que se detuviese. Sí, pero, ¿cómo?

Porque si se detuviese ya no lo sería—no sería tiempo. Entonces, ¿de dónde ese absurdo deseo que todos hemos sentido arrasadoramente alguna vez—de dónde ese contra-sentido?

¿Será en el Arte que se detiene sin dejar de ser él, sin dejar de volar "como saeta o ave"? ¡Ah, esa joven de Vermeer leyendo su carta, leyéndola y leyéndola y leyéndola, siempre con idéntico gusto, a la idéntica luz de su mañana tan fugaz como eterna!

Y si se detiene en el Arte, ¿no tendremos razón en anhelar que lo haga también para nosotros, qué importa cómo?

¿No habrá para nosotros, pobres, siquiera un menudo remanso—en el sueño siquiera?

Dormir, soñar—¡quién sabe![82]

"Time must stop," claims a longing Aldous Huxley. Yes, but how?

Time runs or flies, it flows like rivers into the sea, we already know. "One point is leaving without stopping today." Right, my Don Francisco. Along with Huxley and your humble reader—and what about time in between!—we all want him to stop. Yes, but how?

Because if it stopped it would no longer be—it would not be time. So where does that absurd desire that we have all once felt overwhelming—where did that counter-sense come from?

Is it in Art that it stops without ceasing to be it without ceasing to fly "like a bolt or a bird"? Ah, that young woman from Vermeer reading her letter, reading it and reading it and reading it, always with the same pleasure, in the same light of her morning as fleeting as eternal!

And if it stops at Art, won't we be right to long for it to do it for us too, what does it matter how?

Will there not be for us, poor people, even a small haven—even in the dream?

Sleep, dream—who knows!

Time could also be paused by capturing the past through poetry and by eternalizing the present in words and images. In *Time of Photography* the present, just as it is, is made still.

Ávida vuela la palanca
y entra veloz la luz, el tiempo
preciso y justo de la arena
precipitándose a la trampa. Todo
queda ya igual

—ya para siempre.

Los niños y el resol, la viva espuma,
las nubes en sus coros displicentes,
la dicha inmensa del verano
y el simple estar allí
—tal como era

en aquella otra luz

—en aquel tiempo.[83]

Avidly flies the lever
and the light enters quickly, the time
precise and fair from the sand
rushing into the trap. Everything
remains the same

—forever.

The children and the glare of the sun, the living foam,
the clouds in their careless choruses,
the immense bliss of summer
and just being there

—As it was

in that other light

—at that time.

In capturing the moment, Diego created a form of the present that can be eternal. "Tú eres," he wrote in *A una joven romana*, "tú sólo un instante. Y en ese instante está tu eternidad a salvo" (You just an instant. And in that instant your eternity is safe).[84] The instant becomes eternal when it is noted.[85] The present is expanded from the now into eternity when what surrounds us is noted and the lived experiences are recognized. And what remains with us forever needs special respect and attention.

The Present and Its Possibilities

Diego felt that poetry was hard to define, and he was fond of repeating a Samuel Johnson quote, "Sir, it is easier to say what it is not, than say what is, poetry."[86] But he suggested multiple ways in which poetry could enhance our connectivity to each other, indeed help us form a community.

Poetry is created by attending to what is around us. Diego often said, "La poesía es el acto de atender en toda su pureza" (Poetry is an act of paying attention in all its purity).[87] Listening and observing contribute to a culture of respect.

Poetry is also a means to be a witness and to give testimony of what is.[88] Indeed, the poet has the responsibility of naming what is present and testifying about what surrounds us.

> . . . Y nombraré las cosas, tan despacio
> que cuando pierda el Paraíso de mi calle
> y mis olvidos me la vuelvan sueño,
> pueda llamarlas de pronto con el alba.[89]

> . . . And I'll name things, so slowly
> that when I lose the Paradise of my street
> and my forgetfulness turns it into a dream
> I can call them suddenly at dawn.

Naming things and those around us is a human act of recognizing the "other," a necessary element in building respectful relationships. In Diego's view, poetry also had a social function, and that is communication. In a certain sense, this conception of poetry, while not explicitly political as the *Gaceta* group advocated, does insert art into social reality.

Si la poesía es, ante todo, "el acto de crear," será lícito preguntarnos si todos sentimos o no el impulso o el deseo de crear. Me parece obvia la respuesta en el sentido afirmativo.

. . .

Con lo que llegamos al punto para mí fundamental: el concepto de necesidad. El arte es a un tiempo una necesidad y su respuesta— como el hambre presupone el pan que la satisface, o la sed, el agua.

(. . .)

Ahora bien: ¿necesidad de qué? Pues de comunicarnos—de formar parte, por el ser o
    el saber—del misterio o el enigma de la realidad que nos rodea y cuyo ápice es la
    psique humana en sus aspectos de conciencia y afectividad. No hay cuento fantástico
    tan fantástico como el simple hecho de vivir.[90]

If poetry is, above all, "the act of creating," it will be licit to ask ourselves whether or not we all feel the urge or desire to create. The answer seems to me obvious in the affirmative. . . .

With which we reach the fundamental point for me: the concept of necessity. Art is both a necessity and its response—as hunger presupposes the bread that satisfies it, or thirst, water.

(. . .)

Now, need for what? Well, to communicate—to be a part of something, by being or knowing—of the mystery or the enigma of the reality that surrounds us and whose apex is the human psyche in its aspects of consciousness and affectivity. There is no fantastic tale as fantastic as the simple fact of living.

Communication creates community and allows individuals to feel that they are part of a greater whole. The communicative role of poetry was a theme repeated throughout Diego's work. "Un poema no es más que la felicidad, que una conversación en la penumbra" (A poem is nothing but happiness, but a conversation in the penumbra).[91] In part, this conversation is made possible through poems that can explore and identify human emotions, even those that carry pain.[92]

106 · Democracy and Time in Cuban Thought

Poetry requires an author/writer and audience/readers.

Siempre he pensado que la poesía debe ser como un golpe que lo conmueva a uno, y en esa conmoción está el secreto del asunto; en que un poema debe ser una obra de creación a dos: por una parte el que lo escribe, por otra parte el que lo lee y recrea.[93]

I have always thought that poetry should be like a blow that moves you, and in that commotion is the secret of the matter; in which a poem must be a work of creation for two: on the one hand the one who writes it, on the other hand the one who reads and recreates it.

Diego's views of his readers also point to a sensibility of respect and openness, and to a willingness to allow readers the space to create their own experiences. His is not a didactic approach, but one that makes room for creativity and change.

Tomemos como ejemplo la poesía, ya que debe emplear la materia más huidiza. En un poema habrá los elementos—palabra, ritmo, pausa o silencio—indispensables—los únicos, los necesarios—para que el lector—esto es, el otro—re-cree a partir de ellos la experiencia, o iluminación, original. Si se le da todo, nada tendrá que crear.[94]

Let us take poetry as an example, since it must use the most elusive matter. In a poem there will be the essential elements—word, rhythm, pause or silence—the only ones, the necessary—so that the reader—that is, the other—re-creates from them the original experience, or illumination. If everything is given, nothing will have to be created.

For Diego, reading and interpreting are also creative processes. The reader is given the power to have a voice. Humans can feel and experience reality differently, and this is one of the mysteries of reality. Diego's readers are given the space to have their version of love, of a table, of a cat, of a pineapple.[95]

As with many other poets, there is a democratic impulse in Diego's writings in his ability to see things through distinct points of views. Not only does he grant the reader the right to re-create and reimagine the text, he grants himself, the poet, the right to engage in an exercise to explore diversity of opinion. For instance, in his retelling of fairy tales, Diego sometimes adopted the villain's point of view. In his version of *Little Red Riding Hood,* we see the story through the wolf's gaze.[96]

Diego also made a critical contribution to the ways in which a more expansive and inclusive epistemology can emerge in poetry. Like Vitier and Lezama Lima, he believed that poetry was not only an aesthetic creation, but also a way of acquiring knowledge, for it captured reality and contemplated its meaning.[97] The production of knowledge is an important arena of social struggle—not only does the recognition that human beings have the capacity to add to the body of knowledge go against Catholic teachings (which holds that God is all knowledge), it also sets up a force independent of power structures. In *Aquí un momento* he wrote, "Y pregunto qué sea el lugar donde vivo, éste mi sitio de pensar un momento" (And I wonder what the place is where I live, this place of thinking for a moment).[98] As time flows, and the moment is captured in words, silence brackets the present from the future, creating a time of stillness and contemplation.

> Pero después que todo se acababa,
> las cortezas de fuego entre la espuma,
> se abría el silencio como un mar en calma
> cerrándonos allí como en las islas
> que la serena tarde se ha olvidado.[99]

> But after it was all over,
> the crusts of fire between the foam,
> silence opened like a calm sea
> closing us there as in the islands
> that the serene afternoon has forgotten.

It is in silence that time pauses and creates a moment in which absolutes lose their certainty.[100] It could be said that this is a different kind of waiting than the idle, unproductive present Benjamin outlines and that permits authoritarianism to take root. This waiting is productive and patient.[101] In this still time, a form of dreaming can occur while we are still awake. As such, a future can emerge from a rooted present. In delineating a present in which the future can also coexist, Diego showed an appreciation of a temporality in which a future can be contemplated, in contrast to a present in which needs and desires are simply projected into an unattainable future. Imagination also occurs in the present. Despite the impending coming of winter—death, perhaps—it is necessary to dream while awake.[102] Daydreaming

Figure 3.2. Eliseo Diego. Courtesy of Josefina de Diego.

is an activity that is grounded in the moment, done while one is fully awake, and one that permits rummaging through possibilities.

The Present: Democratic Sensibilities and Some of Its Limitations

There are many conceptions of "the present" in Cuban thought. During the Special Period a form of the present emerged that emphasized immediate gratification. The obvious need for political change in the face of a repressive and authoritarian political apparatus and system contributed to an idle present in which individuals did not feel that they could act. But as we have seen, there is another form of the present that offers a moment to recognize the other and engage with reality. This kind of present is found in Eliseo Diego's appreciations of time and what can occur within time. Here we see the development of the poetic present that Octavio Paz calls for: an alternative to the failed futuristic temporality of the grand narratives of the twentieth century. In Diego's present, the past and the future can coexist. Unlike Arendt's description of modernity's temporality, which abruptly cut ties with the past and moved into a futuristic spectacle leading to totalitarianism, a present that can hold multiple times allows for a richer human experience that does not lend itself as easily to totalizing political structures. In this poetic present, a temporal place exists that allows for the recognition of others as they are. In it, individuals can exist, as they cannot do in temporal spaces that reduce all individuals to categories such as the "masses" or "*el pueblo.*"

For now, a present temporality brings important elements to our discussions. In order to create space for the multiple voices of a diverse society, a recognition of the other as different as he or she may be, is essential for democracy. Communication and deliberations are essential to democracy. Diego's work displays a great appreciation for the need and the ability to communicate through art and poetry. Audiences are given a role in that they are allowed to interpret topics and experiences though their own lenses. Lastly, in Diego's poetic present, there is also a place where we can calmly assess what we have, including the time we have left, and the time that has passed. Contemplation for Arendt and for Diego was a necessary condition for more open societies. After all, democracy is a deliberative process that requires thought, discussions, and compromise.

Most importantly, the poetic present is a time when individual agency can be reclaimed, including in the rewriting of past narratives that have erased dissenting voices. In a more inclusive present, a likewise more inclusive future can be imagined. More democratic forms of creating renditions of the past and laying dreams about the future can emerge in an expansive present. It is in this *entre tiempos* (between times) that more intimate and social relationships can be built. These sensibilities, which contribute to a humanistic and democratic political culture, can thrive in a poetic present.

4

Democratizing the Past

> If we cannot have a future without a past, how are we to integrate that past into our future? The answer is: by giving both of them the time of the present.
>
> Carlos Fuentes, *The Literary Imagination and the Sense of the Past,* 1986

In the work of the poet Eliseo Diego, we appreciated a form of the present that could be inclusive and expansive, and as such more conducive to fostering democratic social sensibilities. Still, temporalities are intertwined, and we may also need to find more open ways of conceiving the past and the future as Carlos Fuentes proposes: locating both in the present.

In this chapter, I explore specific projects aimed at making the past more inclusive. I will consider here a wave of memoirs that have been published in the United States,[1] as well as visual art projects from the island and the United States that are opening the past by questioning history, revising it to be more inclusive, and re-examining its production process, including the very notion of archives, and asking the question of who owns them. Archives are the places in which memory is stored. So the ways in which they are organized and the processes by which materials are chosen to be stored in them directly affect the production of knowledge and our understanding of the past. I end with a discussion of what these projects contribute to our understanding of a more expansive past.

Exile Memoirs: Beyond the Confines of Obligated Memory

As is the case with all wars, the Cuban Revolution generated carefully constructed narratives of its history, with heroes and villains and with starkly cast and carefully scripted storylines. The response of the opposition was to create its own narrative. For many Cuban exiles, the theme of a "Revolution betrayed" turned out to be central in that narrative, as did the idealization of exile as an arena for the Cuban success story. In the United States in particular, Cubans became the golden exiles who thrived despite the loss of a nation, family, property, and imagined futures. The creation of this official exile narrative included a nostalgic retelling of Cuban history to make sure it was never forgotten. This process demanded unanimity in the renditions of the past as well as the present, though it was not always achieved. French philosopher Paul Ricoeur calls this obligated memory, in which what we are expected to remember is not necessarily what happened to us.[2]

The reality, of course, was more complex, as were the human experiences Cuban exiles lived through. Some of these have found themselves into testimonials and memoirs. Memoirs that go against the current do the work of opening history to accommodate experiences outside the militarized memory zones.[3] Indeed, the recent increase in the publication of memoirs worldwide may be what historian Paula Fass has suggested—a manifestation of the rapidly changing temporalities of a globalized world. As she argues, we need to get our stories down before things really change.[4] The passing of the old guard in Cuba hasn't brought about major structural changes to the government, but it has symbolized an end of an era, and many will be compelled to explore their memories of those receding times.

Some of the early cracks in the official Cuban exile narrative surfaced when young Cuban exiles started to visit the island, which was in and of itself an act of defiance. With these organized trips, which in turn evolved into a type of movement, came testimonies of life in the United States that for many, especially those raised outside of the nestled confines of Cuban Miami, included ugly confrontations with racism and discrimination. In *Contra Viento y Marea,* for instance, the poet and scholar Lourdes Casal and a group of editors from *Areíto,* a journal edited by young exiles, gathered personal testimonies from those returning to Cuba with the Antonio Maceo Brigade in the late 1970s and early 1980s.[5] Their return had been an act of defiance against the essence of exile—some of the accounts included experiences with racism and violence—and the stories did not fit neatly into the official narrative, which held that Cubans had been received with open arms, that everyone was thriving, and that life was so much better in the United States.

Several years later, scholar Ruth Behar initiated a project to collect personal narratives of Cuban exiles who continued to have a relationship with the island. Her *Bridges to Cuba,* a two-volume publication of personal narratives, poems, and stories, established a plurality of experiences that constructed alternatives to the tales of survival and success.[6] Longing and nostalgia were shared sentiments, as was the desire to reconnect with the homeland. The book *By Heart/De Memoria: Cuban Women's Journeys in and out of Exile*, which I edited, also provided more nuanced renditions of our exile experiences. It brought together women's personal narratives of encounters with the island from those of us in exile as well as with the returning exiles by those on the island.[7] The book gathers the personal accounts of exiles in the sixties, seventies, eighties, and nineties, and it chronicles the view of those who were on the island during these times. For those of us who had gone back to Cuba, it was important to understand that there was opposition to our return, as well as resentment, from those who had stayed. We were countercultural, and on the island, our activism and cultural proclivities would be met with skepticism. In the exile community, we faced a violent backlash that included bombings and killings. Iraida López's *Impossible Returns: Narratives of the Cuban Diaspora*[8] also examines texts and art of Cuban exiles who returned to Cuba, including documentation about how they were viewed on the island. These memory projects sought to build alternative communities through texts.

As has been noted, the dramatic exodus of 14,000 unaccompanied minors through Operation Pedro Pan in the early 1960s engendered its own deeply militarized memories reflecting the collective coping with the pain arising from the separation of parents and their children. Thus, Pedro Pans became symbolically representative of the origins of a community born of extreme sacrifice. The narrative of the children who had been saved from communism called for presenting their émigré experience as heroic. A code of silence was expected regarding the pain suffered and/or the abuses encountered by these children. Still, there were memoirs like Román de la Campa's *Cuba on My Mind: Journeys to a Severed Nation*.[9] De la Campa returned to Cuba with the first group of the Antonio Maceo Brigade and in his book recounted the complicated politics that framed these returns. Carlos Erie's *Waiting for Snow in Havana: Confessions of a Cuban Boy*[10] presented a more nuanced and complex set of experiences as he recounted how his father, a Havana judge, remained in Cuba as he and his brother were sent to the United States. Flora González's essay "A House on Shifting Sands" beautifully describes how the unmooring caused by the long separation from her parents became a lifelong emotional condition for her.[11]

The Pedro Pan story found its way into other types of cultural productions as well. In theater, Nilo Cruz's *Hortensia and the Museum of Dreams* told the story of how a brother and sister sent alone to the United States bond in intimate ways. Melinda López's *Sonia Flew* revolves around characters who came to the United States as part of Operation Pedro Pan and are all dealing with the lingering emotional fallout of the abrupt separations from their families. Estela Bravo's *Operation Peter Pan: Flying Back to Cuba* and Guillermo Centeno's *Del otro lado del cristal* are films focused on the now-adults' recollection of the pain and dislocation. Both filmmakers were part of the Cuban official world. In Cuba, too, there were theatrical explorations of Operation Pedro Pan, which portrayed the exodus as a sinister plot to rob Cuba of its future.

In the late 1970s, both governments relaxed travel restrictions, and Cuban exiles were allowed to return to the island. They were encouraged to bring with them essential household products the Cuban government was having a hard time providing for the population. These visits heightened frustrations, which in turn increased people's desire to leave the island. The pressure eventually resulted in a massive emigration through the port of Mariel, twenty-five miles west of Havana. Ironically, both the Cuban and the U.S. governments complicated the Mariel boatlift exodus by casting immigrants as criminals and unwanted *escoria*. But Mirta Ojito's *Finding Mañana: A Memoir of a Cuban Exodus* offered the lived version of a twelve-year-old and her middle-class family's journey.[12]

Other memoirs have focused on the cultural dislocations experienced by young exiles and sought to negotiate new identities.[13] Examples of this genre are Pablo Medina's *Exiled Memories: A Cuban Childhood,*[14] Gustavo Pérez Firmat's *Next Year in Cuba: A Cubano's Coming-of-Age in America,*[15] and Richard Blanco's poetic narrative *The Prince of los Cocuyos: A Miami Childhood,*[16] which renders Cuban Miami as a more complex community than the golden exile legend suggests. Blanco's was a working-class upbringing, and through his memories we see the class diversity of Miami Cubans in contrast to the stereotypical image that portrays the exile community as white, conservative, and successful. This memoir genre challenges the idea that Cuban exiles are all the same. We are not, and the differences, whether they be political, racial, or related to sexual orientation, have not been easily accommodated.

Post-millennium, a new wave of memoirs emerged—some written by non-academics, some self-published—indicating a life-cycle phenomenon, as the generation that was in their teens at the time of the 1959 Revolution reached an age of retirement and reflection. Of this group, some reedify the themes of betrayal and success. Others take the reader into the private realm of family pathologies and traumas that happen to play out in a highly politicized environment, thus humanizing an understanding of the exile experience.

Dania Rosa Nasca's *Lights Out: A Cuban Memoir of Betrayal and Survival* is set in Holguín, in eastern Cuba, and documents how one family's life was changed by the Revolution.[17] This memoir, just like Virgil Suárez's *Spared Angola: Memories from a Cuban-American Childhood*,[18] is set mainly in Cuba. Nasca's family, like most Cubans, initially supported the Revolution but joined the opposition early on and decided to leave. At the time, once a family declared its intention to emigrate, its members became persona non grata and lost access to jobs and education. They were identified as enemies of the Revolution and suspicion always followed them. Nasca's memoir has keen observations about how the regime established its power, including by instilling psychological fear. Nasca's father was imprisoned and his small business confiscated. In the book, the author gives us a front-row seat to the dismantling of the small-business sector in Cuba, a process that took almost eight years. This is a special testimony, as this period is not well documented in academic history and certainly not in the popular press.

Another memoir, *My Story: Family, Cuba & Living the American Dream*, by José María de Lasa, was intended as a testament for the author's children and grandchildren, or as a type of family album.[19] As a young man from an upper socioeconomic class and a deeply Catholic family, de Lasa, along with his mother, brother, and sister, participated in the uprising against Batista. They later joined the opposition to Fidel Castro. The memoir offers a window into the involvement of young, upper-class Catholics in the anti-Batista uprising. It could be said that this movement, and its members' commitment and activism around social justice, was a precursor to the Liberation theology movement that came into fruition in Latin America in the 1960s. The schism in the supporters of the Revolution occurred when democracy, in the form of elections, was extracted from the social justice project. De Lasa's memoir also tracks his meteoric rise through the American corporate system, which can be read as a result of hard work, luck, and pre-exile social capital. Of particular interest to those who have studied this period of Cuban history are the candid assessments of the role of the Central Intelligence Agency in the opposition to Fidel Castro. There was no love lost between the young opponents of the Revolution and the CIA, despite recent attempts by some Cuban exiles in Miami to glorify everything related to the United States. Antonio Veciana's memoir, *Trained to Kill: The*

Inside Story of CIA Plots Against Castro, Kennedy, and Che, narrates this complicated relationship.[20]

A Cuban Refugee's Journey to the American Dream: The Power of Education, by Gerardo M. González, explores six decades of a personal story.[21] His family, originally from Placetas, in central Cuba, went into exile in the 1960s. Unlike the more privileged family background of the de Lasas, González's father was a mechanic. While there was an overrepresentation of the Cuban upper and middle classes in the early migratory waves to the United States, other social classes were part of this group as well. Once in Miami, González's father, unable to find work, moved the family north. This second dislocation also marked the young González, as he felt marginalized for being different in terms both of language and culture. Still, he began to find community with other Spanish-speaking kids. This early sense of being "Latino"—even though Latino as a term had not become part of the identity lexicon yet—would later allow him to situate himself in a broader community and dedicate his life to other Latinos. Upon his return to Miami in the late 1960s, he fell into a very diverse group of friends. One persuaded him to go to college. In the memoir, González shared his existential journey poignantly and honestly, including his foray into Eastern religions. He eventually completed a doctorate in education and embarked on a lifelong journey as an educator. At the end of the book, he returns to Cuba, reconnecting with his childhood and narrating the now overfamiliar re-encounters with the homeland.

Similarly, *Dancing with Dictators: A Family's Journey from Pre-Castro Cuba to Exile in the Turbulent Sixties,* by Luis Santeiro, bridges memories from Cuba to U.S. exile.[22] Like other memoirs, his story takes us on a round trip from Cuba to exile and eventually, a visit back. Santeiro writes vividly about early Cuban Miami, his time at Villanova University in Pennsylvania, and his stay with an uncle who lived in New York and who introduced him to theater. A broader project underpins this memoir: The reconciliation of his mother's warm, private memories of her father, President Gerardo Machado, with the disturbing public record the former president imprinted on Cuban history. The memoir travels from Santeiro's early childhood recollections in Cuba to his teenage years in the United States. It is a coming-of-age story that shares with other similar memoirs the typical tug-of-war between the Cuban and the American sides of experiences. To this, Santeiro adds his own journey to understand his family's past. This is not done with sentimentality, but rather based on his own research and difficult discussions with family members. At the end, there is no reconciliation between private and public memoires, but rather a deeper understanding that sometimes these two worlds cannot be reconciled. In Santeiro's memoir, they coexist, and it is important to recognize the tension they cause.

Another more nuanced and less typical memoir is *Adiós, Mi Pequeña Habana*, by Cecilia M. Fernández.[23] This is the antithesis of the golden exile story, as it documents a family's downward spiral in Miami. Shortly after they arrive in the United States and settle in Miami's Little Havana, Cecilia's father leaves her mother for his lover, whom he had also brought from Cuba. The mother suffers from depression and can barely make ends meet or pay close attention to her daughter. This gives young Cecilia room in which to explore Miami and her sexuality away from watchful adult eyes. For young Cuban women in particular, the culture of chaperones and policed sexuality clashed in the 1960s and 1970s with the freer U.S. dating customs and with the so-called sexual revolution of the period. Still, Fernández had to leave Miami to finally achieve what she wanted in life. Attending the University of California, Berkeley, she enters a new world that ultimately brings her into contact with more radical politics.

Another memoir of a broken family is Mia Leonin's *Havana and Other Missing Fathers*,[24] in which Leonin chronicled the search for her father. Attempting to get to know him, she traveled to the many places he had lived, a search that eventually led her to Cuba. This one, like many of the other memoirs, has family separations at its heart.

Marisella Veiga's *We Carry Our Homes With Us: A Cuban American Memoir* offers a unique perspective to exile outside the Miami enclave.[25] Local backlash against Cubans in Florida resulted in a federal relocation program to encourage Cubans to go to other parts of the United States. The Veigas, after a short stay in Miami, decided to move to Minnesota. While the author documented encounters with many American families who were supportive of Cuban refugees, she also wrote that, in Minnesota, her family was seen "as aliens, outsiders." In these new enclaves, Cubans [re]created close-knit communities as they lived near each other and gathered for holidays including Three Kings' Day. Their children, however, quickly incorporated "American ways" as part of a transculturation process. It is precisely that process of becoming bi-cultural that drives this memoir. This openness to other cultures led the author to be at ease with an array of students from many parts of the world when she was at the university. But Veiga's native town of Cojimar is always in the background, anchoring family memories. It is a place she eventually returned to visit.

In *Approaching Freedom: An Exile's Quest for a New Self*,[26] María Nodarse also returns to the island after a long journey that took her family to New Jersey and Miami. She narrates her encounters with racism and stereotypes and describes how she was radicalized while attending Columbia University and how she became estranged from her family and community. In her memoir, she searches for a way in which she can be Cuban and progressive in the United States while maintaining close ties with her family members, who do not share her desire to return to the island.

In *Traveling Heavy: A Memoir in Between Journeys*,[27] Ruth Behar narrates her experiences as the Cuban-born daughter of a Sephardic Jewish father and an Ashkenazi mother. The family settled in New York after leaving Cuba. She, too, traveled the world exploring the disparate parts of her identity, and in the book, gives us a multilayered view of a diverse Cuban exile community. Like many of the other writers, Behar returned to Cuba and established ties with other writers and artists on the island.

Except for de Lasa, who was a bit older when he arrived in the United States, and Nasca, who spent her early adolescence in Cuba, the authors of these memoirs focused on coming of age in exile. The authors' lives unfolded through times of scarcity, cultural dislocations, and in some cases, disintegration of families. All of them suffered from family separations and share a frustration with Americans who romanticize the Cuban Revolution and demonize exiles. Notably, these memoirs challenge the rigid myths of a uniform exile community and by extension of a Cuban nation. And on two fundamental issues, the writers defy U.S.- and island-based stereotypes: They all return to Cuba for visits, and they work to bridge the political divides among Cubans while being sympathetic to the plight of immigrants in the United States. On the other hand, these authors come from very different social, economic, and geographic places, and their lives in the United States yield a variety of human experiences and political outlooks that challenge the dominance of a unitary, politically obligated memory either of Cuba or of exile.

As writing and reading differences in the present become more accepted, so the past becomes a more open and inclusive place. Memory is not history, instead it is a collective process, made up of individual experiences. When historical renditions demand uniformity in remembering events, publicly expressed individual memories are a way of providing more complex views than those prescribed by official "obligated memories."

Art, Memory, and Opening Up the Past

Just as memoirs do, art can play an important role in opening up the past. Through their artistic production, artists are scribes giving us in images what writers record with text. Art, after all, reflects a way of life, and as we look at art, we can imagine what societies in the past were like. Art reflects human imagination. In some artworks, the future is imagined, while in others, the past is reexamined and recast in a new light. Through their art, artists and writers also can rethink the past. Some do it by providing alternative narratives, others by recording what is not permitted, and still others by stamping their personal memories onto a historical narrative. Lastly, some question institutions such as archives and museums that reedify historical memories.

History Revised

By the 2020s, the often-repeated mantra around the importance of history was being widely questioned in Cuba. In a 2023 interview, the renowned writer Leonardo Padura noted, "In Cuba, we are tired of living so much time in History, we want to live in normalcy."[28]

There have been numerous art projects that question the overemphasis of a singular history made by heroes. One art project stands out in regard to its intention to recast the past. That is José Angel Toirac's *Con permiso de la historia* (*With History's Permission*). In this series, Toirac revisited iconic photographs of the Revolution taken by Alberto Korda and Raúl Corrales that exalt the heroism of the guerrillas. He carefully reproduces the composition photographs, introducing new characters. For insatnce in re-creating a photo of a group of guerrilla fighters in the mountains, Toirac replaced the original rebels with fellow artists.

Reynier Leyva Novo also worked with iconic images, but instead of replacing historic characters with contemporary folks, he erased the figures altogether. For instance, in one famous photograph of Fidel Castro standing behind a podium and addressing a crowd, the podium is left empty even as every other detail of the photograph stays the same, including the crowd, the microphone, and the other guests on the podium. There is also the widely published photograph of Castro jumping out of a military tank, supposedly during the Bay of Pigs invasion. Leyva Novo reproduces the tank, but Castro is no longer in the photo.

In a 2012 installation, *El deseo de morir por otros, (The Desire to Die for Others)*, Leyva Novo criticized a version of history that emphasizes war heroes. In what was a foreshadowing of the themes that would drive the protests of July 11, 2021, in Cuba, the installation consisted of replicas of "historical" weapons, revolvers, and machetes once used by noted Cubans fighters. The almost-exact replicas were later displayed in a darkened, somber room in Miami's El Espacio 23, the private museum space of philanthropist and art collector Jorge Pérez.

Leyva Novo goes further in another project called the *Weight of History.* With a software he developed himself, he measures the weight of paper and ink used to publish books written by authoritarian figures. In one series, subtitled *Five Nights,* he uses texts by Hitler, Lenin, Castro, Mao Tse-tung, and Gaddafi. The same amount of ink is used to paint a black rectangle on the wall of the museum—the weight of the ink itself is almost insignificant but the legacy of authoritarianism and censorship is not.[29] In reviewing Leyva Novo's work, art scholar Guillermina De Ferrari noted that in revolutionary Cuba, history is never about the past. It's not only used to legitimize authority, it has also become an arena in which to contest the present.[30]

This absence of an inclusive history has also been a subject of exploration in the exile community. In the late seventies and early eighties, some Cuban Americans who had been born in Cuba and raised elsewhere, turned to art as a way of recapturing their past. Displacement and their condition of exile influenced their work. This does not mean that their artistic production was limited to expositions of nostalgia. In fact, to demonstrate the breadth of styles represented in the production of this generation, art historian and curator Elizabeth Cerejido organized an exhibition, *Radical Convention; Cuban American Art from the 1980s,* which opened at the University of Miami's Lowe Museum in the spring of 2022. Directly debating cultural critics that often dismissed the work of immigrant artists by describing their work as "nostalgic," Cerejido showed that these artists were also working with the traditions of the artistic currents that defined art during this period. And that reducing their artwork to simple longings for the past excluded them from being represented in contemporary art movements.

In terms of exile artists, I will focus my discussion on two of the artists represented in this exhibition, Nereida García Ferraz and María Martínez-Cañas, whose pieces intimately reflect their condition as women exiles whose personal lives were framed by the Cuban Revolution and by the ruptures it produced in their lives. Both studied photography at the

Art Institute of Chicago. García Ferraz went on to work in other mediums, such as sketches and paintings; Martínez-Cañas creates larger photographic montages. While the past, through their childhood memories, is an important source of inspiration for them, their work has been informed by their ongoing efforts to reconcile personal and political histories, questioning in the very borders that separate the two. Both produce pieces that transgress what could be constituted as "the official memory" of the past. I will argue that their paintings and photography also do the work of democratizing the past.

Bringing the Personal into History

For Nereida García Ferraz, the past has played a dominant role in her art, as she was deeply moved by a desire to reconnect and develop a relationship with Cuba. By the time her parents decided to leave the island in the early years of the Revolution, the doors to the United States had already been shut. Until 1970, they lived in a limbo: no longer wanted in Cuba but unable to leave. Those who declared their intent to leave the island were banished to an internal exile of sorts in which they were excluded from active participation in the society. This banishment included the children of the household as well. During this period of her life, García Ferraz trained herself to remember the images she was about to lose. Images became mnemonic devices for her to remember her family life in Cuba.[31]

In the early 1970s, after finally arriving in the United States and during a particularly brutally cold Chicago winter, García Ferraz's father abandoned the family. Her mother and three siblings were left to fend for themselves. For years, García Ferraz carried with her the emotional consequences of her parents' divorce and the family's disintegration. Art became a way for her to remember. She completed her BFA in photography at the School of the Art Institute in Chicago. While she concentrated in photography, she also began to sketch, and eventually to paint with oils on canvas. On colorful images of female bodies, boats, island plant life, and animals, she would write phrases, using text as a way to reconnect to her native language and to embed on the image a more complex story. This work is characterized by longing and nostalgia of a world left behind, but it was also defiant, in that it was a testimony of the refusal to forget.

But her paintings had more to say. They began to reflect her desire to return to the island of her childhood. Each canvas was a journey of return. Travel to the island had been prohibited by both governments. Cubans could leave the homeland, but not return. Family separations grew long. That began to change in 1978 under the Carter administration, when the United States and Cuba negotiated a series of agreements including the release of political prisoners, increased immigration, and the possibility of exiles to return to Cuba for short visits. García Ferraz became part of the Antonio Maceo Brigade, and in 1979, joined a group of almost 200 young Cuban exiles who traveled to the island. These were emotional journeys to the past but also a confrontation with the new Cuba. Influenced by radical politics and perhaps also a need to belong, García Ferraz's return to Cuba, as for many other young exiles, myself included, were filled with nostalgia and longing. On her first trips, García Ferraz used her camera to capture black-and-white images of an island haunted by ruins, exoduses, and memories. She photographed other returning young exiles, as well as her grandmother and aunt, who had never left.

But García Ferraz wanted more than just temporary visits. For her, Cuba had been the only place where her family had been together. In the next several decades, she found ways to stay for longer periods of time. In 2013, as Cuba started granting exiles permission to begin a process of repatriation as part of a new migration reform, García Ferraz secured hers, eventually obtaining a space of her own in Havana. Her work during this time is revealing. At first, her canvases became smaller, perhaps because that made it easier to transport them between Havana and Miami. But perhaps they also became smaller because they were more intimate and explored more explicit memories of her childhood. This period coincided with her mother's death, heightening her need to reconnect with Cuba.

In one of the first series she created in Havana, titled *Havana/Miami*, García Ferraz took pages from old books and glued these to a larger white canvas. On these she drew and painted. The first pieces in the series became vivid fragments of memories of herself and her mother.

Also in the series are images that attempt to recover and express the disintegration of her family and the burden she felt in holding it all together.

In the final piece in the series, García Ferraz paints herself standing on a stack of books, looking at a solitary star similar to the one found on the Cuban flag. Yet in the piece, that solitary star is a gaping hole, an empty promise of hope.

García Ferraz's first works from Cuba challenged renditions of earlier collective narratives that would not allow for personal loss, since loss of any kind was an admission of the failure of the Revolution. In the case of emigration, it would necessarily imply the inability of the nation to hold

Figure 4.1. *Havana/Miami*, Nereida García Ferraz. In the Cuban Heritage Collection, 2018–2020, University of Miami. Courtesy of the artist.

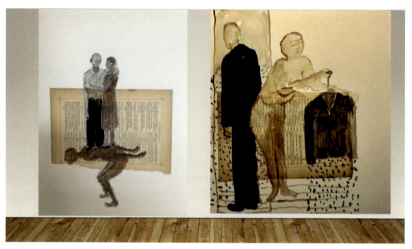

Figure 4.2. *Havana/Miami*, Nereida García Ferraz. In the Cuban Heritage Collection, 2018–2020, University of Miami. Courtesy of the artist.

together its people. By imposing her intimate memories—which had been all but swept away by the official narratives—she recovered her experience of personal loss and "painted" them into a history that had been sanitized by the Revolution.

This work is one that presents history from an individual's perspective, contrasting personal experiences to the "collective" memory imposed by

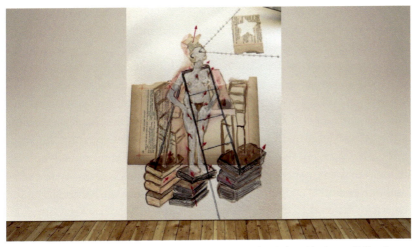

Figure 4.3. *Havana/Miami*, Nereida García Ferraz. In the Cuban Heritage Collection, 2018–2020, University of Miami. Courtesy of the artist.

politics and ideology. It is a way of bringing the individual back into history and in so doing creating room for multiple histories to be told. And in the last painting of this series, she suggests that personal loss is also a loss for the nation.

Contesting the Ways Memories Are Archived

María Martínez-Cañas, an artist who uses a broad range of techniques in her work, explores the past and contests the ways in which it is "archived" and "stored." Martínez-Cañas left Cuba with her family as a three-month-old baby, and therefore has no recollections or conceptual memory of the island. Yet sensory memories, old family photographs, and stories she heard growing up in Miami and Puerto Rico, have helped her to re-create her Cuban past. Her early work explored the intersections between memories and places through the use of maps. She would photograph people and objects and then work with the negatives, cutting them and rearranging them. The final art piece was a developed montage reminiscent of the work of the Cuban artist Wilfredo Lam. She also worked with old Cuban postage stamps, evoking the feeling of a culture beyond immediate reach. As Andy Grundberg wrote, "this work suggests that identity ultimately is not just a receptacle of one's past but something generated by the activity of re-creating the past in the present."[32]

124 · Democracy and Time in Cuban Thought

While much of Martínez-Cañas's work explores national identity, the human body, and intimate spaces like her garden, it is her work with photographs from the personal archive of José Gómez-Sicre that stands out as a project that not only works with the past, but intentionally subverts the role that archives play in legitimizing what we should remember. Gómez-Sicre was for many years the visual arts specialist at the Pan American Union and at the Organization of American States, and became the founding director of the OAS's Museum of Modern Art of Latin America (now Art Museum of the Americas). In that position, he established what eventually became the museum's permanent collection.[33] He was friends with many of Cuba's modernist painters and promoted and exhibited their work throughout the Americas. He worked closely with the Museum of Modern Arts' Alfred H. Barr Jr., then director of collections, Margaret Miller, and Monroe Wheeler to organize and curate MoMA's 1944 exhibition *Modern Cuban Painters*.[34] He was also a close friend of the Martínez-Cañas family. He encouraged Martínez-Cañas to pursue her art when she was a student, and in fact presented her first public exhibition at the OAS museum in 1982. Throughout the years, the two kept in touch.

When Gómez-Sicre died in 1991, his nephew Horacio Gómez-Sicre tried to sell his archive, which consisted of hundreds of boxes filled with personal materials, letters, photos, and exhibition announcements expanding over several decades. Some of these exhibitions were critical in the introduction of modern Latin American art to the United States. Horacio Gómez-Sicre first approached the Nettie Lee Benson Latin American Collection at the University of Texas, the largest Latin American library collection in the world. They were only interested in the letters of Mariano Rodríguez, an internationally known Cuban artist, and in those from Alfred Barr.

Martínez-Cañas's father eventually bought the rest of the archival collection, which included correspondence between Cuban artists and intellectuals of the period; Amelia Peláez and Lydia Cabrera, Cundo Bermúdez's letters, portfolios of Roberto Diago, letters to gallerists and museums about the work of numerous Latin American artists, and hundreds of photos and negatives that Gómez-Sicre had either acquired or taken himself. These primary documents were windows into the world of modern Latin American art and modern art in general, since they also included photos that Gómez-Sicre took of numerous painters in their studios in Paris.

Box by box, Martínez-Cañas's father began sending the documents to her. The first ones, she recalls, arrived in 2001. They contained an unpublished manuscript on Latin American art written by Gómez-Sicre, green scrapbooks filled with newspaper clippings, and thousands of negatives in little transparent envelopes, including images of Alberto Giacometti working in his studio, as well as photos of Picasso, Matisse, Peláez, Bermúdez, Miró, and other artists at work.

Martínez-Cañas says she was not sure what to do with the materials. As she was not inclined to sell them, she tried to donate them to the digital archives project of the Museum of Fine Arts in Houston. The archivists there, according to Martínez-Cañas, were not interested. Gómez-Sicre had been a staunch anti-communist. His archive included materials from artists who had fled the Revolution. This did not fit neatly into the Houston museum's narrative of the revolutionary Latin American artists. She also tried the Benson Library at the University of Texas. They were only interested in a few items. The materials were too Cuban for some museums, too anti-communist for others.

So Martínez-Cañas began working with the files herself. She was fascinated with Gómez-Sicre's gaze. She had known him as a friend and supporter, not as an active photographer. Initially she began to scan his images and to rework them, as she had done in some of her earlier photo-art projects.

The first series that came from the archive, Martínez-Cañas called *Adaptation*. While in Amsterdam in 1951, Gómez-Sicre had been at an exhibition of artists identified with the De Stijl movement, and had taken dozens of photographs. She took fourteen of the photos and digitally removed certain objects from them. The resulting new images became her work.

The next series Martínez-Cañas produced, she titled *Tracings*. This one also contains fourteen pieces, most of them taken in Europe. Unlike *Adaptation*, where parts of the images disappear and the final work is figuratively distinct, in *Tracings* she scanned Gómez-Sicre's photos and then used tracing paper to trace them. The result is a new image where the original fades into the background. She then printed the resulting new image on canvas. The pieces depict a Ferris wheel, girls at a beach, people and pigeons on a plaza, and small bridges. While the original image is left intact in recognition of Gómez-Sicre's gaze, the tracings result in a new work of art.

In the next series, *Vestigios* (2015), Martínez-Cañas went one step further. She recalled, "I started that series by photographing pages—blank pages, or pages that had remnants or stains from things that had been there before."[35] Some of these were from Gómez-Sicre's scrapbooks, and the pages

Figure 4.4. *Tracings* series, *Untitled, (Ferris Wheel)*, 2007, María Martínez-Cañas. Courtesy of the artist.

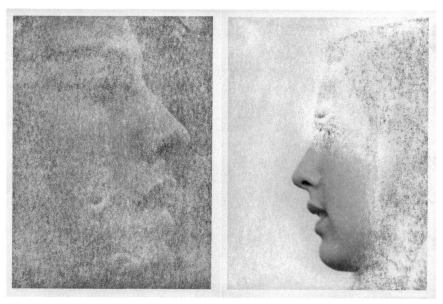

Figure 4.5. From the series *Vestigios, Untitled012, Diptych*, 2007, María Martínez-Cañas. Courtesy of the artist.

Figure 4.6. From the series *Vestigios, Untitled017*, 2015, María Martínez-Cañas. Courtesy of the artist.

still retained some of the little triangle corners used to hold photos. Some of the photos had long fallen out and what remained were pages with shadows left by the photographs that had once been glued to the pages.

In the next series, Martínez-Cañas took a bolder step. She took a newspaper clipping from the files and started to sand it lightly as to create a faded image. She explained what happened next, "Accidentally, I took an original photograph and kept sanding when I realized it. I paused for a minute and then I said to myself, I have nothing to lose."[36] In the end, she sanded down eight silver gelatin photographs. All of them contained images of people, some were facial portraits, while others captured their entire body. The project became about the intentionality of altering the archive. The original images were transformed into new works of art, blurring the lines between what was Gómez-Sicre's work and Martínez-Cañas's.

128 · Democracy and Time in Cuban Thought

Vestigios

In the next series, *Rebus + Diversions* (2016), she continued taking photographs and clippings from the archive and creating collages with empty folders that included images of historical events, such as the opening of the *Modern Cuban Painters* exhibition at MoMA, letters to her family, as well as photos of her family in which she is included. She describes one of the collages: "On the top, that light blue thing is a letter that Gómez-Sicre wrote to my father in 1980, something about my photography—talking about me. I felt, I am going to put myself even more in the personal here."[37]

In another collage, she placed a letter that Gómez-Sicre had written around 1976. "That was a very personal letter that I had had in my files. On top of it—you can barely see it, because it's a little darker—is a 4 × 5 transparency of a painting Cundo [Bermúdez] made of my mother and the three of us [Martínez-Cañas and her sisters]. On the left is a little booklet of an article that Gómez-Sicre wrote about Cundo's work. Then I took a gelatin silver print image of Cundo, and I sanded around and left his face more apparent."[38]

After leaving Cuba, Cundo Bermúdez settled in Washington, D.C. He was a friend of Martínez-Cañas's father, who asked him to paint a portrait of their family. The negative in the collage is a photo that Bermúdez used as the basis for the portrait he painted. Martínez-Cañas told Susan Delson of *Cuban Art News*: "In a way, I feel these works are reactions to my identity. I went back with this series to work—especially in the first ten—with Cuban material, which I have used before in my work. And with the actual materials from the archives."[39]

The materials also included very personal images and letters that referred to her.

Martínez-Cañas's work confronts the past through her memories and through materials from an archive. It raises critical questions about how the past is preserved and how an archive is valued, who owns the archive, and who gets to determine what to do with it.

Martínez-Cañas has given parts of the archive to museums. For instance, a donation to the Smithsonian's National Portrait Gallery included a photograph of Julio López Berenstein, a photographer who in the forties and fifties had photographed many of Cuba's painters and cultural figures, but who died in a Cuban jail after the Revolution. Another was a photograph taken by López Berenstein of Cuban painter Augusto de Castro Tagle, who had become his lover. Gómez-Sicre had shown Berenstein's and Tagle's

Figure 4.7. From the series *Rebus + Diversions, Untitled010*, 2016, María Martínez-Cañas. Courtesy of the artist.

work at the Pan American Union in March–April 1952.[40] Little is known about what led up to Berenstein's death in prison, or what happened to most of his work. Martínez-Cañas insisted that her donation was contingent on exhibiting both photographs together. If Berenstein and Tagle had not been able to be together publicly while they were living, she wanted their portraits to be side by side.[41]

Critics have questioned Martínez-Cañas's "destruction" of archival materials—sanding down the original photos, for example. Some art historians cringed at the idea of these valuable originals being lost. But, she counters, established museums and collections were not interested in them, and the materials seem to have acquired value only once she began to work with them. Martínez-Cañas says she was reworking the archives because she saw herself in them; they were part of who she is. "The *archivo* is an extension of who I am . . . these are people important to my life . . . this work is an exercise in being a Cuban citizen, artist as a Cuban artist . . . personal . . . relationship with an important part of the past, my past . . . that official archivists did not value."[42]

In the end, Martínez-Cañas's work is an aesthetic and political act of recasting the past, an instance of how the personal and the historical come together. In this case, the archival materials include originals about her family

130 · Democracy and Time in Cuban Thought

history, letters to her, and images of her family. While to some they are "history," to Martínez-Cañas they are part of her *personal* history. As such, her reworking of the archive is an act of interjecting her voice into the past. In the act of what some may call destruction of important historical materials, Martínez-Cañas reworked the past and reclaimed her space in it, even as she transformed it and brought it into the present. What some considered an archive important to the public, she saw as personal. Martínez-Cañas intentionally blurs the lines between the personal and the public, making room to recapture her own "history."

Martínez-Cañas and García Ferraz bring the personal into the public discourses of the past, and as such, they rewrite the narrative of a unitary politically obligated memory. By rearranging the past to include personal histories, the past and consequently the present become more open. Martínez-Cañas, in addition, questions the exclusionary practices of official archives and dedicates her work to creating a new archive—one that is personal and all-encompassing.

Toward an Open, Inclusive Past

The past plays a role in politics. Conceptions of the past basically set up the stage for the present and authoritatively determine who is included in it. How then can the past be made more expansive? First, there is the problem of the conception of history itself. History as a unidirectional force toward a determined future leaves out the possibilities of recognizing multiple experiences, particularly when these are uniquely positioned in contrast to each other. History as judge, the type of history we saw Fidel Castro invoke, excludes the possibilities of history as containing multiple and often contradictory experiences. This perspective of history, which is deeply rooted in Christianity, leaves out human beings from the actual building of history. Human agency is missing.

There is also the problem of who gets a role in historical renditions. In the case of Cuba, the past relies on a simplistic narrative and includes very few participants. The totalitarian conception of the past made room only for those whose presence in it did not challenge that the Revolution itself was the culmination of history. Those who did were eliminated—either killed, imprisoned, exiled, or otherwise silenced. Paradoxically, early exile organizations also created a narrative of heroes and villains that mirrored the Revolution's renditions in method, if not in content. This unidimensional view of the past was particularly evident in stories about the Operation Pedro

Pan children and their exodus. Historical facts were replaced with mythology. As such, both the Revolution and its opponents re-historicized events to comport to narrow views that helped sustain limited political dogmas in the present.

A third problem is who gets to tell the stories of the past. The production of historical narratives involves an uneven contribution of competing groups and individuals who have unequal access to the means of such production.[43] It is an often-repeated truth that history is written by the victors, and this may be so. After all, those in power will have direct or indirect influence on the means of production of history, especially in totalitarian regimes. This includes the training of researchers, the control of the publications, access to materials and archives, indeed even the creation of an archive. At the end, the construction of the past is a deeply political process that reflects power struggles.

A final problem is one of repression—the silencing of those who tell stories that contradict official versions. To control the past, it must be policed, and this policing reflects present-day struggles for power. In Cuba, character assassination and banishment from the canons of history have been popular methods of punishing those whose stories are different from the official narrative. As Antón Arrufat—a writer who was marginalized by the Cuban government—so eloquently stated in his poem *Ellos,* the Revolution will write him out of history.[44] A similar process has occurred in the exile community.

How then to recast the past and its reconstructions and remembrances in more democratic ways? To begin with, a more representative understanding of history would not assign to it the role of "judge," but rather that of "facilitator." This would create a space in which contested memories can be debated and reinterpreted; a space in which multiple individuals can "remember" the past. There is no presumption that there is only one conclusive interpretation or judgment of events. Memoirs, as we have seen, provide this kind of space. An individual's memory is made into the main subject of the text, and many memories of the same time period are produced which begin to create a history with an array of elements and perspectives.

The past is a combination of personal and collective experiences. History as a discipline is an "imaginative reconstruction of the past, which is scientific in its determination and artistic in its formulation."[45] This kind of history would give us broad uniformities without claiming them as truths or insisting that everyone experienced them as such. Imagination continues to play a role in conceiving the past without taking away the skill of assem-

132 · Democracy and Time in Cuban Thought

bling an understanding of the past through specific research methods—after all, it is human behavior that is being researched.[46]

In the artwork of Toirac, Leyva Novo, García Ferraz, and Martínez-Cañas, artistic imagination produces images that can bring forth a different past. Toirac and Leyva Novo revise the past, one by inserting new people into "history," the other by imagining a past without the dominant figure of Fidel Castro. If history erased the lived experiences of so many, Leyva Novo seems to say, he can erase Fidel Castro from his own history. García Ferraz explores the loss of her childhood and family in opposition to an island narrative that claimed that emigration purified the nation. Martínez-Cañas reconstructs Gómez-Sicre's gaze, and with his materials creates a new way of thinking about the past. In the process, she "destroys" the existing archive and creates a new one.

Michel de Certeau offers an alternative way of thinking about how to be more inclusive as we try to understand the past. Beyond the monumental stories of heroes and villains, or victors and vanquished, he argues that it is the day-to-day occurrences of everyday life that give meaning to the past.[47] Day-to-day practices and rituals offer a sense of the subjective aspects of the past that allow us to include multiple experiences and multiple actors. It also allows us to understand the emotional work done through the reconstruction of the past, for in seeing ourselves in the past we can better integrate our pasts and presents. This underscores the subjectivity of the past and allows for multiple interpretations of it. This perspective aligns with Hannah Arendt's understanding that the past is an accumulation of experiences.[48] Its renditions need to recognize the multiple experiences and indeed the various dimensions operating to constitute a past.

5

Temporalities and Democracy

I look up to the sky and hope that someday my country does not sacrifice me for my ideas, for my words, for believing in that freedom we all need.

Claudia Padrón, Cárdenas, Cuba

Unlike the past, the future cannot be rewritten—it is yet to be. It can be conjured or imagined. But as we have seen in previous chapters, an open-ended, unmoored future can be the breeding ground for authoritarianism. Democracy needs a relationship with the future that can question the present as well as anticipate and imagine alternatives. But how to imagine a future temporality that does not lead to authoritarian politics? Most importantly, how can hope, a fundamental aspect of a future orientation, be recast as liberating and not as a sentiment to be manipulated? In this concluding chapter, I explore new ways of thinking about the future, and about hope, that may be more conducive to democracy. I will look at some of the contemporary social movements in Cuba to discern the underpinning temporalities of their projects. Are their criticisms of the regime offering a different way of thinking about politics? Are their proposals providing alternative temporal concepts to the overused past and future tropes? I will conclude with a discussion of the impact that an engaged present can have on important aspects of democratic practices and culture, and I will consider what else needs to be incorporated in order to also make the present more inclusive.

A Democratic Future

Democracy as a political system requires a relationship with the present and the future. For example, deliberations are discussions about present-day problems in search of solutions that will be implemented in the future.

134 · Democracy and Time in Cuban Thought

Sociologist Max Weber justly warned that "the proper business of the politician is the future and his responsibility before the future. The failure to use foresight, in other words, is not just a benign failure of intelligence: It is a culpable neglect of future generations."[1]

Perhaps the starting point to rethink a future temporality that may be more conducive to democracy is to study the relationship between present and future. The future cannot be conceived without the present. The promise of *el porvenir* (the still-to-come) is just a possibility, but it does contextualize a "present," since it emanates from it.[2] This is helpful in appreciating that the future is not independent of the present. Instead of thinking about the future as its own temporality, it may be productive to shift the emphasis to the *relationship* between the two. Young people, for instance, do not want to be "future citizens," but rather citizens in the present, and they want their rights realized today, as well as protected tomorrow.[3] From this perspective, the future is rooted in a guarantee given in the present. It reverses the promise of future rights. Rather we have rights today that we can expect to have in the future as well.

Most importantly, future aspirations can provide points of references with which to evaluate the present. Change always implies alternatives that necessarily can only occur in the future.[4] Yet regardless of the starting point, the political impulse toward the future is to change the present. The question is: Are these aspirational changes realistic or just illusionary?

Clearly no one knows exactly what the future will bring. However, rooting the future in critiques of the present can create a realistic roadmap for change. For Walter Benjamin, the appreciation of the future is embedded in his concept of messianic time that moves from an unfulfilled past creating hope for the hopeless.[5] It is a way to break from an empty time into a more productive one.[6] Moments of transition can be filled with expectations, as in Derrida's notion of messianic time that includes a future rooted in the present.[7] Individual agency and voice can also exist in these transitory moments. In fact, multiple voices can emerge.

A parallel concept to the future that is essential to a democratic culture is hope, which necessarily resides in the present but points toward the future—a wish of something to come. There may be a human impulse to hope, and it might be intricately tied to our sense of spirituality and our desire to be healed.[8] Politically, however, hope becomes a vehicle to envision a better life, and as such, it can easily be manipulated to create "false hope." But does hope have to be an empty promise anchored in some future utopia? To answer this, two concepts need to be understood: One is hope itself, and the other is how the future is conceived.

Regarding hope itself: Ernst Bloch believed that what drives human beings is the desire to become.[9] He argued for looking forward, not backward, and most importantly, posited an anchoring of this looking forward in the present. Realistic hope, he proposed, is attached to the present with a nod toward the future.[10] Hope becomes a way to organize and look forward. The Frankfurt School also grappled with the question of how to keep hope alive in the face of the failures of grandly schemed utopias and the world wars. For Max Horkheimer and Theodor W. Adorno, hope did not rely on some unforeseen future but rather on the uncompromising critique of the present.[11] "Hope for better circumstances? If it is not a mere illusion?"[12] Instead, they suggest that future aspirations should emanate from an understanding of deep suffering, not from empty promises. This will give these aspirations a grounding in a situation that requires change. It is a way of grounding the future in the present.

This does not take away the possibility that non-ideological, utopian thinking can be a source of hope. After all, dreaming about the future has been part of the human imagination from Greek and Roman ideals of the golden age, magical kingdoms, and desire for peace. For Arjun Appadurai, hope is tied up with scaled exercises in building, which he calls "the capacity to aspire."[13] He also calls for an examination of the relationship between democracy in today's increasingly unequal world and a more careful understanding of hope. This view is particularly helpful in coming to grips with how a critique of the present can contribute to developing realistic political alternatives.

Ruth Levitas has proposed that desire maybe more inclusive than hope— "the desire for a different, better way of being."[14] She emphasizes this kind of desire over the desire for an alternative to the existing social order. For her, a better life does not necessarily imply a change of the social order. There can also be a relationship between a desire for a better life and happiness. Hope, after all, may be the desire for something over which we have no control.

The second aspect of hope that is important for democracies is the role of the imaginary. The development of future imaginaries, whether in literature, art, or politics, have been posited as alternatives to reality. I have noted that utopian projects mobilized people in a direction of hopelessness, since many of their promises were unattainable. However, intellectu-

136 · Democracy and Time in Cuban Thought

als of various political perspectives have advanced alternative notions of utopia. For example, Marxist philosopher Herbert Marcuse[15] and liberal philosopher John Rawls both proposed the notion of "realistic utopias"[16] that are not disconnected from the possible, which is in part tied to the present. French philosopher Pierre Bourdieu has also called for reasoned utopias, that is, utopias that include elements of the present and are carefully thought through.[17] Bloch, for his part, proposes that utopias can be the analytical tool with which to rethink the present, the emphasis being on the moment, not just a future disconnected from the present. These ways of thinking about utopias suggest that a vision of the future that is realistic and grounded in the present can provide a roadmap for political action and aspirations that are inclusive and possible, and do not easily end up creating false hopes that can be politically manipulated.

Are there ways of thinking about the imagination that do not necessarily lead to empty, wishful thinking? This is particularly important since the imaginary is precisely an exercise in thinking beyond the present. Politically, there are ways to think about the imagination that do not fall into dogmatism. It is in mid-1900s debates about ideology and utopias that we find helpful distinctions. Karl Mannheim believed that utopias were vehicles through which to imagine a future, while ideology was the vehicle for those in power to maintain the status quo. But he gave little thought to how the individual imagination could contribute to social movements.[18] Paul Ricoeur saw that ideology and utopia needed each other. The relationship between "ideology and utopia appears as an interplay of the two fundamental directions of the social imagination. The first tends toward integration, repetition, and a mirroring of the given order. The second tends to bring it astray because it is eccentric."[19] For Ricoeur, the power of social imagination through utopia could be subversive.

Again, Arjun Appadurai insists that the future is a human creation, one based in culture and one in which three human preoccupations—imagination, anticipation, aspiration—work to create it. Imagination is a collective process that comes from culture. He argues that we have the capacity to aspire for an attainable future and is confident that it can be found in culture.[20]

While the defense of utopias seems idealistic, given the extent of the failures of the versions of utopia that emerged in the twentieth century, there are still appeals to save aspects of the imaginary process and perhaps readjust theoretical expectations. José Esteban Muñoz, a theorist of queerness working in the tradition of Bloch, has tried to bring the imaginary back into political movements. "Queerness," he stated, "is essentially a rejection of the here and now and an insistence on the potentiality or concrete possibility of another world."[21] Recognizing the pitfalls of illusion, he called for bringing back imagination to the pragmatic presentism of the gay movement. A more sobering proposal is found in the work of Joshua Foa Dienstag, who looks at how unbridled optimism was built on the flawed assumption of the inevitability of progress and the promise of an orderly march of history into the future. Instead, chaos and disorder abound, he says, and proposes pessimism as a conceptual framework to critically assess the present and avoid falling into the spell of the unknown.[22]

As I have been arguing in this book, the promised future has undermined some of the important elements that could contribute to the building of democratic societies. But is Dienstag's pessimistic realism a reasonable alternative to utopia? Instead, Jerome Binde suggests that what is needed is a realistic utopianism. To achieve this, he advocates for a renewed dialogue between the present and the future that does not foretell nor prescribe the future, but prepares for it.[23] Carlos Fuentes asks, "Can we achieve a less despairing, more modest and reasonable sense of the future, without falling into despair or beatitude once more?"[24] In a more expansive and engaged present, perhaps a more realistic future can be imagined.

A future imagined with modest proposals perhaps requires even greater creative power. Bloch's *The Principle of Hope* is a defense of the analytical power of creative imaginaries, one that also relies on daydreaming as a subversive activity.[25] Daydreaming does not have to be a way of just idly passing time; it can be a productive exercise in which one can dream and think and rethink the present by shattering old ideas about the present and thinking of future possibilities. We found this notion of dreaming while awake in the work of Eliseo Diego, the poet of light and time, who situated imagination in the present.

Perhaps the operative word here is "possibilities," which suggests some assessment in the present of what is truly possible. As Henri Lefebvre noted, ". . . But if what is possible is not certain, if there are several possibilities, how are we to consider the present? With a certain irony."[26] To that, I would add that socially, a more participatory process through which individuals have a say on what is possible can bring forth a more democratic future to all as well.

138 · Democracy and Time in Cuban Thought

The Critique of the Present

One of the most important conclusions drawn from the theoretical discussions about future and hope is that future projects need to be grounded in a critique of the present. These visions can be called realistic utopias in that they do advocate for radical change, but they need to emerge from a critique of the present, not from some predicted evolution of history. Therefore, a more democratic future can begin with a critique of the present, and this is visible in many political and aesthetic projects in Cuba. In this section, we will look at the work of Tania Bruguera, one of the artists who has organized movements for change on the island. I will also examine the projects that emerged during the historic July 11, 2021, protests, with special attention to how hope is constructed in them.

Tania Bruguera[27] was an art student at Havana's Instituto Superior de Arte in the mid-1980s. While there, she was exposed to the groundbreaking work of Ana Mendieta—a Cuban American artist who died at age thirty-six in New York in 1985—through Mendieta's cousin, Raquel Mendieta, a professor at the Instituto. Ana Mendieta was a Pedro Pan who returned to Cuba to work and be part of the artistic movement in her home country. In the early eighties, on a trip in which she met fellow artists, she began art projects in Cuba. These included sand sculptures in Varadero, a beach town where her family had spent their summers, and a series of earth sculptures at the "Cuevas de Jaruco," a group of limestone caves near Havana. Significantly, a century before, the caves had provided shelter for runaway enslaved men who would hide there, their scent lost to the absorbent limestone so that hunting dogs could not track them. After her death, Ana Mendieta's pieces in Cuba were left to decay. Cuba's policies toward the community abroad had changed again, and instead of soliciting exchanges, contact was once again discouraged.

Bruguera learned about Mendieta's work during a period when the Cuban government had imposed a blackout of news about the Cuban American community, and she decided, as an act of defiance, to re-create some of Mendieta's performance work. For her first re-creation, Bruguera chose one of Mendieta's earliest pieces at the University of Iowa. As a form of protest to a campus rape that had occurred while Mendieta was a student, Mendieta would dip her arms in a bucket of blood she obtained from a local butcher, and leaning on a white sheet hung on the wall, with her arms over her head, she would slowly trace the silhouette of her body on the sheet. Bruguera's re-creation brought Mendieta "back to Cuba" and included her in the Cuban present, even though she was being officially erased from the past.

Bruguera's posture of contestation continued. One of her early projects was titled *Memorias de la posguerra,* actually a newspaper dedicated to keeping alive the memory of those who had left the island. In the early 1990s, while the exile community was still shunned as a political entity that corrupted the island, emigration surged. At the time, recognizing the humanity of those who left was seen by the Castro regime as an act of dissidence. After all, according to the official discourse, emigration purified the nation of the unwanted. Yet Cubans of all walks of life wanted to flee. Poorer Cubans cast their destiny to the sea on rickety rafts. Those with some means were able to secure invitations to travel abroad and received exit permits. They would often not return. The impact on the island was undeniable, but the feeling of loss or sadness at seeing friends and relatives leave could not be expressed.

Yet Bruguera's *Memorias de la posguerra,* a "performance" that produced an "art object"—a newspaper—was filled with yearning, loss, and lament over those who were leaving and had left. Bruguera's project wanted to recognize the loss felt by those who stayed behind, who refused to erase their loved ones from history.[28] Two issues were published. They included essays, poetry, and reproductions of works of art. Her piece offered an alternative version to the militarized rhetoric used by the government to continuously mobilize the population, which cast émigrés as traitors and enemies. Instead of heroism and sacrifice, Bruguera highlighted the losses caused by war.

After the publication of her newspapers, Bruguera was detained and questioned by state security. It was her first time in detention, but it would not be the last. She continued to work with the theme of emigration. In a subsequent installation, she captured the loss experienced by those on the island as their friends and relatives threw themselves to sea on homemade rafts in the early nineties. No one really knows how many died in the effort to flee. Bruguera conceived of a project like the Vietnam Veterans Memorial in Washington, D.C., a wall on which families could share the names of relatives who had perished trying to cross the Florida Straits. This project was censored by the Cuban government, so instead, Bruguera built *La tabla de salvación (Lifeline,* 1994), a black marble slab symbolic of a raft. She propped the slab against a wall in a Havana gallery and lined it with candles that reflected onto the shiny black surface, a memorial to those who drowned trying to escape.[29]

140 · Democracy and Time in Cuban Thought

Her work grew more critical of the government. Her subsequent performances included biting critiques of the failure of the Revolution itself. In one installation set in a dark tunnel, Bruguera played videos of Fidel Castro speaking about heroism and sacrifice as spectators walked on rotting stalks of sugar cane. Only if they looked behind them could the spectators see that there were two naked men closely watching their progress. This was first performed at La Cabaña, the fortress that had been used as a political prison and execution site in the early 1960s. Eventually the Museum of Modern Art in New York acquired it for their permanent collection.

Her performances continued as she expanded her themes to include censorship, interrogations, and acts against humanity. Many of the themes referenced historical events; all obviously questioned and confronted the ways in which the Cuban government maintained control over the population—their actions and thoughts. Often, Bruguera's performances centered her body and the many ways that others attempted to control it. She protested against censorship by tying herself to a wall and placing a gag over her mouth.

In what has become one of the most referenced performances worldwide, she focused on the lack of freedom of speech on the island. During the 10th Havana Biennial in 2009, Bruguera placed a platform in a public space, provided a microphone, and invited people to say whatever they wanted for a few minutes. A white dove was placed on the shoulders of the speakers. This was a direct mocking of the myths created around Fidel Castro—sometimes by *santeros* (santería priests)—including one that related how two doves had come to rest on a young Fidel's shoulder as he addressed the nation after the triumph of the Revolution. When the speakers were done, two actors in military uniform escorted them off stage. The piece is titled *Taitlin's Whisper*, in reference to Vladimir Taitlin's unrealized monument to the Third International.[30] Organizers of the Biennial seemed to have been taken by surprise when several people took the opportunity to call for democracy.

Bruguera attempted to stage another version of *Taitlin's Whisper* in the 2014 Havana Biennial.[31] She invited participants to come to the Plaza of the Revolution, and specifically to the pillar that has a statue of José Martí, a structure that had become one of the icons of the Cuban Revolution even though it was built during Batista's regime. But on her way to the plaza, she was detained and prohibited from going through with her project.

The following year, she launched another project to encourage people to reflect on the nature of the totalitarian nature of the government. From her home in Havana, she invited people to an open studio reading of Hannah Arendt's *The Origins Totalitarianism*. Friends, other artists, and curators stopped by and read for a total of 100 hours.[32] At the end of the reading, as Bruguera stepped outside her house, a book in one hand and a dove in the other, she was detained by the secret police, which had surrounded her house. However, the performance made a point: The Cuban regime had roots similar to those of other totalitarian governments. Curiously, the theme of the Biennial was *"entre la idea y la experiencia"* (between the idea and the experience), juxtaposing the future and the present. Bruguera presented a biting critique of the present instead.

The performance was cleverly scheduled for May 20, which had been Cuba's Independence Day until the regime changed it to July 26 to mark the attack on the Moncada barracks. On that same day, Bruguera launched the Instituto de Artivismo Hannah Arendt (Hannah Arendt Artivism Institute), an organization dedicated to promoting peaceful civic engagement and advocacy.[33] Alluding to the literacy campaign of 1961, when the government sent thousands of young people to the countryside to teach peasants how to read and write, Bruguera proposed a civil rights literacy campaign to give people tools with which to engage in meaningful political change.

Bruguera's work is an exercise in democracy. She uses images of the past and interplays them with the present thus providing a critical view of the "now." This critical perspective of the present can create a space in which new ideas can emerge. Obviously, the political challenge is how to create political change in which these new ideas can be implemented.

Figure 5.1. Tania Bruguera, 100 horas de lectura de *Los orígenes del totalitarismo* de Hannah Arendt, 2015. Courtesy of photographer Leandro Feal.

Cuba Entre Tiempos, Again

Six decades after gaining power, the Revolution has deployed both the future and the past in an attempt to sustain its viability. It can be said that the Revolution's decline has accelerated the competition among multiple temporalities. In 2019, the government launched a massive campaign to persuade people to vote for a new constitution. The new document was controversial, since it reedified socialism and one-party rule. While it offered protection for certain rights, such as speech and artistic creation, those protections were all qualified by language that made it illegal to criticize the government or socialism. The slogan for the campaign was *El futuro que aún puede ser* (the future that can still be). Once again, the future was being deployed to justify the present, although, tellingly, the slogan included the tacit admission that the promises made in the past were still unfulfilled. A year later, Raúl Castro resigned from his formal role in the government, and Miguel Díaz-Canel was named president during the Party Congress. In an interesting temporal switch, the slogans went from relying on the future to laying claim to the future because of the past. The new military elite tried to find legitimacy in its connections to the "historic" leadership. Their claim to be the heirs of the revolutionary spirit relied on the notion of "continuity"—the mantle that Fidel Castro had inherited from Martí, in turn passed to Raúl Castro from Fidel, and now to Díaz-Canel from Raúl. It could be said that the new leaders were inheriting the past. Their promise was to maintain the status quo, the continuity of socialism, and of one-party rule. The new slogan: "*Somos Cuba: Continuidad de la Revolución y su legado histórico*" (We are Cuba: The continuity of the revolution and its historic legacy).

Yet the ongoing economic crisis in the island demanded more than continuity, and the reactions to the new slogan was widespread skepticism. On social media, Cubans asked, continuity of what? Repression, inequalities, lack of basic freedoms and material conditions? On the streets of Miramar, a privileged neighborhood in Havana, the party slogan was edited to include the words Patria y vida, Homeland and Life.

Patria y vida, a rap song that honors the artists of the San Isidro neighborhood who had protested against new restrictions on artistic creation, quickly became the soundtrack of an incipient social movement seeking political changes. Instead of continuity, the song demands room for a new generation, "*Tú, cinco nueve, yo doble dos. Ya se acabó. Sesenta trancado el dominó*" (You, five nine, me, double two. It's all over now! Sixty years of a game that is stuck). The song, clearly located in the present, asks that those in power walk through poor neighborhoods, which do not reflect the future promised by the Revolution. *"Hoy yo te invito a caminar por mis solares. Pa' demostrarte de qué sirven tus ideales"* (Today, I invite you to walk through my tenements. To show you what your ideals are good for). The song is also a critique of official narratives, as protesters demand to tell their own stories.

In contrast to another government slogan, *Somos Cuba* (We are Cuba), the performers of *Patria y vida* put forth a different view of the nation based on an appreciation of difference, and demand that it should be respected. *"Somos humanos aunque no pensemos iguales. No nos tratemos ni dañemos como animales"* (We are human, though you and I do not think the same. Let's not demean ourselves or treat ourselves like animals). *Que no siga corriendo la sangre, por querer pensar diferente. ¿Quién les dijo que Cuba es de ustedes? Si mi Cuba es de toda mi gente* (No longer shall flow the blood, Of those who dare to think differently, Who told you Cuba is yours? Indeed, Cuba is for all my people).

The song's title, *Patria y vida*, is an alternative to the slogan with which Castro traditionally used to end his speeches, *Patria o muerte. Venceremos* (Homeland or death. We will triumph). *Patria y vida* directly confronts this message. The slogan grounds the movement in a defense of the nation, but instead of glorifying death, it is a freeing call for life and nation. *"¡No más mentiras! ¡Mi pueblo pide libertad, no más doctrinas!¡Ya no gritemos 'Patria o Muerte' sino 'Patria y Vida'! Y empezar a construir lo que soñamos, lo que destruyeron con sus manos"* (No more lies! My people demand freedom! No more doctrines! No longer shall we cry, 'Homeland or death' But 'Homeland and life'! And begin to build what we dreamed of. What they destroyed with their hands). The song's temporality is clearly distinct from the official past and future.

The governmental actions that spurred the creation of various citizen organizations, including the Movimiento San Isidro (San Isidro Movement, MSI), was the decree that all art projects had to be submitted to the government for approval. On November 9, 2020, Denis Solis, a rapper, was arrested by security forces who broke into his home without a warrant. A group of artists from the San Isidro Movement staged a hunger strike, which was forcibly ended. This was followed by a protest on November 27, 2020, in front of the Ministry of Culture, in which artists, journalists, and activists demanded freedom of creation and the right to dissent. Some of the activists coalesced and formed another group, 27 of November (27N).

Their platform based their call for freedom of expression and association on the International Bill of Human Rights, as well as on the Constitution of the Republic of Cuba that had been approved on April 19, 2019. Their vision for Cuba is located in a detailed critique of the present Cuban political system and on the aspiration for a democratic future. "We are committed to addressing the current suffering of Cuban society and its aspirations for a future of democracy and welfare. . . . We want a country that is inclusive, democratic, sovereign, prosperous, equitable, and transnational."[34] Their vision of building a future relies on action in the present. "Cuba needs a change, and for this it needs to build a more participatory citizenry with greater degree of awareness that the political and economic future of this country depends on us."[35]

Their stated political principles included an appreciation of the heterogeneity of ideas. "We need to reaffirm ourselves as people who are different from each other, as ecumenical, tolerant citizens, respectful of the opinions of others. Consequently, we advocate for laws that guarantee our right to develop as a heterogeneous society, where laws created for the benefit of the majority do not restrict or disregard the rights of minorities."[36]

There is also a commitment to social justice. "We aspire to work for a society with social justice and welfare, where every Cuban can live in Cuba / in their country from the fruits of their labor, where the productive forces are liberated [and] leave behind the misery and shortages imposed by the incompetence of the prevailing system. We want to guarantee the right to a dignified life, which should guarantee, among other things, healthcare and public education."[37]

The social protesters of the summer of 2021 also expressed hope even as the word hope itself had come under suspicion. Why hope if everything was fine? In the late 1990s, when the Cuban government permitted the opening of restaurants in people's homes called *paladares,* a friend of mine had just inherited the home of a lady whom he had cared for. Her name was Esperanza (Hope). He decided to open a *paladar* and named it after her to honor her memory. Within weeks, he was visited by state security and questioned as to why he had named his restaurant *Esperanza.* The word had become prohibited; it was subversive because it could imply that there was something wrong with the present.

Still, the desire for change entails a level of hope, which of course inherently contains a critique of the present. For instance, Claudia Padrón, a young visual artist from Cárdenas, one of the epicenters of the social movements of the summer of 2021, describes her feelings after the protests in a text that accompanies one of her photographs:

Termina de llover. Camino es busca de un destello de inspiración. Hay un silencio, las voces permanecen a oscuras dentro de las casas. Quedaron algunas puertas semiabiertas, todos cuentan su versión de ese día, una nieta les narra a sus abuelos que jamás se había sentido tan viva, tan libre en su propia tierra . . . sonrío, continúo mi viaje. Pienso en los desaparecidos, me duele como si fueran mi familia, los hermanos que nunca tuve. Miro al cielo y espero que un día mi patria no me sacrifique por mis pensamientos, por mis palabras, por creer en esa libertad que todos necesitamos.

The rain has stopped. I go out in search of a glimmer of inspiration. There is a silence, the voices remain in the dark inside the houses. Some doors are slightly open, everyone relates their version of that day. A granddaughter whispers to her grandparents that she has never felt so alive, so free in her own land . . . I smile and continue my journey. I think of the disappeared, it hurts me as if they were my family, the brothers I never had. I look up to the sky and hope that someday my country does not sacrifice me for my ideas, for my words, for believing in that freedom we all need.

In this passage, Padrón locates herself in the present as she critically speaks about the disappeared. But her yearning for a more open society is also looking to the future, and it is expressed in terms of hope. It is an aspiration that does not necessarily call for social change, but it does locate the individual in a more desirable political space.

Today's call for freedom by young people is rooted in Cuba's long political struggle—one that has not just been against foreign intervention, but has also included a search for democratic alternatives. Even in the days of the War of Independence from Spain, the platform of the *independentistas* (those in favor of independence) included freedom for enslaved people and democratic alternatives to monarchy and colonial ruling practices. In fact, Fulgencio Batista's violation of the 1940 Cuban Constitution and its protections of social justice *and* democracy, was the primary *raison d'être* for the armed insurrection that led to his overthrow. And while we can debate how much social justice has been delivered, or sustained, by the Revolution, it is painfully obvious that its promise of democracy was never kept. Free elections have never been held, and dissenters have been submitted to summary trials, long prison terms, and many executions. Repression and banishment have been the tools to keep a mostly white regime in power

Figure 5.2. *Infinite Ocean, Cárdenas*, 2021, Claudia Padrón. Courtesy of the artist.

and in control of a population whose proportion of Black Cubans, by some assessments, may be upward of 50 percent of the island residents.

While it is impossible to predict how events will unfold in Cuba, what is certain is that the search for social justice and democracy is still alive in the opposition to the regime. Even though the historic July 11, 2021, protests—in which thousands of Cubans throughout the island flooded the streets of their cities and towns to protest government repression and general economic conditions—and its aftermath have underscored the racial inequalities in Cuba and have called for a more democratic society, a deeper understanding of the nature of racism, of how it is embedded in both Cuban history and in the Revolution itself is still lacking. These new civic movements would do well to heed the words of Enrique Patterson, a philosopher and former professor at the University of Havana who went into exile in the early 1990s. In his book, *La soledad histórica y otros ensayos (Historic Solitude and Other Essays)*, Patterson documents the whiteness of the colonial era, the independence movement, the Republic, and the Revolution. In conclusion, any democratic project moving forward that understands the failings of socialism needs to develop a liberal notion of democracy, which is necessary to defend individual liberties, but it also has to be cognizant of the racism in its historical tradition.

The new advocates for democracy in Cuba have been met with brutal repression. A year after the marches, over 700 mostly young people including a dozen minors, were still in prison, with sentences ranging from five to thirty years. These included Luis Manuel Otero Alcántara the artist of the project *La bandera es de todos* and Maykel Osorbo, one of the composers of *Patria y vida*. Others were forced into exile. The prospects of change dimmed as the government continued wrapping itself in a rhetoric that roots its legitimacy in the past and once again promised a better future. Government and party officials ignored the protesters' calls, which highlighted the untenable present, one marked by poverty, inequality, and repression as Cuban protesters squarely situated their demands in a critique of the present with alternative visions for the future.

Signs of democratic movements are also visible in the exile community. Even as antidemocratic movements were on the upswing in the United States and particularly in the state of Florida, groups such as the Miami Freedom Project, Cuban American Women for Democracy, and Raíces Cubanas are providing alternative politics anchored in the here and now. And culturally the Pérez Art Museum is contributing to a more unified vision of what constitutes the Cuban nation promoting projects to create bridges between the island and the diaspora as well as highlighting the contribution of Black artists.

The Poetic Present and Democracy: A More Inclusive Temporality

Let's now look at how the temporality of the poetic present can encourage a more democratic society. As has been noted, individual agency and accountability do not occur in the past or the future; if political projects are lodged in those temporalities, individuals lose their voice. The present, as discussed in a previous chapter, has multiple forms, not all of which create more open political environments. The poetic present—a temporality in which individuals can engage respectfully—which is found in the work of Eliseo Diego, does provide elements that can contribute to a more democratic space, although there is the question of how past systemic exclusions can be successfully addressed in a poetic engagement paradigm.

The structure of democratic deliberations can take many forms, but there are key elements that are necessary for anyone of those forms to function. Among them are informed participation, respect for the individual, and respect of others, particularly those in minority positions, however those positions are defined. All of these elements are necessary conditions for a more participatory public space that is conducive to forming meaningful relations. Keeping in mind that a democratic system works on the majority principle, it must also include safeguards for those in the minority. A culture is needed that recognizes and tolerates differences. And this is the kind of vision that was promoted by Cuban protesters in the summer of 2021.

On the aspect of thoughtful deliberations, the poetic present provides a space in which contemplation can occur. It is the gap between the past and the future. In modernity, as the past loses power to anchor the present, the past became a less dominant force in politics, and time accelerates, pushing us to a future. Arendt paused and explored the space in between. This space can be passive or productive. It is a temporal space in which action and feelings emerge. It is also the space where Arendt, in her book *Between Past and Future,* suggested that thinking occurs.[38] Obviously thinking is an important component of thoughtful deliberations. In the poetic present, the politics of patience can be practiced as well.[39] Eliseo Diego also saw the present as a stage in which to pause and take stock of what is around us. It is a space in which contemplation can occur. However, the fact that there is a space in which deliberations may occur does not necessarily mean that they *will* occur.

Arendt also believed that an educated public was needed for political deliberations. Thinking was an act that required training, and on that point, the work of American pragmatists like John Dewey may be helpful. For Dewey, democracy required an informed citizenry, a notion he explored in his book *Democracy and Education.*[40] Social decisions, he wrote, are complex, and an uneducated people could be manipulated. Education also socializes individuals into acting together and exploring issues together, thus creating a more engaged public. José Martí is another thinker who linked the happiness of the nation to the level of education of its population.

Another important aspect of the poetic present is that it is a space from which past and future temporalities can be made more inclusive. American pragmatists such as George Mead appreciated that individuals act with others in a social medium that is in part constructed by notions of time.[41] The present, for Mead, was the temporal place in which the past and the future were constructed. History is written from a future/present temporality, and it will be as inclusive or exclusive as the present is. And just as the past could be conjured in a more inclusive way, a more inclusive future could also be imagined. Politics, after all, is a social act, and the construction of an imaginary is also social. The question becomes how inclusive is this process of imagining? Recognizing individual voices in the present allows these voices to gain access to new ways of thinking about the past and the future. Democracy thrives when individual voices are heard and when there is a shared sense of the past as well as a sense of inclusion in the construction of the future. These more inclusive processes create community.

As we have seen, time conceived as a linear progression limits the possibilities of more fluid social interactions.[42] In contrast, in an engaged present, multiple times can be appreciated. Time can be multi-dimensional as well as multi-directional. For example, younger generations can be at ease learning and respecting traditions while previous generations can be respectful of the ideas of a younger generation. The "old" is not pitted against the "new." Generational conflict, often violent, reflects clashes between past and future projects, as if time could only hold one temporality at a time. Perhaps, instead of temporal clashes, there can be reflexive and intentional accommodations of multiple temporalities.

A consequence of the perception of time as a rushed linear progression was the obliteration of the individual. The "masses" or "*el pueblo*" replaced the individual as a political actor. But democracy requires a certain level of individuation. Rights and responsibilities are lodged in the individual, even as individuals can be constituted in a "class" or group. The process of going from "Us" to "I" is aided by a temporality that pauses in the in-between space of the present. This is not a proposition to hyper-individualize human beings but rather to recognize differences and respect individual voices so a repurposed "Us" can be constructed.

In this discussion, we could interrogate the concept of the *compañero* (companion, comrade, partner), a term that is widely—almost universally—used in revolutionary Cuba. *Compañero* stands in contrast to the term *ciudadano* (citizen) and inserts a term that renders the individual an apolitical actor. In contrast, the notion of a "citizen" is embedded with rights and responsibilities, a political actor, not just a personal one.

It is important to note that there have been two main schools of thought about whether we should think in terms of sameness or differences. One of the precepts of democratic thought is precisely that we are all equal, a proposition that is the foundation to the idea that everyone has the same rights and opportunities. In contemporary theory, philosophers Slavoj Žižek[43] and Alain Badiou[44] have advocated for sameness. They are deeply suspicious of identity politics, they say, because identity politics has often created an othering based on the superiority of one group over another. The othering process justifies oppression, and indeed, historically, the notion of one group's superiority over another has been the justification for enslavement, oppression, and occupation.

In the Cuban experience, this was precisely José Martí's position. When the War of Independence from Spain began, Cuba was still a society based on slavery, a system that many of those involved in the early independence movement wanted to retain. Cuba's "Lone Star" conspiracy in the mid-1800s—inspired by Texas, which sought to separate from Mexico so that it could maintain slavery—wanted the island independent from Spain so that it could then be annexed to the South of the United States and retain slavery. Indeed, Cuba's flag, also consisting of white and blue stripes and a solitary star, was inspired by the Texas flag. But the Lone Star conspiracy failed. When Martí resuscitated the independence movement, he advocated not only for an end to slavery but also for the inclusion of Blacks into the Rebel Army. He promoted Antonio Maceo to the position of general, signaling that Blacks would be welcomed as equals. In turn, Blacks became the backbone of the independence movement.

The myth of the colorblind society was based precisely on the worthy philosophical precepts of the notion that "all men are created equal." However, the legacy of slavery and the memory that is engraved on the bodies and experiences of people who were enslaved, and on their descendants, cannot be wished away. Moreover, that legacy is also a source of cultural production and pride for people who carry this history. Denying it not only devalues the pain but it erases the resilience it may have spurred.

When the United States intervened in Cuba's independence movement, it introduced segregation measures that sparked widespread rioting. During the early Republic, Blacks in Cuba had the opportunity to organize freely, and it was though associations of Blacks that advocacy for racial equality took hold. Eventually, this advocacy led to the inclusion of anti-discrimination laws into the Constitution of 1940.

This historically important development was to be followed up with specific laws and regulations that could define what constituted discrimination. This never happened. After the Revolution, the entire Constitution of 1940 was suspended and with it all the pending regulatory projects related to it. Instead, Fidel Castro reclaimed the intellectual legacy of Martí's raceless vision: Since everyone was Cuban, there was no need for organizing along color lines. All forms of independent organizing, including Black societies, were dismantled and banned.[45] Even forms of Black cultural expressions inspired by the civil rights movement Fidel Castro had so enthusiastically applauded during his visit to New York City in 1960 were punished. When the Revolution itself was the embodiment of Cuba's historic aspirations, there was no need to organize for social justice. Once again, Black Cubans were denied their past and deprived of the ability to pursue their contemporary struggle. But as philosopher Enrique Patterson decries, the price for becoming human was that Blacks lost their race.[46]

The consolidation of an ideology that wiped out individual experiences also contributed to denying Blacks the ability to continue to organize. Che Guevara's insistence that "the masses" needed to be led by the "enlightened comrades" was elitist and racist, given that almost all the commanders of the Revolution were white, and the majority of the "masses" Black. The "masses" were undifferentiated. As such, they were stripped of distinguishing characteristics, such as race, class, gender, age, or religion, that informed people's personal histories and influenced their position in society. In many ways, the Revolution rolled back the gains that Blacks had made in their efforts to be seen as both Cuban and Black. The state's operating philosophical precepts were based on a colorblind notion of nation. But this idea misses that we are also different in a multiplicity of ways, that structural inequalities create differences as well, and that these differences allow us to see our individuality. For philosopher Emmanuel Levinas, this awareness of difference occurs in the instant—in a form of the present. Without disregarding important criticism about Levinas's inconsistent application of rights to all groups,[47] I would like to suggest that democracy also needs the recognition of the other based on difference. Propositions like "We are all Cuban," regardless of race, obliterates the existing racism and discrimination along with the history of Afro-Cubans who were enslaved. Anne Phillips, a feminist political theorist, has argued that there cannot be a differentiated unity, for unity implies subordination to the whole. She is not suggesting that

152 · Democracy and Time in Cuban Thought

there cannot be coalitions, or unity defined in more inclusive terms, but that calls for unity may result in obliterating the individual. The alternative to unity does not necessarily have to be hyper-individualized politics. Most importantly, she argues against the either/or proposition between sameness and difference—alterity and sameness.[48] For Cuba, it means that people can be both Cuban and Black. Social theorist Chantal Mouffe has made similar arguments in commenting on the tension inherent in postmodernism—a system that also emphasized sameness while acknowledging individualism. She noted that those with privilege and power can argue sameness, and in so doing, obliterate the impact that differential structures have on those who have historically been left out.[49]

I would suggest that the problem is not the recognition of difference, rather it is the imposition of hierarchy of one category over another. Can we imagine a society where we all did the same thing, spoke just one language? Only an authoritarian form of government could impose "sameness." Still the recognition of universality is also necessary—it is universality that allows for respecting differences, since it values all human lives.[50] In the poetic present, differences are recognized, setting a temporal stage for thoughtful deliberation among individuals who are different yet still share a common humanity.

The work of Caribbean philosopher Charles Mills becomes critically important to understanding the limitations of both the liberal project that argued for the individual and the Marxist project that argued for class. While liberalism and Marxism are seemingly at odds with each other, Mills contends, they share the same philosophical roots, that is, European enlightenment. Both are rational projects conceived as liberatory—one frees the individual and the other liberates an oppressed class. Liberalism relied on the notion of the social contract, of a covenant between individuals and the state. But Blacks were not included in the notion of "individuals." With that in mind, Mills reframes the social contract as the "Racial contract," and demonstrates that the goal of liberalism was to create European global economic dominance and national white privilege.[51] Marxism, on the other hand, predicted that workers would be liberated through a revolutionary process that would bring the working class to power.[52] Leading the vanguard were the white workers of Europe, thus privileging "whiteness," just as liberalism does.

While noting the racist origins of both projects, Mills concludes that at least in liberalism there is a better chance of including Blacks, because the individual is allowed to freely express themselves and as such differences can be a basis for organizing. In Marxism, the obliteration of the individual and the imposition of a universal "class" makes it impossible to organize along any other dimension. As we have seen, the poetic present does create a temporal space in which individuals can exist, it can also be a space that recognizes individual differences.

The Elusive Present

The central theme of this book has been temporalities and their impact on political projects. Cuba provides a case study on how temporalities influence the construction of political projects that either limit or create opportunities for individual engagement. The work of Hannah Arendt on the rise of totalitarianism in modernity has contributed to the conceptual scaffolding of this inquiry. She observed how modernity cut off the past and rushed toward the future obliterating opportunities for individual engagement without which democracy is impossible. As Austrian writer Stefan Zweig observed, the acceleration of time destroyed the present, and consequently the individual as well.[53] The masses replaced individuals. In this unmoored time when members of society were subsumed into one category that obliterated their individualism, totalitarianism could take root.

Political projects such as the Cuban Revolution promised a more open, democratic, and egalitarian society. Instead, an authoritarian government took hold that consolidated a military elite that did not serve the nation but rather enriched itself through partnerships with foreign investors.[54] In part its temporal settings contributed to this. The Revolution relied on the past as a way of legitimizing its aspirations. The unfulfilled mandate of the past was summoned to guide the revolutionary process. Fidel Castro became heir to a project that was still incomplete. His promise of bringing forth an independent nation was lodged in past struggles that had not yielded fruit. But nation-building itself was a futuristic project, as was the building of a socialist society.

The Revolution also took on a unique temporality of a "permanent revolution," and as such became frozen in a past that continued to repeat itself. Even though the original leadership hung on to power for more than half a century, the Revolution itself was not eternal. Yet it has often been presented as an ongoing process that reaches back to the wars of independence and marches forward into the future.

At the end, twentieth-century socialist projects did not bring forth more inclusive and egalitarian economic systems. Indeed, many became totalitarian. Cuba was no exception. The era after the collapse of socialism became known as the end of ideas. Perhaps a better description would be the end of the promise of a better future. The idea of communism grows out of an illusion, one that promised a better global system. It is an illusion that gave hope in times of devastating world wars. This is not to say that ideals had not swept social and political movements in the past. Indeed, the French Revolution itself was imbued with ideas to be realized in the future. The difference is that in communism, the state and its government managed the future by promoting illusions, organized them, mobilized them, and made them part of the ordinary. In slogans such as *Pioneros por el comunismo, ¡Seremos como el Che!* (Pioneers for socialism; We will be like Che), past and future melded into the quotidian.[55]

In reality, socialism was not the only ideological system that failed. Democratic institutions that melded with capitalist economic systems did not bring forth their promise of equal opportunities, either. Some of the world's strongest democratic countries waged wars abroad, denying others the freedoms and practices they supposedly defended for their own countries. The end of the Cold War was most visibly represented by the fall of the Berlin Wall, which was popularly read as the triumph of the West over the East. But it meant much more than that. Indeed, it marked the end of the future as a political temporality and questioned the Enlightenment and rationalism in general.[56] Rational projects, with their willful orientation toward the future, were often replaced by a return to the past. In recent decades, for example, a religious revival has emerged worldwide. Regaining what had been lost has become a rallying cry for political mobilization throughout the world.

The void left by the end of the future was also filled by a "fall into the present," a pragmatic orientation toward the now fueled by global markets.[57] Socialist regimes embraced market-Leninism, capitalism with authoritarian states, or state capitalism. Capitalist institutions fought against state regulations, and any consideration of the impact that their actions could have either on societies or the environment were replaced by the immediate goal of maximizing profits.

A present without a past, or without at least an understanding of the past, can lead to an inactive pessimism.[58] Without an inclusive past and a shared realistic future, the present can become a series of spectacles. In recent years, catastrophes—wild fires, rising seas, and uncontrolled violence—sucked the world into a despairing present, one unable to offer time for contemplation or space for individual voices. And a health emergency, the COVID-19 pandemic, obliterated our customary sense of time altogether, as what we had learned to experience as rapid time grew long and slow, and the world as we had known it became a very distant past. A "new" present emerged, unmoored from the past and without a future in sight.

The collapse of the Soviet Union in the 1990s threw Cuba into the vortex of an idle present. Waiting, for many, was waiting for the death of Fidel Castro. Yet when he died, there was no major upheaval. Stuck in time, more specifically stuck in the present, Cuba's political institutions and political culture was unable to change. A younger military generation continued to perform the past while still promising a better future. But while the death of Fidel Castro may not have set off institutional changes, it did reset the temporal construct of *La Espera* (The Wait). What happens after the event you have been waiting for occurs? As the Cuban-born cultural critic Iván de la Nuez has noted, "We are not waiting for the future for the simple reason that it is already here and it is what we have today."[59] In Cuba, that future did not turn out to be the promised land, rather it was marked by inequality and maintained through repression, perhaps a future that repeated the past.

Václav Havel observed that after the fall of communism, history needed to make up for lost time. There was a rushing away from authoritarian regimes where time had stopped. Post-Soviet changing times were, in fact, "a change in time."[60] We might call these times *entre tiempos* (between times), a time of transition that has the potential of restructuring our perceptions of time and politics, one that has been called messianic time.[61] Another way of appreciating this *entre tiempos* is what Giorgio Agamben refers to as the time that remains, a time in which various temporalities and the concepts and practices that grew from specific time periods are reexamined and restructured and a new synthesis can occur.[62] The present can open opportunities for essential activities conducive to democracy to materialize. We can say that this aptly describes the opposition in Cuba during the early 2020s. It is impossible to predict whether they will succeed, but there at least seemed to be a public awareness of the need for a more democratic political culture even among the protesters themselves.

In this time that remains, the engaged present, the poetic present suggested by Octavio Paz and evidenced in the works of Eliseo Diego, can emerge. Indeed, in literature and art, in this case specifically in poetry, a distinct temporality can materialize.[63] Poetry and poets after all have played a critical role in the formation of the nation as well as in its identity. In the early 1800s, the Cuban-born poet Gertrudis Gómez de Avellaneda imagined the nation from abroad in her poem *Al partir* (On leaving).[64] In 1845, the mixed-race poet Concepción Valdés, known as Plácido, was executed for his challenge to the Spanish authority. The injustice of this was captured in his last poem, published in the United States under the title *Plácido's Last Song*.[65] José Martí, one of the intellectuals of the War of Independence, was also a poet, and his work became intricately tied to notions of *cubanidad* (Cubanness). And many ideological struggles of the 1900s were played out in literary magazines.

But what exactly is the relationship between this poetic present and democracy, when democracy is also linked to future outcomes? As I have laid out, key elements necessary for the development of a more democratic culture require the present and cannot only rely on a promised future. By appreciating an open present, both the past and the future can be more democratic. This reexamination may yield new propositions about time itself and its relationship to politics.

It is also in the present that change and action occurs. Centering political projects in the present allows for agency to be exercised, not remembered or anticipated. It also allows for a recognition of the other as an individual, with the capacity to see sameness and respect differences. We see this in the politics and ideas of the opposition in Cuba. It is in the temporal space of the present that inclusivity can be practiced, not imagined.

Along strident political discourses, in Cuba, poetry has functioned to create a space of contemplation and reflection. In so doing, it has created alternative temporalities conducive to a more open political culture. Since poetry played such an important role in the formation of the Cuban nation, perhaps poets and artists can also contribute to its future by helping to create a temporal space in which individuals are respected and their differences recognized. This time, the poetic present, which has been elusive, can be democracy's time.

Notes

Preface

1 "Remarks by President Obama at the First Plenary Session of the Summit of the Americas," April 11, 2015, https://obamawhitehouse.archives.gov/the-press-office/2015/04/11/remarks-president-obama-first-plenary-session-summit-americas (accessed February 16, 2023).
2 María de los Ángeles Torres, *The Lost Apple: Operation Pedro Pan, Cuban Children in the U.S., and the Promise of a Better Future* (Boston: Beacon Press, 2003).
3 María de los Ángeles Torres, Irene Rizzini, and Norma Del Río, *Citizens in the Present: Youth Civic Engagement in the Americas* (Urbana: University of Illinois Press, 2013).

Introduction

1 Félix Varela, *Escritos políticos* (La Habana: Editorial Ciencias Sociales, 1977).
2 José Martí, *Selected Writings* (New York: Penguin Press, 2002).
3 Alejandro de la Fuente, *A Nation for All: Race, Inequality, and Politics in Twentieth-Century Cuba* (Chapel Hill: University of North Carolina Press, 2011).
4 Julia Sweig, *Inside the Cuban Revolution: Fidel Castro and the Urban Underground* (Cambridge: Harvard University Press, 2004).
5 Javier Figueroa de Cárdenas, *El sueño inconcluso: La historia del Directorio Revolucionario Estudiantil, 1959–1966* (Miami: Ediciones Universal, 2022).
6 Figueroa de Cárdenas, *El sueño inconcluso*, 41.
7 Carlos Moore, *Castro, the Blacks, and Africa* (Los Angeles: UCLA Center for African-American Studies, 1988).
8 Abel Sierra Madero, *El cuerpo nunca olvida: Trabajo forzado, hombre nuevo y memoria en Cuba (1959–1980)* (Ciudad de Mexico: Rialta Ediciones, 2022).
9 Madeline Cámara, "Vocación de Casandra: La poética en 'El ángel agotado' de María Elena Cruz Varela," *Cuban Studies* 29 (1999): 83–104.
10 Madeline Cámara, "Grafoscopio: MADELINE CAMARA: MEMORIA DE MARQUÉS RAVELO," May 23, 2018. https://grafoscopio.blogspot.com/2018/05/madeline-camara-memoria-de-marques.html, accessed February 15, 2023.

158 · Notes to Pages 6–11

11 José Manuel Pallí, Esq. "Analysis: Understanding Payá and his Varela Project," August 21, 2012, https://www.cubastandard.com/analysis-understanding-osvaldo-paya-and-his-varela-project/, accessed February 15, 2023.

12 Jorge Olivera, interview by author, April 18, 2022.

13 Jonathan Watts, "Cuban dissident Oswaldo Payá's death 'no accident' claims daughter," *The Guardian*, July 23, 2012.

14 Louis Pérez Jr., *The Structure of Cuban History* (Chapel Hill: University of North Carolina Press, 2015).

15 Fidel Castro, *"History Will Absolve Me,"* (La Habana: Instituto Cubano del Libro, 1973). Fidel Castro's speech on October 16, 1953.

16 José Quiroga, *Cuban Palimpsests* (Minneapolis: University of Minnesota Press, 2005).

17 George Gudsorf, *Mythe et metaphysique,* cited in Fernando Aínsa, "Imagen y la posibilidad de la utopía en 'Paradiso,' de Lezama Lima," *Revista Iberoamericana* XLIX, 123–124 (April–September 1983): 263–277.

18 José Martí, *La Edad de Oro*. Miami: Ediciones Universal, 1988; Philip S. Foner, (ed.), *On Education: Articles on Educational Theory and Pedagogy and Writing for Children from the Age of Gold* (New York: Monthly Review Press, 1979).

19 *Granma,* Headlines, December 27, 1987.

20 Abilio Estévez, *Tuyo es el reino* (Barcelona: Tusquets Editores, SA, 1997).

21 Pedro Juan Gutiérrez, *Dirty Havana Trilogy,* trans. Natasha Wimmer (New York: Farrar, Straus and Giroux, 2001).

22 Zoé Valdés, *La nada cotidiana* (Barcelona: Editorial Planeta, 1996).

23 Quiroga, *Cuban Palimpsests,* 2005.

24 Rolando Estévez, "Gerundios para la espera (Verbs for Waiting): A Visual Coda," in *The Portable Island: Cubans at Home in the World,* edited by Ruth Behar and Lucía Suárez (New York: Palgrave Macmillan, 2008), 235–247.

25 Walter Benjamin, *Selected Writings,* vol. 1, edited by Howard Eiland and Michael W. Jennings (Cambridge, MA & London: Harvard University Press, 1991–1999), 395.

26 Paul Miller, "Blancas y Negras: Carpentier and the Temporalities of Mutual Exclusion," *Latin American Literary Review* 29, 58 (July–December 2001): 23–45.

27 Fernando Aínsa, "Imagen y la posibilidad de la utopía en 'Paradiso,' de Lezama Lima," *Revista Iberoamericana* XLIX, 123–124 (April–September 1983): 263–277.

28 Walter Benjamin, *Illuminations: Essays and Reflections,* edited by Hannah Arendt (New York: Harcourt, Brace, Jovanovich, 1968).

29 Achy Obejas, *Ruins* (New York: Akashic Books, 2009).

30 Sally Mann, *Still Time* (New York: Aperture Foundation, 2008).

31 Merriam-Webster, "democracy," https://www.merriam-webster.com/dictionary/democracy, accessed July 1, 2023.

32 Julio Antonio Fernández Estrada, "The July 11th Protests in Cuba: The Opinion of Julio Antonio Fernández Estrada," https://www.youtube.com/watch?v=qJbRjwrVkZc&t=2s, accessed February 16, 2023. Also Yunior García, "The 11J detainees in Cuba: Testimony of Yunior García Aguilera," https://www.youtube.com/watch?v=IFHd9qMfga4 (accessed February 16, 2023).

Notes to Pages 11–18 · 159

33 Samuel A. Chambers, "Untimely politics *avant la lettre:* The temporality of social formations," *Time & Society* 20, 2 (July 2011): 197–223.

34 David Couzens Hoy, *The Time of Our Lives: A Critical History of Temporality* (Cambridge: MIT Press, 2012), xvii.

35 Chambers, "Untimely politics *avant la lettre*," 218.

36 Chambers, "Untimely politics *avant la lettre*," 199.

37 Stephen Hawking, *A Brief History of Time* (New York: Bantam, 1998).

38 Carlo Rovelli, *Seven Brief Lessons on Physics* (New York: Riverhead Books, 2016), 60.

39 Nathan Widder, *Reflections on Time and Politics* (University Park: Pennsylvania State University Press, 2008), 13.

40 Russell West-Pavlov, *Temporalities* (New York: Routledge, 2013), 34.

41 West-Pavlov, *Temporalities,* 43.

42 Martin Heidegger, *Being and Time* (New York: Harper Perennial Modern Classics, 2008).

43 Johannes Fabian, *Time and the Other: How Anthropology Makes Its Object* (New York: Columbia University Press, 2014).

44 Octavio Paz, "Interview," *New Perspectives Quarterly* 4, 1 (Winter 1987).

45 Alfred Gell, *The Anthropology of Time: Cultural Constructions of Temporal Maps and Images* (London: Bloomsbury Academic, 2001).

46 Carl Goldberg, "Time in Psychoanalysis: Some Contradictory Aspects" (Book Review), *American Psychological Association,* http://www.apadivisions.org/division -39/publications/reviews/time-contradictory.aspx, accessed September 2, 2020.

47 Hannah Arendt, *The Origins of Totalitarianism* (New York: Harcourt, 1968).

48 Katherine Bermingham, "Time for Arendt," *Amor Mundi,* https://hac.bard.edu/ amor-mundi/time-for-arendt-2019-08-02, accessed February 16, 2023.

49 Eyal Chowers, "Gushing Time: Modernity and the Multiplicity of Temporal Homes," *Time & Society* 11, 2–3 (September 2002): 233–249.

50 Hannah Arendt, *The Human Condition* (Chicago: University of Chicago Press, 1958), 242–243.

51 Hannah Arendt, *Between Past and Future* (New York: Viking Press, 1961).

52 Arendt, *The Origins of Totalitarianism,* Chapter 13.

53 Kathrin Braun, "Biopolitics and Temporality in Arendt and Foucault," *Time & Society* 16, 1 (March 2007): 12; and Arendt, *Origins of Totalitarianism.*

54 Braun, "Biopolitics and Temporality," 13.

55 Walt W. Rostow, *The Stages of Economic Growth: A Non-Communist Manifesto* (Cambridge: Cambridge University Press, 1960).

56 Karl Marx, *The Communist Manifesto,* Marxist Internet Archive, https://www .marxists.org/archive/marx/works/1848/communist-manifesto/ch01.htm, accessed July 27, 2020.

57 Braun, "Biopolitics and Temporality," 13.

58 Arendt, *The Human Condition.*

59 West-Pavlov, *Temporalities,* 45.

60 Iain Macdonald, "Adorno's Modal Utopianism: Possibility and Actuality in Adorno and Hegel," *Adorno Studies* 1, 1 (January 2017): 11.

160 · Notes to Pages 18–25

61 John Rawls, *The Law of Peoples* (Cambridge: Harvard University Press, 1999).

62 Arjun Appadurai, *The Future as Cultural Artifact: Essays on the Global Condition* (London: Verso, 2013).

63 Braun, "Biopolitics and Temporality," 10.

64 Couzens Hoy, *Time of Our Lives*, 45, 155.

65 Quoted in Gary Smith Chowers (ed.), *Benjamin: Philosophy, Aesthetics, History* (Chicago: University of Chicago Press, 1989), 244.

66 Kia Lindroos, *Now-time Image-space: Temporalization of Politics in Walter Benjamin's Philosophy of History and Art* (Jyväskylä: SoPhi Academic Press, 1998).

67 Svetlana Boym, *The Future of Nostalgia* (New York: Basic Books, 2001), 23.

68 Néstor García Canclini, *Hybrid Cultures: Strategies for Entering and Leaving Modernity* (Minneapolis: University of Minnesota Press, 2005).

69 Javier Santiso, "The Fall into the Present: The Emergence of Limited Political Temporalities in Latin America," *Time & Society* 7, 1 (March 1998): 25–54.

70 George Herbert Mead, *The Philosophy of the Present* (New York: Prometheus Books, 2002).

71 David R. Maines et al., "The Sociological Import of G. H. Mead's Theory of the Past," *American Sociological Review* 48, 2 (1983): 161–173.

72 Octavio Paz, "In Search of the Present," Nobel Prize Acceptance Speech, 1990, https://www.nobelprize.org/prizes/literature/1990/paz/lecture/, accessed February 21, 2023.

73 Eliseo Diego, *Un hondo bosque de sueños: Notas sobre literatura para niños* (La Habana: Ediciones Unión, 2008).

Chapter 1. The Past

1 Paula Rosas, "En Cuba estamos cansados de vivir tanto tiempo en la Historia y queremos vivir en la normalidad," BBC News *Mundo*, January 27, 2023, https://www.bbc.com/mundo/noticias-64189085, accessed February 26, 2023.

2 Michael Bustamante, *Cuban Memory Wars: Retrospective Politics in Revolution and Exile* (Chapel Hill: University of North Carolina Press, 2021).

3 Parts of the following discussion appeared in María de los Ángeles Torres, "History Will Absolve Me," in Alan West-Durán, (ed.), *Cuba* (New York: Charles Scribner's Son, 2012).

4 Michel-Rolph Trouillot, *Silencing the Past: Power and the Production of History* (Boston: Beacon Press, 1995), 26.

5 Paul Ricoeur, *Memory, History, Forgetting*, trans. Kathleen Blamey and David Pellauer (Chicago: University of Chicago Press, 2004).

6 Hannah Arendt, *Between Past and Future* (New York: Penguin Classics, 2006).

7 Benedict Anderson, *Imagined Communities: Reflections on the Origin and Spread of Nationalism* (London: Verso Books, 1983).

8 Maurice Halbwachs. *On Collective Memory*, trans. Lewis A. Coser (Chicago: University of Chicago Press, 1992), 40.

9 Halbwachs, *On Collective Memory*, 50.

10 Pierre Nora, *Rethinking France: Les Lieux de mémoire,* trans. Mary Trouille (Chicago: University of Chicago Press, 2001–2006).

11 Alejandro Madrid, *Sounds of the Modern Nation: Music, Culture, and Ideas in Post-Revolutionary Mexico* (Philadelphia: Temple University Press, 2008).

12 Paul Connerto, *How Societies Remember* (London: Cambridge University Press, 1989).

13 Pierre Nora, "Between Memory and History: Les Lieux de Mémoire," *Representations* 26 (Spring, 1989): 7–24.

14 Louis A. Pérez Jr., *The Structure of Cuban History: Meanings and Purpose of the Past* (Chapel Hill: University of North Carolina Press, 2015).

15 Pérez, *Structure of Cuban History,* 2.

16 Pérez, *Structure of Cuban History,* 50.

17 Zygmunt Bauman, "Time and Space Reunited," *Time & Society* 9, 2/3 (June 2000): 171–185,

18 Pérez, *Structure of Cuban History,* 34.

19 Pérez, *Structure of Cuban History,* 131.

20 Torres, "History Will Absolve Me."

21 Gary Daynes, "Finding Meaning in Moncada: Historical Memory in Revolutionary Cuba," *Caribbean Quarterly* 42, 1, (March 1996): 1–13.

22 Fidel Castro Speeches, LANIC, University of Texas, http://lanic.utexas.edu/project/castro/db/1959/19590514.html, accessed February 16, 2023.

23 Fidel Castro, *History Will Absolve Me* (La Habana: Instituto Cubano del Libro, 1973).

24 Fidel Castro, "Ceremony Marking the Centennial of Cuba's Struggle for Independence, 1968," LANIC, University of Texas, http://lanic.utexas.edu/project/castro/db/1968/19681011.html, accessed September 2, 2020.

25 Leonel Antonio de la Cuesta (ed.), *Constituciones Cubanas desde 1812 hasta nuestro tiempos* (New York: Ediciones Exilio, 1974).

26 Castro, *History Will Absolve Me.*

27 Nicola Miller, "The Absolution of History: Uses of the Past in Castro's Cuba," *Journal of Contemporary History* 38, 1 (2003): 147–162.

28 Carlo Ginzburg, "Checking the Evidence: The Judge and the Historian," *Critical Inquiry* 18, 1, (Autumn 1991): 79–92.

29 Arendt, *Between Past and Future.*

30 Roy Medvedev, *Let History Judge,* trans. George Shriver (New York: Columbia University Press, 1989).

31 Rafael Rojas, *La máquina del olvido: Mito, historia y poder en Cuba* (Ciudad de México: Taurus, 2011).

32 Rojas, *La máquina del olvido,* 113.

33 Manuel Moreno Fraginals, *Historia como arma: Y otros estudios sobres esclavos, ingenios y plantaciones* (Madrid: Crítica, 2003).

34 Arendt, *Between Past and Future.*

35 Lillian Guerra, *Heroes, Martyrs, and Political Messiahs in Revolutionary Cuba, 1946–1958* (New Haven: Yale University Press, 2018).

162 · Notes to Pages 34–44

36 Raquel Mendieta, *Cultura, lucha de clases y conflicto racial, 1878–1895* (La Habana: Editorial Pueblo y Educación, 1989).
37 Guerra, *Heroes,* 7.
38 Guerra, *Heroes,* 25.
39 Julia Sweig, *Inside the Revolution: Fidel Castro and the Urban Underground* (Cambridge: Harvard University Press, 2002).
40 Rojas, *La máquina del olvido,* 69.
41 Herbert Müller, *Uses of the Past: Profiles of Former Societies* (New York: Oxford University Press, 1952), 347.
42 Hannah Arendt, *The Origins of Totalitarianism* (New York: Harcourt, Brace, Jovanovich, 1968).
43 Rojas, *La máquina del olvido,* 56.
44 Ulises Schmill, *Las revoluciones: Teoría jurídica y consideraciones sociológicas* (Madrid: Trotta, 2009), quoted in Rojas, *La máquina del olvido,* 70.
45 Rafael Rojas, *Isla sin fin: contribución a la crítica del nacionalismo cubano* (Miami: Universal Press, 1999), 86.
46 Fidel Castro Speeches, "July 27, 1959, Castro Agrees to Return to Premiership," LANIC, University of Texas, http://lanic.utexas.edu/project/castro/db/1959/19590514.html, accessed February 16, 2023.
47 Orlando Jiménez Leal and Manuel Zayas, *El Caso PM: Cine, poder y censura* (Madrid: Editorial Hypermedia, 2014).
48 Fidel Castro, "Palabras a los intelectuales. 1961," *Se dice cubano* 9 (2016), http://www.uneac.org.cu/sites/default/files/pdf/publicaciones/boletin_se_dice_cubano_no.9.pdf, accessed September 2, 2020.
49 Nora, "Between Memory and History," 26.
50 Trouillot, *Silencing the Past.*
51 Edmundo Desnoes, *Memorias del subdesarrollo* (Madrid: Mono Azul, 2011).
52 María de los Ángeles Torres, *In the Land of Mirrors: Cuban Exile Politics in the United States* (Ann Arbor: University of Michigan Press, 1999).
53 Torres, *In the Land of Mirrors,* Chapter 4.
54 Grupo Areíto, *Contra viento y marea: Jóvenes cubanos hablan desde su exilio en Estados Unidos* (Ciudad de México: Siglo XXI, 1978).
55 Jesús Díaz, dir., *55 Hermanos,* Production ICAIC, 1978, https://www.youtube.com/watch?v=MJUSCWl6VY8, accessed February 16, 2023.
56 María de los Ángeles Torres, "Donde los fantasmas bailan el guaguancó: Where Ghosts Dance el Guaguanco," in *By Heart/De Memoria: Cuban Women's Journeys In and Out of Exile,* edited by María de los Ángeles Torres (Philadelphia: Temple University Press, 2003), 23–57.
57 VerbiClara, "La Operación Pedro Pan y los niños cubanos," June 2, 2009, https://verbiclara.wordpress.com/2009/06/02/la-operacion-peter-pan-y-los-ninos-cubanos/, accessed February 16, 2023.
58 "Testimony of Rev. Bryan Walsh, National Conference of Catholic Charities," Cuban Refugee Problems: Hearings Before the Subcommittee to Investigate Problems Connected with Refugees and Escapees. Committee on the Judiciary, US Senate,

Notes to Pages 44–53 · 163

87th Congress, First Session, 1961 (Washington DC: US Government Printing Office, 1962).

59 Sergio López Miró, "El lado oscuro de Pedro Pan," *El Miami Herald*, November 29, 1990.

60 *Escape from Havana: An American Story*, CNBC, May 2010, https://www.cnbc.com/escape-from-havana-an-american-story/, accessed February 16, 2023.

61 Letter to CNBC from Board of Directors of Operation Pedro Pan Group, Inc., June 15, 2010, http://pedropan.org/content/letter-cnbc-board-directors-operation-pedro-pan-group-inc, accessed February 16, 2023.

62 Antón Arrufat, *Repaso final* (La Habana: Ediciones, 1964), "Ellos."

63 Press release, Governor Ron DeSantis, https://www.flgov.com/2022/02/07/governor-ron-desantis-faith-leaders-and-pedro-pans-biden-border-crisis-is-harming-children/, accessed February 16, 2023.

64 Syra Ortiz-Blanes and Bianca Prado-Ocasio, "Debate with DeSantis over unaccompanied minors divides Miami's Pedro Pan Cubans," *The Miami Herald*, February 7, 2022, https://www.miamiherald.com/article258035883.html, accessed February 16, 2023.

65 Victor Andrés Triay, *Fleeing Castro: Operation Pedro Pan and the Cuban Children's Program* (Gainesville: University Press of Florida, 1999).

66 Lindsey Dodd, "Small Fish, Big Pond: Using a Single Oral Narrative to Reveal Broader Social Change," in *Memory and History: Understanding Memory as Source and Subject*, edited by Joan Tumbley (Abingdon: Routledge, 2013), 37.

Chapter 2. The Future

1 Alejo Carpentier, *Lo real maravilloso* (Ciudad de México: Universidad Nacional Autónoma de México, 2004).

2 Diego Petersen Farah, "Cuba: El futuro es cosa del pasado," *Nexos*, September 1, 2014, http://www.nexos.com.mx/?p=22328, accessed September 2, 2020.

3 Sergio Fontanella, "Margin and Utopia by Pedro Pablo Oliva," *On Cuba*, August 2015, oncubamagazine.com, accessed September 2, 2020.

4 Iván de la Nuez, *Iconocracia: An Image of Power and the Power of Images in Contemporary Cuban Photography* (Nashville: Turner, 2016), Chapter 3.

5 Andrea O'Reilly Herrera, *Cuba: IDEA of a Nation Displaced* (Albany: State University of New York, 2007).

6 Nikolas Kompridis, "The Idea of a New Beginning: A Romantic Source of Normativity and Freedom," in *Philosophical Romanticism*, edited by Nikolas Kompridis (Abingdon: Routledge, 2006), 32–59.

7 Junger Habermas. *Philosophical Discourses of Modernity* (Cambridge: Harvard University Press, 1987).

8 Reinhart Koselleck, *Futures Past: On the Semantics of Historical Times* (New York: Columbia University Press, 2006).

9 Henri Lefebvre, *Introduction to Modernity*, trans. John Moore (London: Verso, 1995), 168–238.

164 · Notes to Pages 54–58

10 Armin Nassehi, "No Time for Utopia: The Absence of Utopian Contents in Modern Concepts of Time," *Time & Society* 3, 1, (February 1994): 47.

11 Hannah Arendt, *The Origins of Totalitarianism* (New York: Harcourt, Brace & World, 1968), 461–462.

12 Leo Marx and Bruce Mazlish, (eds.), *Progress: Fact or Illusion?* (Ann Arbor: University of Michigan Press, 1998).

13 Walter Benjamin, *Illuminations: Essays and Reflections* (New York: Schocken Books, 1969), 261.

14 Giuseppe Tassone, *A Study on the Idea of Progress in Nietzsche, Heidegger, and Critical Theory* (New York: E. Mellen Press, 2002).

15 Karl Popper, *The Poverty of Historicism* (New York: Routledge, 1957).

16 Steven Goldman, "Progress: Fact or Illusion?" *Technology & Culture* 41, 1 (2000): 116–117.

17 Lewis Mumford, *Technics and Civilization* (Chicago: University of Chicago Press, 2010), 429–432.

18 Richard Shorten, "Conceptions of 'the political': A note on contrasting motifs in Hannah Arendt's treatment of totalitarianism," *Journal for Political Thinking* 2, 1 (September 2006).

19 Steven Hutchinson, "Mapping Utopias," *Modern Philology* 85, 2 (November 1987): 170–185.

20 Nassehi, "No Time for Utopia," 47.

21 Gregory Claeys and Lyman Tower Sargent, *The Utopia Reader* (New York: New York University Press, 1999), 6.

22 Phillip E. Wegner, *Imaginary Communities: Utopia, the Nation, and the Spatial Histories of Modernity* (Los Angeles: University of California Press, 2002).

23 Lewis Mumford, *The Story of Utopias* (New York: Viking Press, 1962).

24 Michel Foucault, *The Order of Things: An Archaeology of the Human Sciences* (New York: Vintage Books, 1994).

25 Benedict Anderson, *Imagined Communities: Reflections on the Origin and Spread of Nationalism* (London: Verso, 2006).

26 Louis A. Pérez Jr., *The Structure of Cuban History: Meanings and Purpose of the Past* (Chapel Hill: University of North Carolina Press, 2013), 62.

27 Georg Wilhelm Friedrich Hegel, *The Philosophy of History* (New York: Dover Publication, 1956), 17.

28 Wegner, *Imaginary Communities,* 63.

29 Lillian Guerra, *The Myth of José Martí: Conflicting Nationalisms in Early Twentieth-Century Cuba* (Chapel Hill: University of North Carolina Press, 2005).

30 Pérez, *Structure of Cuban History,* 56.

31 Simón Bolívar, *El Libertador: Writings of Simón Bolívar,* trans. Frederick Fornoff (New York: Oxford University Press, 2003).

32 Philip Foner (ed.), *José Martí, Our America: Writings on Latin America and the Struggle for Cuban Independence* (New York: Monthly Review Press, 1977).

33 José Martí, *Nuestra América,* http://www.josemarti.cu/publicacion/nuestra-america-version-ingles/, accessed February 17, 2023.

Notes to Pages 58–66 · 165

34 Martí, *Nuestra América*.
35 María de los Ángeles Torres, a version of the following appeared as an essay in *Cuba* (New York: Charles Scribner's Son, 2012)
36 José Martí, *La Edad de Oro* (Miami: Ediciones Universal, 1988).
37 José Martí, *On Education: Articles on Educational Theory and Pedagogy and Writings from the Age of Gold,* edited by Philip S. Foner (New York: Monthly Review Press, 1979), 34.
38 Martí, *On Education,* 35.
39 Martí, *On Education,* 166.
40 Leonel Antonio de la Cuesta (ed.), *Constituciones cubanas desde el 1812 hasta nuestros días* (Miami: Ediciones Exilio, 1974), 253–254.
41 Martí, *La Edad de Oro,* 11.
42 Martí, *La Edad de Oro,* 12.
43 Kim Beauchesne and Alessandra Santos, *Utopian Thought in Latin America* (New York: Palgrave MacMillan, 2011).
44 John Reed, *Ten Days that Shook the World* (New York: Penguin, 1977); John Reed, *Insurgent Mexico* (Greenwood: Greenwood Press, 1914).
45 José Carlos Mariátegui, *Seven Interpretive Essays on Peruvian Reality,* trans. Marjorie Urquidi (Austin: University of Texas Press, 1971).
46 Irene Rizzini, "The Child-Saving Movement in Brazil: Ideology in the Late Nineteenth and Early Twentieth Centuries," in *Minor Omissions: Children in Latin American History and Society,* edited by Tobias Hecht (Madison: University of Wisconsin Press, 2002), 165–180.
47 Gabriela Mistral, *Selected Prose and Prose-Poems,* trans. Stephen Tabscott (Austin: University of Texas Press, 2010).
48 José Vasconcelos, *La Raza Cósmica,* trans. Didier Jaen (Baltimore: Johns Hopkins University Press, 1997).
49 Evita Perón, *Historia del peronismo* (Buenos Aires: Ediciones Mundo Peronista, 1951).
50 Robert Whitney, "The Architect of the Cuban State: Fulgencio Batista and Populism in Cuba, 1937–1940," *Journal of Latin American Studies* 32, 2 (May 2000): 435–459.
51 Fidel Castro, Speech on the Second Anniversary of the Revolution, January 5, 1961, LANIC, University of Texas, http://lanic.utexas.edu/project/castro/db/1961/19610105.html accessed February 17, 2023.
52 Erik Ching, Christina Buckley, and Angélica Lozano-Alonso, "The Socialist Utopia: Che Guevara and the Cuban Revolution," in *Reframing Latin America: A Cultural Theory Reading of the Nineteenth and Twentieth Centuries,* edited by Erik Ching, Christina Buckley, and Angélica Lozano-Alonso (Austin: University of Texas Press, 2007), 237–259.
53 *The Che Guevara Reader* (Melbourne: Ocean Press, 2005).
54 Ernesto Guevara, "Socialism and Man in Cuba. March 1965," Marxist Internet Archive, https://www.marxists.org/archive/guevara/1965/03/man-socialism.htm, accessed February 17, 2023.
55 Guevara, "Socialism and Man in Cuba."

166 · Notes to Pages 67–77

56 Guevara, "Socialism and Man in Cuba."
57 Guevara, "Socialism and Man in Cuba."
58 Guevara, "Socialism and Man in Cuba."
59 Perón, *Historia del peronismo.*
60 Guevara, "Socialism and Man in Cuba."
61 Guevara, "Socialism and Man in Cuba."
62 Guevara, "Socialism and Man in Cuba."
63 Guevara, "Socialism and Man in Cuba."
64 Guevara, "Socialism and Man in Cuba."
65 Guevara, "Socialism and Man in Cuba."
66 Guevara, "Socialism and Man in Cuba."
67 Guevara, "Socialism and Man in Cuba."
68 Richard Fagen, *The Transformation of Political Culture in Cuba* (Palo Alto: Stanford University Press, 1969).
69 Graciella Cruz-Taura, "Revolution and Continuity in the History of Education in Cuba," November 2008, https://www.ascecuba.org/asce_proceedings/revolution-and-continuity-in-the-history-of-education-in-cuba/, accessed February 17, 2023.
70 Andy Gomez and Paul Webster Hare, "How Education Shaped Communist Cuba," *The Atlantic,* https://www.theatlantic.com/education/archive/2015/02/how-education-shaped-communist-cuba/386192/, accessed February 17, 2023).
71 Deborah Shnookal, *Operation Pedro Pan and the Exodus of Cuba's Children* (Gainesville: University of Florida Press, 2020), 21.
72 Ada Ferrer, *Cuba: An American History* (New York: Scribner, 2021), 386.
73 Guevara, "Socialism and Man in Cuba."
74 Guevara, "Socialism and Man in Cuba."
75 Guevara, "Socialism and Man in Cuba."
76 Guevara, "Socialism and Man in Cuba."
77 Guevara, "Socialism and Man in Cuba."
78 Lost Apple Documentary, https://www.youtube.com/watch?v=WKoJKF-FtS4, accessed February 17, 2023.
79 Jorge Castañeda, *Utopia Unarmed: The Latin American Left After the Cold War* (New York: Random House, 1994).
80 Stephen R. Graubard, "Preface to the Issue 'Utopia,'" *Daedalus* 94, 2, (Spring 1965): iii–vi.
81 Crane Brinton, "Utopia and Democracy," *Daedalus* 94, 2 (Spring 1965): 348–366.
82 Fredric Jameson, "Review: Of Islands and Trenches: Naturalization and the Production of Utopian Discourse," *Diacritics* 7, 2 (Summer 1977): 2–21.
83 Karl Popper, *Open Society and Its Enemies* (Princeton: Princeton University Press, 2013).
84 Francis Fukuyama, *The End of History and the Last Man* (New York: Free Press, 1992).
85 Perry Anderson, "Homeland," *New Left Review,* 81 (May-June 2013): 5–32.

Notes to Pages 77–82 · 167

86 Russell Jacoby, *The End of Utopia: Politics and Culture in an Age of Apathy* (New York: Basic Books, 1999).
87 Douglas Kellner, "Ernst Bloch, Utopia and Ideology Critique," *Illuminations: The Critical Theory Project*, https://pages.gseis.ucla.edu/faculty/kellner/Illumina%20 Folder/kell1.htm, accessed February 17, 2023.

Chapter 3. The Present

1 Jerome Binde, "Toward an Ethics of the Future," *Public Culture* 12, 1 (2000): 51–72.
2 Carlos Fuentes, "Remember the Future," *Salmagundi*, 68/69 (1985/1986); and "The Literary Imagination and the Sense of the Past," *Salmagundi* 68/69 (Fall 1985–Winter 1986): 333–352.
3 Norbet Lechner, "Chile 2000: Las sombras del mañana," http://www.revistaei.uchile .cl/index.php/REI/article/viewFile/15352/27344, accessed February 17, 2023.
4 Václav Havel, "Address of the President of Czechoslovakia Václav Havel to a Joint Session of the United States Congress, Washington, D.C., February 21, 1990," https://www.muzeuminternetu.cz/offwebs/czech/347.htm, accessed February 17, 2023.
5 Jorge Luis Borges, *Utopía de un hombre que está cansado / A Weary Man's Utopia. Book of Sand* (Buenos Aires: Emcee, 1975).
6 Jorge G. Castañeda, *Utopia Unarmed: The Latin American Left After the Cold War* (New York: Vintage Press, 1992).
7 Lucía Suárez, "Ruin Memory: Havana Beyond the Revolution," *Canadian Journal of Latin American and Caribbean Studies* 39, 1 (2014): 38–55.
8 Achy Obejas, *Ruins* (New York: Akashic Books 2009).
9 Abilio Estévez, *Los palacios distantes* (Barcelona: Tusquets Editores S.A., 2002).
10 Iván de la Nuez, "El hombre nuevo ante el futuro," *La Habana Elegante*, 2003, http:// www.habanaelegante.com/Summer2003/VerbosaNuezAguilera.html, accessed February 17, 2023.
11 Ruth Behar, "Post-Utopic Cuba: The Erotics of Power and Cuba's Revolutionary Children," in *The Elusive Nation*, edited by Damián Fernández and Madeline Cámara Betancourt (Gainesville: University of Florida Press, 2000), 140.
12 Anke Birkenmaier and Esther Whitfield (eds.), *Havana Beyond the Ruins: Cultural Mappings after 1989* (Durham: Duke University Press, 2011).
13 Javier Santiso, "The Fall Into the Present: The Emergence of Limited Political Temporalities in Latin America," *Time & Society* 7, 1 (March 1998): 25–54.
14 Sarah Waterlow, "Aristotle's Now," *The Philosophical Quarterly* 34, 135 (1984): 104–128.
15 St. Augustine, *City of God*, Book 11 (Hyde Park: New City Press, 2013).
16 Arthur N. Prior, "The Notion of the Present," in *The Study of Time*, edited by J. T. Fraser, F. C. Haber, and G. H. Müller (Berlin: Springer, 1972).
17 David R. Maines, Noreen M. Sugrue, and Michael A. Katovich, "The Sociological Import of G. H. Mead's Theory of the Past," *American Sociological Review* 48, 2 (1983): 161–73.

168 · Notes to Pages 82–89

18 Michael G. Flaherty and Gary A. Fine, "Present, Past and Future," *Time & Society* 10, 147 (2001): 147–161.

19 Walter Benjamin, *Illuminations: Essays and Reflections*, edited by Hannah Arendt (New York: Harcourt, Brace, Jovanovich, 1968), 260–261.

20 Benjamin, *Illuminations*, 262.

21 Benjamin, *Illuminations*, 263.

22 Jacques Derrida, *Speech and Phenomena: And Other Essays on Husserl's Theory of Signs* (Chicago: Northwestern University Press, 1973).

23 Roland Barthes, *Camera Lucida: Reflections on Photography*, trans. Richard Howard (New York: Hill and Wang, 1981).

24 Marcel Proust, *Remembrance of Things Past*, 3 Volumes (New York: Vintage, 1981).

25 Giorgio Agamben, *The Time That Remains: A Commentary on the Letter to the Romans* (Palo Alto: Stanford University Press, 2005).

26 Octavio Paz, "In Search of the Present," Nobel Prize Acceptance Speech, 1990, https://www.nobelprize.org/prizes/literature/1990/paz/lecture/, accessed February 17, 2023.

27 Paz, "In Search of the Present."

28 Paz, "In Search of the Present."

29 Paz, "In Search of the Present."

30 Paz, "In Search of the Present."

31 Paz, "In Search of the Present."

32 Hannah Arendt, Between the Past and Future: Eight Exercises in Political Thought (New York: Viking Press), 13.

33 Fidel Castro, Palabras a los intelectuales, June 30, 1961, http://www.fidelcastro.cu/es/discursos/conclusion-de-las-reuniones-con-los-intelectuales-cubanos-efectuadas-en-la-biblioteca, accessed February 17, 2023.

34 Iván de la Nuez, *Iconocracia: An Image of Power and the Power of Images in Contemporary Cuban Photography* (Nashville: Turner, 2016).

35 *Granma*, Headline, December 27, 1986.

36 Raquel Mendieta, "Only Fragments of Memories," in *By Heart/De Memoria: Cuban Women's Journeys In and Out of Exile*, edited by María de los Ángeles Torres (Philadelphia: Temple University Press, 2003), 146.

37 Mendieta, "Only Fragments," 149.

38 Interview with Pedro Juan Gutiérrez by Nazma Muller, http://caribbeanreviewofbooks .com/crb-archive/14-november-2007/i-live-a-simple-life/, accessed February 17, 2023.

39 Esther Whitfield, "The Body Impolitic of *Trilogía sucia de La Habana*," *Revista de Estudios Hispánicos* 36, 2 (May 2002): 329–351.

40 Francisco Leal, "*Trilogía sucia de La Habana* de Pedro Juan Gutiérrez: Mercado, crimen y abyección," *Taller de Letras*, 37 (2005): 51–66.

41 Charles Trumbull, "Prostitution and Sex Tourism in Cuba," November 2001, https://www.ascecuba.org/asce_proceedings/prostitution-and-sex-tourism-in-cuba/, accessed February 17, 2023.

Notes to Pages 90–97 · 169

42 Rafael Rojas, *El arte de la espera: Notas al margen de la política cubana* (Madrid: Colibrí, 1998).

43 Rojas, *El arte de la espera*, 145.

44 Zoé Valdés, *La nada cotidiana* (Barcelona: Editorial Planeta, 1996).

45 Valdés, *La nada cotidiana*, 15.

46 Dinora Cardoso and Ynés Oggel, "Self-Actualization is Paradise in 'La nada cotidiana' by Zoé Valdés," *Journal of Caribbean Literatures* 6, 2 (Fall 2009): 65–75.

47 Valdés, *La nada cotidiana*, 30.

48 Mendieta, "Only Fragments," 148.

49 James M. Griesse, "From Heaven to Hell: Revolutionary Dreams and Dystopia in Zoé Valdés's *La nada cotidiana*," *L'Érudit Franco-Espagnol* 1 (Spring 2012): 122–123; Ana García Chichester, "Virgilio Piñera and the Formulation of a National Literature," *CR: The New Centennial Review* 2, 2 (2002): 231–251.

50 Rolando Estévez, "Gerundios para la espera (Verbs for Waiting): A Visual Coda," in *The Portable Island: Cubans at Home in the World*, edited by Ruth Behar and Lucía Suárez (New York: Palgrave Macmillan, 2008), 235–247.

51 Ruth Behar, "Waiting," in *The Portable Island: Cubans at Home in the World*, eds. Ruth Behar and Lucía Suárez (New York: Palgrave Macmillan, 2008), 233–235.

52 Fina García Marruz, *No, No Memoria*, https://www.isliada.org/poetas/fina-garcia -marruz/, accessed February 17, 2023.

53 Josefina de Diego, *El reino de mi abuelo* (Ciudad de México: Ediciones de Equilibrista, 1993).

54 Katerina Gonzalez Seligmann, *Writing the Caribbean in Magazine Time* (New Brunswick: Rutgers University Press, 2021).

55 Glenn Chambers, "The Rise of Son and the Legitimatization of African-Derived Culture in Cuba, 1908–1940," *Callaloo* 30, 2 (2007): 497–507.

56 Gonzalez Seligmann, *Writing in the Caribbean*.

57 Jesús Barquet, "El Grupo Orígenes ante el negrismo," *Afro-Hispanic Review* 15, 2 (1996).

58 Enrique Patterson, "Lezama y la Torre de Marfil," in *La soledad histórica y otros ensayos* (Philadelphia: Eniola Publishing, 2022), 44.

59 Lucía Ballester Ortiz, "Gastón Baquero: Testament and Word," *Islas 49,* https://www .angelfire.com/planet/islas/English/v1n4-pdf/49-51.pdf, accessed February 17, 2023.

60 Gastón Baquero, *Indios, blancos y negros en el caldero de América* (Madrid: Ediciones de Cultura Hispánica, 1991).

61 Irlemar Chiampi, "La revista Orígenes ante la crisis de la modernidad," *Capa* 1, 1 (2002): 1–16.

62 Manuel Gayol, "José Lezama Lima y la búsqueda de los orígenes," *Hispanic LA*, December 2010, http://www.hispanicla.com/jose-lezama-lima-y-la-busqueda-de-los -origenes-16659, accessed February 17, 2023.

63 Jorge Luis Arcos, *La solución unitiva: Sobre el pensamiento poético de José Lezama Lima* (La Habana: Editorial Academia, 1990).

170 · Notes to Pages 97–105

64 Jorge Luis Arcos, *Orígenes: La pobreza irradiante* (La Habana: Editoriales Letras Cubanas, 1994), 105.

65 Arcos, *Orígenes*, 102.

66 Arcos, *Orígenes*, 102.

67 Rafael Rojas, *Essays in Cuban Cultural Intellectual History* (New York: Palgrave MacMillan, 2008), 70.

68 Eliseo Diego, *Por los extraños pueblos*. (Impresores Ucar, García, S.A., 1958), 76.

69 Eliseo Diego, *Un hondo bosque de sueños: Notas sobre literatura para niños* (La Habana: Ediciones Unión, 2008), 87.

70 Eliseo Diego, "Único y curioso libro del Ajedrez," in *Muestrario del mundo o Libro de las Maravillas de Boloña* (La Habana: Editorial Letras Cubanas, 1968), 28.

71 Fina García Marruz, "Del tiempo largo," https://www.poeticous.com/fina-garcia -marruz/del-tiempo-largo?locale=es, accessed February 17, 2023.

72 Ivette Fuentes, *A través de su espejo: Sobre la poética de Eliseo Diego* (La Habana: Letras Cubanas, 2006), 52.

73 Eliseo Diego, "Las ropas," in *Por los extraños pueblos* (La Habana: Impresores Ucar, García, S.A., 1958), 71.

74 Eliseo Diego, "Imaginemos un tiempo," in *Los días de tu vida* (La Habana: Ediciones Unión, 1977), 57.

75 Eliseo Diego, "El domingo," in *Por los extraños pueblos*, 46.

76 Eliseo Diego, "Coplas del tiempo," in *Muestrario del mundo o Libro de las Maravillas de Boloña*, 30.

77 Eliseo Diego, *El Oscuro esplendor* (La Habana: Ediciones BELIC, Cuadernos Girón, 1966), 19.

78 Eliseo Diego, "El día de hoy," in *Libro de quizás o de quién sabe* (La Habana: Editorial Letras Cubanas, 1989), 42.

79 Eliseo Diego, "Comienza un lunes," https://www.poeticous.com/eliseo-diego/ comienza-un-lunes?locale=es, accessed February 22, 2023.

80 Mark Weiss (ed.), *The Whole Island: Six Decades of Cuban Poetry, A Bilingual Anthology,* trans. Mark Weiss (Oakland: University of California Press, 2009), 157.

81 Eliseo Diego, "Tiempo de la siesta," in *Los días de tu vida*, 29.

82 Diego, "El día de hoy," 42.

83 Eliseo Diego, "Tiempo de la fotografía," in *Los días de tu vida*, 32.

84 Eliseo Diego, "A una joven romana," in *En otro reino* (La Habana: Ediciones Unión, 1999), 56.

85 Enrique Sainz, *Prologue to Eliseo Diego, Poesía Completa* (La Habana: Editorial Letras Cubanas, 1983).

86 Eliseo Diego, *Ensayos* (La Habana: Ediciones Unión, 2006), 258.

87 Diego, *Por los extraños pueblos,* 69.

88 Diego, *Por los extraños pueblos,* 69.

89 Eliseo Diego, *El silencio de las pequeñas cosas* (La Habana: Instituto Cubano del Libro, 1993), 10.

90 Eliseo Diego, *El día de hoy*, 42.

Notes to Pages 105–112 · 171

91 Eliseo Diego, "No es más," in *El oscuro esplendor* (La Habana: Ediciones BELIC, Cuadernos Girón, 1966), 127.
92 Eliseo Diego, "*La necesidad de la poesía,*" in *Libro de quizás y de quién sabe* (La Habana: Editorial Letras Cubanas, 1989).
93 Eliseo Diego, *Por los extraños pueblos,* 83.
94 Eliseo Diego, *El día de hoy,* 42.
95 Eliseo Diego, *Versiones* (La Habana, Ediciones Unión, Colección Contemporáneos, 1970).
96 Eliseo Diego and Mark Weiss, "Eliseo Diego and Fairy Tales," *Marvels & Tales* 23, 2 (2009): 391–398.
97 Arcos, *Orígenes,* 97.
98 Eliseo Diego, "*Aquí un momento,*" in *En la calzada de Jesús del Monte* (La Habana: Ediciones Orígenes, 1949), 19–27.
99 Eliseo Diego, *Las islas, Por los extraños pueblos,* 78–79.
100 Diego, "Decíamos que sí, que lo sabíamos," in *Los días de tu vida,* 83.
101 Giovanni Gasparini, "On Waiting," *Time & Society* 4, 1 (1995): 29–45.
102 Eliseo Diego, "Vienen noticias del atroz invierno," in *Muestrario del mundo o Libro de las maravillas de Boloña,* 30.

Chapter 4. Democratizing the Past

1 A version of this appeared in *Cuban Studies,* 50, 2021.
2 Paul Ricoeur, *Memory, History, Forgetting* (Chicago: University of Chicago Press, 2006).
3 Myra Mendible, "Imagining Cuba: Storytelling and the Politics of Exile," in *Telling Stories to Change the World: Global Voices on the Power of Narrative to Build Community and Make Social Justice Claims,* edited by Rickie Solinger, Madeline Fox, and Kayhan Iran (New York: Routledge, 2008).
4 Paula Fass, "The Memoir Problem," *Reviews in American History* 34, 1 (2006): 107–123.
5 Grupo Areíto, *Contra viento y marea* (La Habana: Casa de las Americas, 1978).
6 Ruth Behar (ed.), *Bridges to Cuba/Puentes a Cuba* (Ann Arbor: University of Michigan Press, 1995).
7 María de los Ángeles Torres (ed.), *By Heart/De Memoria: Cuban Women's Journeys In and Out of Exile* (Philadelphia: Temple University Press, 2003).
8 Iraida López, *Impossible Returns: Narratives of the Cuban Diaspora* (Gainesville: University of Florida Press, 2015).
9 Román de la Campa, *Cuba on My Mind: Journeys to a Severed Nation* (New York: Verso, 2000).
10 Carlos Eire, *Waiting for Snow in Havana: Confessions of a Cuban Boy* (New York: Simon and Schuster, 2003).
11 Flora González Mandri, "A House on Shifting Sands," in *Bridges to Cuba/Puentes a Cuba,* edited by Ruth Behar (Ann Arbor: University of Michigan Press, 1995), 76–79.

172 · Notes to Pages 113–119

12 Mirta A. Ojito, *Finding Mañana: A Memoir of a Cuban Exodus* (New York: Penguin Books, 2005).

13 Isabel Álvarez-Borland, *Cuban-American Literature of Exile: From Person to Persona* (Charlottesville: University Press of Virginia, 1998).

14 Pablo Medina, *Exiled Memories: A Cuban Childhood* (New York: Persea Books, 2002).

15 Gustavo Pérez Firmat, *Next Year in Cuba: A Cubano's Coming-of-Age in America* (Houston: Arte Público Press, 2006).

16 Richard Blanco, *The Prince of los Cocuyos: A Miami Childhood* (New York: Ecco/Harper Collins, 2014).

17 Dania Rosa Nasca, *Lights Out: A Cuban Memoir of Betrayal and Survival* (North Charleston: CreateSpace Independent Publishing Platform, 2016).

18 Virgil Suárez, *Spared Angola: Memories from a Cuban-American Childhood* (Houston: Arte Público Press, 1997).

19 José María de Lasa, *My Story: Family, Cuba & Living the American Dream* (Miami: Ediciones Universal, 2018).

20 Antonio Veciana and Carlos Harrison, *Trained to Kill: The Inside Story of CIA Plots against Castro, Kennedy, and Che* (New York: Skyhorse, 2017).

21 Gerardo M. González, *A Cuban Refugee's Journey to the American Dream: The Power of Education* (Bloomington: Well House Books, Indiana University Press, 2018).

22 Luis Santeiro, *Dancing with Dictators: A Family's Journey from Pre-Castro Cuba to Exile in the Turbulent Sixties* (New York: Luis Santeiro, 2017).

23 Cecilia M. Fernández, *Leaving Little Havana: A Memoir of Miami's Cuban Ghetto* (Orlando: Beating Windward Press, 2013).

24 Mia Leonin, *Havana and Other Missing Fathers* (Tucson: University of Arizona Press, 2016).

25 Marisella Veiga, *We Carry Our Homes with Us: A Cuban American Memoir* (St. Paul: Minnesota Historical Society Press, 2016).

26 María Nodarse, *Approaching Freedom: An Exile's Quest for a New Self* (New York: Nook Book, 2018).

27 Ruth Behar, *Traveling Heavy: A Memoir in between Journeys* (Durham: Duke University Press, 2014).

28 Paula Rosas, "En Cuba estamos cansados de vivir tanto tiempo en la Historia y queremos vivir en la normalidad," *BBC News Mundo*, January 27, 2023, https://www.bbc.com/mundo/noticias-64189085, accessed February 17, 2023.

29 Reynier Leyva Novo: *The Weight of History, Five Nights*, https://hirshhorn.si.edu/explore/reynier-leyva-novo-the-weight-of-history-five-nights/, accessed February 17, 2023.

30 Guillermina De Ferrari, "Opacity and Sensation in Reynier Leyva Novo's Historical Installations," *InVisible Culture: An Electronic Journal for Visual Culture*, April 2015, https://ivc.lib.rochester.edu/opacity-and-sensation-in-reynier-leyva-novos-historical-installations/, accessed February 17, 2023.

Notes to Pages 120–134 · 173

31 Nereida García Ferraz, "Not the Golden Age," in *By Heart/De Memoria: Cuban Women's Journeys In and Out of Exile*, edited by María de los Ángeles Torres (Philadelphia: Temple University Press, 2003), 57–74.

32 Andy Grundberg, "A Storm of Images: The Photographs of María Martínez-Cañas," https://mariamartinez-canas.com/A-Storm-of-Images-The-Photographs-of-Maria -Martinez-Canas-by-Andy, accessed April 16, 2020.

33 Olga U. Herrera, "AMA and the Concept of Latin American Art," in *Art of the Americas: Collection of the Art Museum of the Americas of the Organization of Americans States* (Washington, DC: AMA, 2017), 40–47.

34 Olga U. Herrera, *American Interventions and Modern Art in South America* (Gainesville: University Press of Florida, 2017), 217.

35 María Martínez-Cañas, interview by author, March 2017.

36 María Martínez-Cañas, interview by author, March 2017.

37 María Martínez-Cañas, interview by author, March 2017.

38 María Martínez-Cañas, interview by author, March 2017.

39 Susan Delson, "In the Studio with María Martínez-Cañas, Personal history and Cuban art history merge in recent works," *Cuban Art News*, March 9, 2017, https://cubanartnews.org/2017/03/09/in-the-studio-with-maria-martinez-canas/, accessed September 2, 2020.

40 The exhibition titled *Personalities in the Americas: Photographs by Berenstein-Tagle* was presented in the main building of the OAS, March 17–April 12, 1952.

41 María Martínez-Cañas, interview by author, March 2017.

42 María Martínez-Cañas, interview by author, March 2017.

43 Michel-Rolph Trouillot, *Silencing the Past: Power and Production of History* (Boston: Beacon Press, 1995).

44 Jesús J. Barquet, "El 'caso' se investiga: Antón Arrufat y Los siete contra Tebas," http://cdigital.uv.mx/bitstream/123456789/871/2/2000115P59.pdf, accessed February 17, 2023.

45 Wilhelm Dilthey, *Pattern and Meaning in History: Thoughts on History and Society* (New York: Harper Torchbooks, 1961), 43.

46 Dilthey, *Pattern and Meaning in History*, 44.

47 Michel de Certeau, *The Writing of History*, trans. Tom Conley (New York: Columbia University Press, 1988).

48 Hannah Arendt, *Between Past and Future* (New York: Penguin Classics, 2006).

Chapter 5. Temporalities and Democracy

1 Max Weber, quoted in Arjun Appadurai, *Globalization* (Durham: Duke University Press, 2001), 96.

2 Delmiro Rocha, "Pensar el porvenir. La disyunción futuro/porvenir en la deconstrucción de J. Derrida," *Revista Internacional de Filosofía*, Suplemento 3 (2010): 117–123.

3 María de los Ángeles Torres, Irene Rizzini, and Norma Del Río, *Citizens in the Pres-*

174 · Notes to Pages 134–136

ent: Civically Engaged Youths in the Americas (Urbana: University of Illinois Press, 2013).

4 Fredric Jameson, *Archaeologies of the Future: The Desire Called Utopia and Other Science Fictions* (New York: Verso, 2007).

5 Walter Benjamin, *Illuminations: Essays and Reflections* (New York: Schocken Books, 1969), 261.

6 Sami R. Khatib, "A Non-Nullified Nothingness: Walter Benjamin and the Messianic," *Stasis, International Journal in social and political philosophy and theory* 1, 1 (Fall 2013): 82–108.

7 Jacques Derrida, *Specters of Marx: The State of the Debt, the Work of Mourning & the New International* (New York: Routledge Press, 2006); For a comparative study of Derrida and Benjamin, see Owen Ware, "Dialectic of the Past/Disjuncture of the Future: Derrida and Benjamin on the Concept of Messianism," *Journal of Religious Theory* 5, 2 (April 2004): 99–114.

8 Gloria Anzaldúa, *Light in the Dark/Luz en lo Oscuro: Rewriting Identity, Spirituality, Reality,* edited by AnaLouise Keating (Durham: Duke University Press, 2015); Pedro Luis Entralgo, *La espera y la esperanza: Historia y teoría del esperar humano* (Madrid: Alianza Editorial, 1984).

9 Ernst Bloch, "Introduction," *The Principle of Hope,* Vol. 1 (Cambridge: MIT Press, 1995).

10 Kathi Week, *The Problem with Work: Feminism, Marxism, Antiwork Politics, and Postwork Imaginaries* (Durham: Duke University Press, 2011).

11 Adriana S. Benzaquén, "Thought and Utopia in the Writings of Adorno, Horkheimer, and Benjamin," *Utopian Studies* 9, 2 (1998): 149–161.

12 Max Horkheimer and Theodor W. Adorno, *Dialectic of Enlightenment,* trans. John Cumming (New York: Continuum, 1991), 225, quoted in Benzaquén, "Thought and Utopia," 160.

13 Arjun Appadurai, "The Capacity to Aspire: Culture and the Terms of Recognition," in *Culture and Public Action,* edited by Vijayendra Rao and Michael Walton (Palo Alto: Stanford University Press, 2004), 59–84.

14 Ruth Levitas, *The Concept of Utopia* (Oxford: Peter Lang Press, 2010), 209.

15 Herbert Marcuse, "The End of Utopia, 1967." Marxists Internet Archive, https://www.marxists.org/reference/archive/marcuse/works/1967/end-utopia.htm, accessed September 2, 2020.

16 John Rawls, *The Law of Peoples* (Cambridge: Harvard University Press, 1999).

17 Pierre Bourdieu, "A Reasoned Utopia and Economic Fatalism," *New Left Review,* Issue 227 (January 1998): 125.

18 Karl Mannheim (ed.), *Ideology and Utopia: An Introduction to the Sociology of Knowledge* (Eastford: Martino Fine Books, 2015).

19 Paul Ricoeur, *Lectures on Ideology and Utopia* (New York: Columbia University Press, 1986).

20 Arjun Appadurai, *The Future as Cultural Artifact: Essays on the Global Condition* (London: Verso, 2013), 179.

Notes to Pages 137–150 · 175

21 José Esteban Muñoz, *Cruising Utopia: The Then and There of Queer Futurity* (New York: New York University Press, 2009).

22 Joshua Foa Dienstag, *Pessimism: Philosophy, Ethic, Spirit* (Princeton: Princeton University Press, 2009).

23 Jerome Binde, "Toward an Ethics of the Future," *Public Culture* 12, 1 (Winter 2000): 51–72.

24 Carlos Fuentes, "Remember the Future," *Salmagundi*, 68/69 (Fall 1985–Winter 1986): 333–352.

25 Bloch, *The Principle of Hope*, Vol. 1.

26 Henri Lefebvre, *Introduction to Modernity*, trans. John Moore (London: Verso, 1995).

27 Tania Bruguera, *Tania Bruguera* (Chicago: Lowitz and Sons, 2005).

28 Tania Bruguera, *Memorias de la Postguerra*, November 1993.

29 Juan Antonio Molina, "Entre la Ida y el Regreso. La experiencia del otro en la memoria," October 1996, http://taniabruguera.com/cms//422-1-Entre+la+Ida+y+el+Regreso+La+experiencia+del+otro+en+la+memoria.htm, accessed September 2, 2020.

30 Christian Viveros-Faune, "How Tania Bruguera's 'Whisper' Became the Performance Heard Around the World," *Artnet News*, January 8, 2015, https://news.artnet.com/art-world/how-tania-brugueras-whisper-became-the-performance-heard-round-the-world-213637/amp-page, accessed February 21, 2023.

31 Olga Viso, "Tania Bruguera: Artivism and Repression in Cuba," 2015, https://walkerart.org/magazine/tania-bruguera-artivism-gerardo-mosquera-cuba, accessed February 21, 2023.

32 Gerardo Mosquera, "Taitlin Shouts," 2015, https://walkerart.org/magazine/tania-bruguera-artivism-gerardo-mosquera-cuba, accessed February 20, 2023.

33 Tania Bruguera, 2019, Visible, https://www.visibleproject.org/blog/project/the-institute-of-artivism-hannah-arendt-instar/, accessed February 19, 2023.

34 Manifesto 27 de noviembre, https://artistsatriskconnection.org/story/cubas-27n-movement-releases-manifesto, accessed February 19, 2023.

35 Manifesto 27 de noviembre.

36 Manifesto 27 de noviembre.

37 Manifesto 27 de noviembre.

38 Hannah Arendt, *Between Past and Future* (New York, Penguin Classics, 1977).

39 Arjun Appadurai, "Deep Democracy: Urban Governmentality and the Horizon of Politics," *Environment and Urbanization* 13, 2, (October 2001).

40 John Dewey, *Democracy and Education* (New York: MacMillan Company, 1916).

41 George Herbert Mead, *The Philosophy of the Present* (New York: Prometheus, 2002).

42 Owen Ware, "Dialectic of the Past/Disjuncture of the Future: Derrida and Benjamin on the Concept of Messianism," *Journal for Cultural and Religious Theory* 5, 2 (April 2004): 99–114.

43 Slavoj Žižek, "Neighbors and Other Monsters: A Plea for Ethical Violence," in *The Neighbor: Three Inquiries in Political Theology*, edited by Slavoj Žižek, Eric L. Sant-

176 · Notes to Pages 150–156

ner, and Kenneth Reinhard (Chicago: The University of Chicago Press, 2005), 134–90.

44 Alain Badiou, *Ethics: An Essay on the Understanding of Evil*, trans. Peter Hallward (London: Verso, 2001).

45 Enrique Patterson, *La soledad histórica y otros ensayos* (Philadelphia: Eniola Publishing, 2021).

46 Patterson, *La soledad histórica y otros ensayos.*

47 Zahi Zalloua, "The Ethics of Trauma/The Trauma of Ethics," in *Terror, Theory and the Humanities*, edited by Jeffrey R. Di Leo and Uppinder Mehan (Ann Arbor: Open Society Press, 2012), 223–243.

48 Anne Phillips, *The Politics of Presence* (Oxford: University of Oxford Press, 1995).

49 Chantal Mouffe, "Feminism, Citizenship, and Radical Democratic Politics," in *Feminists Theorize the Political,* edited by Judith Butler and Joan W. Scott (New York: Routledge Press, 2013), 369–385.

50 María de los Ángeles Torres, "Multiculturalism and Democracy," in *Our Diverse Society: Race and Ethnicity—Implications for 21st Century American Society,* edited by David W. Engstrom and Lissette Piedra, (Washington, DC: NASW Publishers, 2006), 161–182.

51 Charles Mills, *The Racial Contract* (Ithaca: Cornell University, 1997), 31.

52 Charles Mills, *From Class to Race: Essays in White Marxism and Black Radicalism* (Lanham: Rowman and Littlefield, 2003), 127.

53 Stefan Zweig, *The World of Yesterday* (Lincoln: University of Nebraska Press, 2013).

54 Armando Chaguaceda, "Cuba: A Critique of Despotic Reason," *Dialektika*, February 18, 2023, https://en.dialektika.org/society-politics/cuba-a-critique-of-despotic-reason/, accessed February 22, 2023.

55 Motto of the Organización de Pioneros José Martí.

56 Binde, "Towards an Ethics of the Future," 51–72.

57 Javier Santiso, "The Fall Into the Present: The Emergence of Limited Political Temporalities in Latin America," *Time & Society* 7, 1 (1998): 25–54.

58 Joshua Foa Dienstag, "Nietzsche's Dionysian Pessimism," *The American Political Science Review* 95, 4 (December 2001): 923–937.

59 Iván de la Nuez, *Iconocracia: An Image of Power and the Power of Images in Contemporary Cuban Photography* (Nashville: Turner Publishers, 2016).

60 Leszek Koczanowicz, *Politics of Time: Dynamics of Identity in Post-Communist Poland* (New York: Berghahn Books, 2008).

61 Owen Ware, "Dialectic of the Past/Disjuncture of the Future," 99–114, http://www.jcrt.org/archives/05.2/ware.pdf, accessed February 19, 2023.

62 Giorgio Agamben, *The Time That Remains: A Commentary on the Letter to the Romans* (Palo Alto: Stanford University Press, 2005).

63 Bill Ashcroft, "African futures: The necessity of utopia," *International Journal of African Renaissance Studies—Multi-, Inter- and Transdisciplinarity* 8, 1 (2013): 94–114.

64 Gertrudis Gómez de Avellaneda, "Al partir," *All Poetry*, https://allpoetry.com/Al-Partir#orig_86021123, accessed February 19, 2023.

65 "Plácido's Last Song," https://aadl.org/signalofliberty/SL_18450106-p1-02, accessed February 19, 2023.

Bibliography

Agamben, Giorgio. *The Time That Remains: A Commentary on the Letter to the Romans.* Palo Alto: Stanford University Press, 2005.

Aínsa, Fernando. "Imagen y la posibilidad de la utopía en 'Paradiso,' de Lezama Lima." *Revista Iberoamericana* XLIX, 123–124 (Abril–Septiembre 1983): 263–77.

Aguila León. *Todo en su tiempo.* Miami: Ediciones Universal, 1997.

Álvarez-Borland, Isabel. *Cuban-American Literature of Exile: From Person to Persona.* Charlottesville: University Press of Virginia, 1998.

Anderson, Benedict. *Imagined Communities: Reflections on the Origin and Spread of Nationalism.* London: Verso Books, 1983.

Anderson, Perry. "Homeland." *New Left Review* 81 (May–June 2013): 532.

Anzaldúa, Gloria. *Light in the Dark/Luz en lo Oscuro: Rewriting Identity, Spirituality, Reality.* Edited by AnaLouise Keating. Durham: Duke University Press, 2015.

Appadurai, Arjun. *Modernity at Large: Cultural Dimensions of Globalization.* Minneapolis: University of Minnesota Press, 1996.

———. "Deep Democracy: Urban Governmentality and the Horizon of Politics." *Environment and Urbanization* 13, 2, (October 2001).

———. "The Capacity to Aspire: Culture and the Terms of Recognition." In *Culture and Public Action,* edited by Vijayendra Rao and Michael Walton, 59–84. Palo Alto: Stanford University Press, 2004.

———. *The Future as Cultural Artifact: Essays on the Global Condition.* London: Verso, 2013.

Arcos, Jorge Luis. *La solución unitiva: Sobre el pensamiento poético de José Lezama Lima.* La Habana: Editorial Academia, 1990.

———. *Orígenes: La pobreza irradiante.* La Habana: Editoriales Letras Cubanas, 1994.

Arendt, Hannah. *The Human Condition.* Chicago: University of Chicago Press, 1958.

———. *The Origins of Totalitarianism.* New York: Harcourt, Brace & World, 1968.

———. *Between Past and Future.* New York: Penguin Classics, 2006.

Aron, Raymond. *Politics and History.* New York: Routledge, 1983.

Arrufat, Antón. *Repaso final.* La Habana: Ediciones Revolución, 1964.

Ashcroft, Bill. "African futures: The necessity of utopia." *International Journal of African Renaissance Studies—Multi-, Inter- and Transdisciplinarity* 8, 1 (2013): 94–114.

178 · Bibliography

Badiou, Alain. *Ethics: An Essay on the Understanding of Evil.* Translated by Peter Hallward. London: Verso, 2001.

Ballester Ortiz, Lucía, "Gastón Baquero: Testament and Word." *Islas 49,* https://www.angelfire.com/planet/islas/English/v1n4-pdf/49-51.pdf, accessed February 20, 2023.

Baquero, Gastón (1991). *Indios, blancos y negros en el caldero de América.* Madrid: Ediciones de Cultura Hispánica, 1991.

Barquet, Jesús J. "El Grupo Orígenes ante el negrismo." *Afro-Hispanic Review* 15, 2 (1996).

———. "El 'caso' se investiga: Antón Arrufat y Los siete contra Tebas." *La Palabra y el Hombre* 115 (July–September 2000): 59–69.

Barthes, Roland. *Camera Lucida: Reflections on Photography.* Translated by Richard Howard. New York: Hill and Wang, 1981.

Beauchesne, Kim, and Alessandra Santos (eds.) *The Utopian Impulse in Latin America.* New York: Palgrave MacMillan, 2011.

Behar, Ruth (ed.) *Bridges to Cuba/Puentes a Cuba.* Ann Arbor: University of Michigan Press, 1995.

———. "Post-Utopia: The Erotics of Power and Cuba's Revolutionary Children." In *Cuba, the Elusive Nation: Interpretations of National Identity,* edited by Damián J. Fernández and Madeline Cámara Betancourt, 134–154. Gainesville: University Press of Florida, 2000.

———. "Waiting." In *The Portable Island: Cubans at Home in the World,* edited by Ruth Behar and Lucía Suárez (New York: Palgrave/MacMillan, 2008), 233–235.

———. *Traveling Heavy: A Memoir in between Journeys.* Durham: Duke University Press, 2014.

Benjamin, Walter. *Illuminations: Essays and Reflections.* Edited by Hannah Arendt. New York: J. Houghton Mifflin Harcourt, 1969.

———. *Selected Writings,* 4 vols, edited by Howard Eiland and Michael W. Jennings. Cambridge: Harvard University Press, 1991–1995.

Benzaquén, Adriana S. "Thought and Utopia in the Writings of Adorno, Horkheimer, and Benjamin." *Utopian Studies* 9, 2 (1998): 149–161.

Bermingham, Katherine. "Time for Arendt." *Amor Mundi,* https://hac.bard.edu/amor-mundi/time-for-arendt-2019-08-02, accessed February 16, 2023.

Binde, Jerome, "Toward and Ethics of the Future." *Public Culture* 12, 1 (Winter 2000): 51–72.

Birkenmaier, Anke, and Esther Whitfield, (eds.) *Havana Beyond the Ruins: Cultural Mappings after 1989.* Durham: Duke University Press, 2011.

Blanco, Richard. *The Prince of Los Cocuyos: A Miami Childhood.* New York: Ecco/HarperCollins, 2014.

Bloch, Ernst. *The Principle of Hope.* Vol. 1. Cambridge: MIT Press, 1995.

Bolívar, Simón. *El Libertador: Writings of Simón Bolívar.* Translated by Frederick Fornoff. New York: Oxford University Press, 2003.

Borges, Jorge Luis. *Utopía de un hombre que está cansado / A Weary Man's Utopia. Book of Sand.* Buenos Aires: Emcee, 1975.

Bourdieu, Pierre. "A Reasoned Utopia and Economic Fatalism." *New Left Review* 227 (Jan. 1998).

Boym, Svetlana. *The Future of Nostalgia*. New York: Basic Books, 2001.

Braun, Kathrin. "Biopolitics and Temporality in Arendt and Foucault." *Time & Society* 16, 1 (March 2007): 5–23.

Brinton, Crane. "Utopia and Democracy." *Daedalus* 94, 2 (Spring 1965): 348–66.

Bruguera, Tania. *Tania Bruguera*. Chicago: Lowitz and Sons, 2005.

———. *Memorias de la Postguerra*, November 1993. https://taniabruguera.com/, accessed February 16, 2023.

Bustamante, Michael. *Cuban Memory Wars: Retrospective Politics in Revolution and Exile*. Chapel Hill: University of North Carolina, 2021.

Cámara, Madeline, "Vocación de Casandra: La poética en 'El ángel agotado' de María Elena Cruz Varela." *Cuban Studies* 29 (1999): 83–104.

———. "Memoria de Marqués Ravelo," http://grafoscopio.blogspot.com/2018/05/madeline-camara-memoria-de-marques.html, accessed February 20, 2023.

Cardoso, Dinora, and Ynés Oggel. "Self-Actualization is Paradise in 'La nada cotidiana' by Zoé Valdés." *Journal of Caribbean Literatures* 6, 2 (Fall 2009): 65–75.

Carpentier, Alejo. *Viaje a la semilla*. Tafalla: Editorial Txalaparta, 2003.

———. *Lo real maravilloso*. Ciudad de México: Universidad Nacional Autónoma de México, 2004.

Casal, Lourdes, *Palabras juntan revolución*. La Habana: Casa de las Américas, 1981.

Castañeda, Jorge. *Utopia Unarmed: The Latin American Left After the Cold War*. New York: Random House, 1994.

Castro, Fidel. "July 27, 1959, Castro Agrees to Return to Premiership," http://lanic.utexas.edu/project/castro/db/1959/19590514.html, accessed September 2, 2020.

———. "Speech on the Second Anniversary of the Revolution, January 5, 1961," http://lanic.utexas.edu/project/castro/db/1961/19610105.html, accessed September 2, 2020.

———. "Palabras a los intelectuales." June 30, 1961, http://www.fidelcastro.cu/es/discursos/conclusion-de-las-reuniones-con-los-intelectuales-cubanos-efectuadas-en-la-biblioteca, accessed February 17, 2023.

———. "Ceremony Marking the Centennial of Cuba's Struggle for Independence, 1968," http://lanic.utexas.edu/project/castro/db/1961/19610105.html, accessed September 2, 2020.

———. *History Will Absolve Me*. La Habana: Instituto Cubano del Libro, 1973.

Chaguaceda, Armando. Cuba: A Critique of Despotic Reason, *Dialektika*, February 18, 2023, https://en.dialektika.org/society-politics/cuba-a-critique-of-despotic-reason/, accessed February 22, 2023.

Chambers, Glenn. "The Rise of Son and the Legitimatization of African-Derived Culture in Cuba, 1908–1940." *Callaloo* 30, 2 (2007): 497–507.

Chambers, Samuel A. "Untimely politics *avant la lettre*: The temporality of social formations." *Time & Society* 20, 2 (July 2011): 197–223.

180 · Bibliography

Chiampi, Irlemar. "La revista Orígenes ante la crisis de la modernidad." *Brazilian Journal of Latin American Studies* 1, 1 (2002): 1–16, http://www.revistas.usp.br/prolam/article/view/81746/85066, accessed February 20, 2023.

Chichester, Ana García. "Virgilio Piñera and the Formulation of a National Literature." *CR: The New Centennial Review* 2, 2 (2002): 231–251.

Ching, Erik, Christina Buckley, and Angélica Lozano-Alonso (eds.) "The Socialist Utopia: Che Guevara and the Cuban Revolution." In *Reframing Latin America: A Cultural Theory Reading of the Nineteenth and Twentieth Centuries,* 237–259. Austin: University of Texas Press, 2007.

Chowers, Eyal. "Gushing Time: Modernity and the multiplicity of temporal homes." *Time & Society* 11, 2/3 (September 2002): 233–49.

Conde, Yvonne. *Operation Pedro Pan: The Untold Exodus of 14,048 Cuban Children.* New York: Routledge, 1999.

Claeys, Gregory, and Lyman Tower Sargent (eds.) *The Utopia Reader.* New York: New York University Press, 1999.

Connerto, Paul. *How Societies Remember.* London: Cambridge University Press, 1989.

Couzens Hoy, David. *The Time of Our Lives: A Critical History of Temporality.* Cambridge: MIT Press, 2012.

Dallmayr, Fred. "The Discourse of Modernity: Hegel and Habermas." *The Journal of Philosophy* 84, 11 (November 1987): 682–692.

Daynes, Gary. "Finding Meaning in Moncada: Historical Memory in Revolutionary Cuba," *Caribbean Quarterly* 42, 1 (March 1996).

de Certeau, Michel. *The Writing of History.* Translated by Tom Conley. New York: Columbia University Press, 1988.

de Diego, Josefina. *El reino de mi abuelo.* Ciudad de México: Ediciones de Equilibrista, 1993.

de Ferrari, Guillermina. "Opacity and Sensation in Reynier Leyva Novo's Historical Installations." *InVisible Culture: An Electronic Journal for Visual Culture,* April 2015, https://ivc.lib.rochester.edu/opacity-and-sensation-in-reynier-leyva-novos-historical-installations/, accessed February 20, 2023.

de la Campa, Román. *Cuba on My Mind: Journeys to a Severed Nation.* New York: Verso, 2000.

de la Cuesta, Leonel Antonio (ed.) *Constituciones cubanas desde el 1812 hasta nuestros días.* Miami: Ediciones Exilio, 1974.

de la Fuente, Alejandro. *A Nation for All: Race, Inequality and Politics in Twentieth Century Cuba.* Chapel Hill: University of North Carolina Press, 2011.

de la Nuez, Iván. *El hombre nuevo ante el futuro.* La Habana: La Habana Elegante, 2003.

———. *Postcapital: Crítica del futuro.* Barcelona: Instituto de Cultura y Linkgua, 2007.

———. *Iconocracia: An Image of Power and the Power of Images in Contemporary Cuban Photography.* Nashville: Turner, 2016.

de Lasa, José María. *My Story: Family, Cuba & Living the American Dream.* Miami: Ediciones Universal, 2018.

Delson, Susan, "In the Studio with María Martínez-Cañas, Personal history and Cuban art history merge in recent works." *Cuban Art News,* March 9, 2017, https://

cubanartnews.org/2017/03/09/in-the-studio-with-maria-martinez-canas/, accessed September 2, 2020.

Derrida, Jacques. *Speech and Phenomena: And Other Essays on Husserl's Theory of Signs.* Chicago: Northwestern University Press, 1973.

———. *Specters of Marx: The State of the Debt, The Work of Mourning & the New International.* New York: Routledge Press, 2006.

Desnoes, Edmundo. *Memorias del subdesarrollo.* Madrid: Mono Azul, 2011.

Dewey, John. *Democracy and Education.* New York: MacMillan Company, 1916.

Diego, Eliseo. *Aquí un momento, en la calzada de Jesús del Monte.* La Habana: Ediciones Orígenes, 1949.

———. "Testamento," http://www.los-poetas.com/e/diego1.htm#TESTAMENTO, accessed February 20, 2023.

———. "Las ropas." *Por los extraños pueblos.* La Habana: Impresores Ucar, García, S.A., 1958.

———. "El domingo." *Por los extraños pueblos.* La Habana: Impresores Ucar, García, S.A., 1958.

———. *El oscuro esplendor.* La Habana: Ediciones BELIC, Cuadernos Girón, 1966.

———. "No es más." *El oscuro esplendor.* La Habana: Ediciones BELIC, Cuadernos Girón, 1966.

———. "Coplas del tiempo." *Muestrario del mundo o Libro de las maravillas de Bolania.* La Habana: Editorial Letras Cubanas, 1968.

———. "Vienen noticias del Atroz Invierno." *Muestrario del mundo o Libro de las maravillas de Bolania.* La Habana: Editorial Letras Cubanas, 1968.

———. *Versiones.* La Habana: Ediciones Unión, Colección Contemporáneos, 1970.

———. "Imaginemos un tiempo." *Los días de tu vida.* La Habana: Ediciones Unión, 1977.

———. "Tiempo de la siesta." *Los días de tu vida.* La Habana: Ediciones Unión, Colección Contemporáneos, 1977.

———. "Decíamos que sí, que lo sabíamos." *Los días de tu vida.* La Habana: Ediciones Unión, 1977.

———. "Tiempo de la fotografía." *Los días de tu vida.* La Habana: Ediciones Unión, Colección Contemporáneos, 1977.

———. "Único y curioso libro del Ajedrez." *Muestrario del mundo o Libro de las maravillas de Bolania.* La Habana: Editorial Letras Cubanas, 1979.

———. *Biografía, A través de mi espejo.* La Habana: Ediciones Unión, Colección Contemporáneos, 1981.

———. *El día de hoy, Libro de quizás o de quién sabe.* La Habana: Editorial Letras Cubanas, 1989.

———. *El silencio de las pequeñas cosas.* La Habana: Instituto Cubano del Libro, 1993.

———. *A una joven romana, en otro reino.* La Habana: Ediciones Unión, 1999.

———. *Por los extraños pueblos.* La Habana: Impresores Ucar, García, S.A., 1958.

———. *Las islas.* La Habana: Ediciones Unión, 2001.

———. *Ensayos.* La Habana: Ediciones Unión, 2006.

———. *Un hondo bosque de sueños: Notas sobre literatura para niños.* La Habana: Ediciones Unión, 2008.

182 · Bibliography

Diego, Eliseo, and Mark Weiss. "Eliseo Diego and Fairy Tales," *Marvels & Tales* 23, 2 (2009): 391–98.

Dienstag, Joshua Foa. "Nietzsche's Dionysian Pessimism," *The American Political Science Review* 95, 4 (December 2001): 923–937.

———. *Pessimism: Philosophy, Ethic, Spirit.* Princeton: Princeton University Press, 2009.

Dilthey, Wilhelm. *Pattern and Meaning in History. Thoughts on History and Society.* New York: Harper Torchbooks, 1961.

Dodd, Lindsey. "Small fish, big pond: using a single oral narrative to reveal broader social change." In *Memory and History: Understanding Memory as Source and Subject,* edited by Joan Tumbley, 34–49. Abingdon: Routledge, 2013.

Duany, Jorge, "From the Cuban Ajiaco to the Cuban-American Hyphen: Changing Discourses of National Identity on the Island and in the Diaspora," 1997, https://scholarship.miami.edu/esploro/search/outputs?query=any,contains,Jorge%20duany&page=1&sort=rank&scope=Research&institution=01UOML_INST, accessed February 20, 2023.

Dussel, Enrique. *Philosophy of Liberation.* New York: Orbis Books, 1985.

Eire, Carlos. *Waiting for Snow in Havana: Confessions of a Cuban Boy.* New York: Simon and Schuster, 2003.

Espinosa Domínguez, Carlos. "Advertencias del rehabilitado: El hallazgo de unos poemas de Antón Arrufat que nunca se han publicado en Cuba, pone en evidencia la mano de la censura que los eliminó del libro del cual formaban parte." *Cuba Encuentro,* https://www.cubaencuentro.com/cultura/articulos/advertencias-del-rehabilitado-276207, 2012, last accessed February 21, 2023.

Entralgo, Pedro Luis. *La espera y la esperanza: Historia y teoría del esperar humano.* Madrid: Alianza Editorial, 1984.

Escape from Havana: An American Story, CNBC, 2010, https://www.cnbc.com/escape-from-havana-an-american-story/, last accessed February 21, 2023.

Estévez, Abilio. *Tuyo es el reino.* Barcelona: Tusquets Editores, SA., 1997.

———. *Los palacios distantes.* Barcelona: Tusquets Editores S.A., 2002.

Estévez, Rolando. "Gerundios para la espera (Verbs for Waiting): A Visual Coda." In *The Portable Island: Cubans at Home and Abroad,* edited by Ruth Behar and Lucía Suárez, 235–47. New York: Palgrave MacMillan, 2008.

Fabian, Johannes. *Time and the Other: How Anthropology Makes Its Object.* New York: Columbia University Press, 2014.

Fagen, Richard. *The Transformation of Political Culture in Cuba.* Palo Alto: Stanford University Press, 1969.

Farah, Diego Petersen. "Cuba: El futuro es cosa del pasado." *Nexos,* Septiembre 1, 2014, https://www.nexos.com.mx/?p=22328, accessed February 21, 2023.

Fass, Paula. "The Memoir Problem." *Reviews in American History* 34, 1 (2006): 107–123.

Fernández, Cecilia M. *Leaving Little Havana: A Memoir of Miami's Cuban Ghetto.* Orlando: Beating Windward Press, 2013.

Fernández Estrada, Julio Antonio, "The July 11th Protests in Cuba: The Opinion of Julio Antonio Fernandez Estrada," https://www.youtube.com/watch?v=qJbRjwrVkZc&t=2s, accessed February 16, 2023.

Ferrer, Ada. *Cuba: An American History.* New York: Scribner, 2021.

Figueroa de Cárdenas, Javier. *El sueño inconcluso: La historia del Directorio Revoluciona-rio Estudiantil, 1959–1966.* Miami: Ediciones Universal, 2022.

Press release, Governor Ron DeSantis, https://www.flgov.com/2022/02/07/governor-ron-desantis-faith-leaders-and-pedro-pans-biden-border-crisis-is-harming-children/, accessed February 16, 2023.

Flaherty, Michael G., and Gary A. Fine. "Present, Past and Future." *Time & Society* 10, 147 (2001): 147–61.

Fontanella, Sergio. "Margin and utopia by Pedro Pablo Oliva." *On Cuba,* September 24, 2013, https://oncubanews.com/en/styles-trends/technologies-of-communication-and-media/margin-and-utopia-by-pedro-pablo-oliva/, accessed February 21, 2023.

Foner, Philip S. (ed.) *Our America: Writings on Latin America and the Struggle for Cuban Independence.* New York: Monthly Review Press, 1977.

———. *On Education: Articles on Educational Theory and Pedagogy and Writing for Children from the Age of Gold.* New York: Monthly Review Press, 1979.

Foucault, Michel. *The Order of Things: An Archaeology of the Human Sciences.* New York: Vintage Books, 1994.

Fuentes, Carlos. "Remember the Future." *Salmagundi* 68/69 (Fall 1985–Winter 1986): 338–343.

———. "The Literary Imagination and the Sense of the Past." *Salmagundi* 68/69 (Fall 1985–Winter 1986): 333–52.

Fuentes, Ivette. *A través de su espejo: Sobre la poética de Eliseo Diego.* La Habana: Letras Cubanas, 2006.

Fukuyama, Francis. *The End of History and the Last Man.* New York: Free Press, 1992.

Furet, François. *The Passing of an Illusion: The Idea of Communism in the Twentieth Century.* Chicago: University of Chicago Press, 1999.

García, Yunior. "The 11J detainees in Cuba: Testimony of Yunior García Aguilera," https://www.youtube.com/watch?v=IFHd9qMfga4, accessed February 16, 2023.

García Canclini, Néstor. *Hybrid Cultures: Strategies for Entering and Leaving Modernity.* Translated by Christopher L. Chiappari and Silvia L. López. Minneapolis: University of Minnesota Press, 2005.

García Ferraz, Nereida. "Not the Golden Age." In *By Heart/De Memoria: Cuban Women's Journeys In and Out of Exile,* edited by María de los Ángeles Torres, 57–74. Philadelphia: Temple University Press, 2003.

García Marruz, Fina. *No, No Memoria,* https://www.isliada.org/poetas/fina-garcia-marruz/, accessed February 20, 2023.

———. *Del tiempo largo,* https://www.poeticous.com/fina-garcia-marruz/del-tiempo-largo?locale=es, accessed February 20, 2023.

Gasparini, Giovanni. "On Waiting." *Time & Society* 4, 1 (1995): 29–45.

Gayol, Manuel. "José Lezama Lima y la búsqueda de los orígenes." *Hispanic LA* (December 2010), http://www.hispanicla.com/jose-lezama-lima-y-la-busqueda-de-los-origenes-16659, accessed February 17, 2023.

Gell, Alfred. *The Anthropology of Time: Cultural Constructions of Temporal Maps and Images.* London: Bloomsbury Academic, 2001.

184 · Bibliography

Ginzburg, Carlo. "Checking the Evidence: The Judge and the Historian." *Critical Inquiry* 18, 1 (Autumn, 1991): 79–92.

Goldberg, Carl. "Time in Psychoanalysis: Some Contradictory Aspects" (Book Review), *American Psychological Association*, http://www.apadivisions.org/division-39/publications/reviews/time-contradictory.aspx, accessed September 2, 2020.

Goldman, Steven. "Progress: Fact or Illusion?" *Technology & Culture* 41, 1 (2000): 116–17.

Gómez-Sicre, José. *Personalities in the Americas: Photographs by Berestein-Tagle, March 17-April 12, 1952.* Exhibition catalog, Washington, D.C.: Pan American Union, 1952.

González, Gerardo M. *A Cuban Refugee's Journey to the American Dream: The Power of Education.* Bloomington: Well House Books, Indiana University Press, 2018.

González Mandri, Flora. "A House on Shifting Sands." In *Bridges to Cuba/Puentes a Cuba,* edited by Ruth Behar, 76–79. Ann Arbor: University of Michigan Press, 1995.

González Seligmann, Katerina. *Writing the Caribbean in Magazine Time.* New Brunswick: Rutgers University Press, 2021.

Graubard, Stephen R. "Preface to the Issue 'Utopia.'" *Daedalus* 94, 2 (Spring 1965): iii–vi.

Griesse, James M. "From Heaven to Hell: Revolutionary Dreams and Dystopia in Zoé Valdés's *La nada cotidiana,*" *L'Érudit Franco-Espagnol* 1 (Spring 2012): 112–24.

Grundberg, Andy. "A Storm of Images: The Photographs of María Martínez-Cañas," https://www.mariamartinez-canas.com/A-Storm-of-Images-The-Photographs-of-Maria-Martinez-Canas-by-Andy, accessed February 21, 2023.

Grupo Areíto. *Contra viento y marea: Jóvenes cubanos hablan desde su exilio en Estados Unidos.* Ciudad de México: Siglo XXI, 1978.

Guerra, Lillian. *The Myth of José Martí: Conflicting Nationalisms in Early Twentieth Century Cuba.* Chapel Hill: University of North Carolina Press, 2005.

———. *Heroes, Martyrs and Political Messiahs in Revolutionary Cuba, 1946–1958.* New Haven: Yale University Press, 2018.

Guevara, Ernesto Che. "Man and Socialism in Cuba. Letter to Carlos Quijano." In *Che Guevara Reader,* edited by David Deutschmann. Melbourne: Ocean Press, 2005.

———. "Socialism and Man in Cuba, March 1965." Marxists Internet Archive, https://www.marxists.org/archive/guevara/1965/03/man-socialism.htm, accessed February 21, 2023.

Gusdsorf, George. *Mythe et metáphysique.* Paris: Flammarion, 1993.

Gutiérrez, Pedro Juan. *Dirty Havana Trilogy.* Translated by Natasha Wimmer. New York: Farrar, Straus and Giroux, 2001.

Habermas, Jürgen. *The Philosophical Discourses of Modernity.* Translated by Frederick Lawrence. Cambridge: MIT Press, 1987.

Halbwachs, Maurice. *On Collective Memory.* Translated by Lewis A. Coser. Chicago: University of Chicago Press, 1992.

Havel, Václav. "Address of the President of Czechoslovakia Václav Havel to a Joint Session of the United States Congress, Washington, D.C., February 21, 1990," https://www.muzeuminternetu.cz/offwebs/czech/347.htm, last accessed February 21, 2023.

Hawking, Stephen. *A Brief History of Time.* New York: Bantam, 1998.

"Headlines." *Granma,* December 27, 1987.

Bibliography · 185

Hegel, Georg Wilhelm Friedrich. *The Philosophy of History*. New York: Dover Publication, 1956.

Heidegger, Martin. *Being and Time*. New York: Harper Perennial Modern Classics, 2008.

Herrera, Andrea O'Reilly. *Cuba: Idea of a Nation Displaced*. Albany: State University of New York, 2007.

Herrera, Olga U. *American Interventions and Modern Art in South America*. Gainesville: University Press of Florida, 2017.

———. "AMA and the Concept of Latin American Art." In *Art of the Americas: Collection of the Art Museum of the Americas of the Organization of Americans States*, 40–47. Washington, D.C.: AMA, 2017.

Horkheimer, Max, and Theodor W. Adorno. *Dialectic of Enlightenment*. Translated by John Cumming. New York: Continuum, 1991.

Hutchinson, Steven. "Mapping Utopias." *Modern Philology* 85, 2 (November 1987): 170–185.

Jacoby, Russell. *The End of Utopia: Politics and Culture in an Age of Apathy*. New York: Basic Books, 1999.

———. *Picture Imperfect: Utopian Thought for an Anti-Utopian Age*. New York: Columbia University Press, 2005.

Jameson, Frederic. "Review: Of Islands and Trenches: Naturalization and the Production of Utopian Discourse." *Diacritics* 7, 2 (Summer, 1977): 2–21.

———. *Archaeologies of the Future: The Desire Called Utopia and Their Science Fictions*. London: Verso, 2005.

Jiménez Leal, Orlando, and Manuel Zayas. *El Caso PM: Cine, poder y censura*. Madrid: Editorial Hypermedia, 2014.

José Toirac: Waiting for the Right Time. Pan American Art Projects, November 2019–January 2020, https://panamericanart.com/wp-content/uploads/2019/11/Esperando-el-momento-correcto.pdf, accessed February 21, 2023.

Kellner, Douglas. "Ernst Bloch, Utopia and Ideology Critique." Illuminations: The Critical Theory Project, https://pages.gseis.ucla.edu/faculty/kellner/Illumina%20Folder/kell1.htm, accessed February 21, 2023.

Khatib, Sami R. "A Non-Nullified Nothingness: Walter Benjamin and the Messianic in Stasis." *Stasis* 1, 1 (Fall 2013): 82–108.

Knausgaard, Karl Ove. "My Saga," Part 1. *New York Times Magazine*, February 25, 2015.

Koczanowicz, Leszek. *Politics of Time: Dynamics of Identity in Post-Communist Poland*. New York: Berghahn Books, 2008.

Kompridis, Nikolas. "The Idea of a New Beginning: A Romantic Source of Normativity and Freedom." In *Philosophical Romanticism*, edited by Nikolas Kompridis, 32–59. Abingdon: Routledge, 2006.

Koselleck, Reinhart. *Futures Past: On the Semantics of Historical Time*. Translated by Keith Tribe. New York: Columbia University Press, 2004.

Laín, Pedro. *Espera y esperanza*. Madrid: Obras Plenitud, 1956.

Leal, Francisco. "Trilogía sucia de La Habana de Pedro Juan Gutiérrez: Mercado, crimen y abyección." *Taller de Letras* 37 (2005): 51–66.

186 · Bibliography

Lechner, Norbert. "Chile 2000: Las sombras del mañana." *Estudios Internacionales* 27, 105 (January–March 1994): 3–11.

Lefebvre. Henri. *Introduction to Modernity.* Translated by John Moore. London: Verso, 1995.

Leonin, Mia. *Havana and Other Missing Fathers.* Tucson: University of Arizona Press, 2016.

Levinas, Emmanuel. *Time and the Other.* Translated by Richard Cohen. Pittsburgh: Duquesne Press, 1987.

Levitas, Ruth. *The Concept of Utopia.* Oxford: Peter Lang Press, 2010.

Leyva-Pérez, Irina. "Revisiting History: A Conversation with Meira Marrero and José Angel Toirac." *Art Pulse,* December 3, 2013, http://artpulsemagazine.com/revisiting -history-a-conversation-with-meira-marrero-and-jose-angel-toirac, accessed February 21, 2023.

Lindroos, Kia. *Now-time Image-space: Temporalization of Politics in Walter Benjamin's Philosophy of History and Art.* Jyväskylä: SoPhi Academic Press, 1999.

Lindsey, Dodd. "Small fish, big pond: Using a single oral narrative to reveal broader social change." In *Memory and History: Understanding Memory as Source and Subject,* edited by Joan Tumblety, 44–59. Abingdon: Routledge, 2013.

López, Iraida. *Impossible Returns: Narratives of the Cuban Diaspora.* Gainesville: University of Florida Press, 2015.

López Miró, Sergio. "El lado oscuro de Pedro Pan." *El Miami Herald,* November 29, 1990.

Lost Apple Documentary, https://www.youtube.com/watch?v=WKoJKF-FtS4, accessed February 21, 2023.

Macdonald, Iain. "Adorno's Modal Utopianism: Possibility and Actuality in Adorno and Hegel." *Adorno Studies* 1, 1 (January 2017): 1–12.

Madrid, Alejandro. *Sounds of the Modern Nation: Music, Culture, and Ideas in Post-Revolutionary Mexico.* Philadelphia: Temple University Press, 2008.

Maines, David R., Noreen M. Sugrue, and Michael A. Katovich. "The Sociological Import of G. H. Mead's Theory of the Past." *American Sociological Review* 48, 2 (1983): 161–73.

Mann, Sally. *Still Time.* New York: Aperture Foundation, 2008.

Mannheim, Karl (ed.) *Ideology and Utopias: An Introduction to the Sociology of Knowledge.* Eastford: Martino Fine Books, 2015.

Marcuse, Herbert. "The End of Utopia, 1967." Marxists Internet Archive, https://www .marxists.org/reference/archive/marcuse/works/1967/end-utopia.htm, accessed February 21, 2023.

Mariátegui, José Carlos. *Seven Interpretive Essays on Peruvian Reality.* Translated by Marjorie Urquidi. Austin: University of Texas Press, 1971.

Martí, José. *Nuestra América* (English versión), 1891. http://www.josemarti.cu/ publicacion/nuestra-america-version-ingles/, accessed June 2023.

———. *Selected Writings* (New York: Penguin Press, 2002).

———. *La Edad de Oro.* Miami: Ediciones Universal, 1968.

Marx, Karl. *The Manifesto of the Communist Party.* Marxists Internet Archive, https://

www.marxists.org/archive/marx/works/1848/communist-manifesto/ch01.htm, accessed July 2020.

Marx, Leo, and Bruce Mazlish (eds.) *Progress: Fact or Illusion?* Ann Arbor: University of Michigan Press, 1998.

Mead, George Herbert. *The Philosophy of the Present.* New York: Prometheus Books, 2002.

Medina, Pablo. *Exiled Memories: A Cuban Childhood.* New York: Persea Books, 2002.

Medvedev, Roy. *Let History Judge.* Translated by George Shriver. New York: Columbia University Press, 1989.

Mendible, Myra. "Imagining Cuba: Storytelling and the Politics of Exile." In *Telling Stories to Change the World: Global Voices on the Power of Narrative to Build Community and Make Social Justice Claims,* edited by Rickie Solinger, Madeline Fox, and Kayhan Irani, 239–248. New York: Routledge, 2008.

Mendieta, Raquel. *Cultura, lucha de clases y conflicto racial, 1878–1895.* La Habana: Editorial Pueblo y Educación, 1989.

———. "Only Fragments of Memories." In *By Heart/De Memoria: Cuban Women's Journeys In and Out of Exile,* edited by María de los Ángeles Torres, 133–150. Philadelphia: Temple University Press, 2003.

Miller, Nicola. "The Absolution of History: Uses of the Past in Castro's Cuba." *Journal of Contemporary History* 38, 1 (2003): 147–62.

Miller, Paul. "Blancas y Negras: Carpentier and the Temporalities of Mutual Exclusion." *Latin American Literary Review* 29, no. 58 (July–Dec. 2001): 23–45.

Mills, Charles. *The Racial Contract.* Ithaca: Cornell University, 1997.

———. *From Class to Race: Essays in White Marxism and Black Radicalism.* Lanham: Rowman and Littlefield, 2003.

Mistral, Gabriela. *Selected Prose and Prose-Poems.* Translated by Stephen Tabscott. Austin: University of Texas Press, 2010.

Molina, Juan Antonio. "Entre la Ida y el Regreso. La experiencia del otro en la memoria," October 1996, https://taniabruguera.com/entre-la-ida-y-el-regreso-la-experiencia-del-otro-en-la-memoria/, accessed September 2020.

Moore, Carlos. *Castro, the Blacks and Africa.* Los Angeles: UCLA Center for Afro-American Studies, 1988.

Moreno Fraginals, Manuel. *La historia como arma: Y otros estudios sobres esclavos, ingenios y plantaciones.* Madrid: Crítica, 2003.

Mosquera, Gerardo, 2015, "Taitlin Shouts," 2015, https://walkerart.org/magazine/tania-bruguera-artivism-gerardo-mosquera-cuba, accessed February 20, 2023.

Mouffe, Chantal. "Feminism, Citizenship, and Radical Democratic Politics." In *Feminists Theorize the Political,* edited by Judith Butler and Joan W. Scott, 369–385. New York: Routledge Press, 2013.

Müller, Herbert J. *The Uses of the Past: Profiles of Former Societies.* New York: Oxford University Press, 1952.

Muller, Nazma. "'I live a simple life' Pedro Juan Gutiérrez talks to Nazma Muller about writing, poverty, and the dangers of autobiography." *The Caribbean Review of Books*

188 · Bibliography

(November 2007), http://caribbeanreviewofbooks.com/crb-archive/14-%20%20%20 %20november-2007/i- live-a-simple-life/, accessed February 21, 2023.

Mumford, Lewis. *The Story of Utopias*. New York: Viking Press, 1962.

———. *Technics and Civilization*. Chicago: University of Chicago Press, 2010.

Muñoz, José Esteban. *Cruising Utopia: The Then and There of Queer Futurity*. New York: New York University Press, 2009.

Nasca, Dania Rosa. *Lights Out: A Cuban Memoir of Betrayal and Survival*. North Charleston: CreateSpace Independent Publishing Platform, 2016.

Nassehi, Armin. "No Time for Utopia: The Absence of Utopian Contents in Modern Concepts of Time." *Time & Society* 3, 1 (February 1994): 47–78.

Nodarse, María. *Approaching Freedom: An Exile's Quest for a New Self*. New York: Nook Book, 2018.

Nora, Pierre. "Between Memory and History: Les Lieux de Mémoire." *Representations* 26 (Spring, 1989): 7–24.

Nora, Pierre, and David P. Jordan (eds.) *Rethinking France: Les Lieux de mémoire, Vol. 1: The State*. Translated by Mary Trouille. Chicago: University of Chicago Press, 2001–2006.

Obama, Barack. "Remarks by President Obama at the First Plenary Session of the Summit of the Americas," April 11, 2015, https://obamawhitehouse.archives.gov/the -press-office/2015/04/11/remarks-president-obama-first-plenary-session-summit -americas, accessed February 21, 2023.

Obejas, Achy. *Ruins*. New York: Akashic Books, 2009.

Ojito, Mirta A. *Finding Mañana: A Memoir of a Cuban Exodus*. New York: Penguin Books, 2005.

Pallí, José Manuel, Analysis: Understanding Payá and his Varela Project, https://www .cubastandard.com/analysis-understanding-osvaldo-paya-and-his-varela-project/, August 21, 2012.

Patterson, Enrique. *La soledad histórica y otros ensayos*. Philadelphia: Eniola Publishing, 2021.

Paz, Octavio. "Interview." *New Perspectives Quarterly* 4, 1 (Winter 1987).

———. "In Search of the Present." Nobel Prize Acceptance Speech, 1990, https://www .nobelprize.org/nobel_prizes/literature/laureates/1990/paz-lecture.html, accessed February 21, 2023.

Pedro Pan Organization. http://pedropan.org/content/letter-cnbc-board-directors -operation-pedro-pan-group-inc, accessed February 16, 2023.

Pérez, Louis A., Jr. *The Structure of Cuban History: Meaning and Purposes of the Past*. Chapel Hill: University of North Carolina Press, 2015.

Pérez Firmat, Gustavo. *Next Year in Cuba: A Cubano's Coming-of-Age in America*. Houston: Arte Público Press, 2006.

Perón, Evita. *Historia del peronismo*. Buenos Aires: Ediciones Mundo Peronista, 1951.

Phillips, Anne. *Democracy and Difference*. University Park: Pennsylvania State University Press, 1993.

———. *The Politics of Presence*. Oxford: University of Oxford Press, 1995.

Pletsch, Carl E. "History and Friedrich Nietzsche's Philosophy of Time." *History and Theory* 16, 1 (February 1977): 30–39.

Popper, Karl. *The Poverty of Historicism.* New York: Routledge, 1957.

———. *Open Society and Its Enemies.* Princeton: Princeton University Press, 2013.

Prior, Arthur N. "The Notion of the Present." In *The Study of Time*, edited by J. T. Fraser, F. C. Haber, and G. H. Müller, 320–323. Berlin: Springer Verlag, 1972.

Proust, Marcel. *Remembrance of Things Past*, 3 Vols. New York: Vintage, 1981.

Quijano, Aníbal. "Modernity, Identity and Utopia in Latin America." *Boundary* 2, 20 (Autumn 1993): 140–155.

Quiroga, José. *Cuban Palimpsests.* Minneapolis: University of Minnesota Press, 2005.

Rawls, John. *The Law of Peoples.* Cambridge: Harvard University Press, 1999.

Reed, John. *Insurgent Mexico.* Greenwood: Greenwood Press, 1914.

———. *Ten Days that Shook the World.* New York: Penguin, 1977.

Ricoeur, Paul. *Lectures on Ideology and Utopia.* New York: Columbia University Press, 1986.

———. *Memory, History, Forgetting.* Chicago: University of Chicago Press, 2006.

Rizzini, Irene. "The Child-Saving Movement in Brazil: Ideology in the Late Nineteenth and Early Twentieth Centuries." In *Minor Omissions: Children in Latin American History and Society*, edited by Tobias Hecht, 165–180. Madison: University of Wisconsin Press, 2002.

Rocha, Delmiro. "Pensar el porvenir. La disyunción futuro/porvenir en la deconstrucción de J. Derrida." *Revista Internacional de Filosofía*, Suplemento 3 (2010): 117–123.

Rodríguez Acevedo, Cruz Javier. "La esperanza en el humanismo de Laín Entralgo." *Relectiones, Revista Interdisciplinar de Filosofía y Humanidades* (November 2016): 45–63.

Rojas, Rafael. *El arte de la espera: Notas al margen de la política cubana.* Madrid: Colibrí, 1998.

———. *Isla sin fin: Contribución a la crítica del nacionalismo cubano.* Miami: Universal Press, 1999.

———. *José Martí: La invención de Cuba.* Madrid: Editorial Colibrí, 2008.

———. *Essays in Cuban Cultural Intellectual History.* New York: Palgrave MacMillan, 2008.

———. *Las Repúblicas del Aire: Utopía y desencanto en la revolución de Hispanoamérica.* Ciudad de México: Taurus, 2009.

———. *La máquina del olvido: Mito, historia y poder en Cuba.* Ciudad de México: Taurus, 2011.

Rosas, Paula. "En Cuba estamos cansados de vivir tanto tiempo en la Historia y queremos vivir en la normalidad." BBC News Mundo, January 27, 2023, https://www.bbc.com/mundo/noticias-64189085, accessed February 26, 2023.

Rostow, Walt W. *The Stages of Economic Growth: A Non-Communist Manifesto.* Cambridge: Cambridge University Press, 1960.

Rovelli, Carlo. *Seven Brief Lessons on Physics.* New York: Riverhead Books, 2016.

Sainz, Enrique. Prologue to *Eliseo Diego, Poesía Completa.* La Habana: Editorial Letras Cubanas, 1983.

190 · Bibliography

Santeiro, Luis. *Dancing with Dictators: A Family's Journey from Pre-Castro Cuba to Exile in the Turbulent Sixties*. New York: Luis Santeiro, 2017.

Santiso, Javier. "The Fall into the Present: The Emergence of Limited Political Temporalities in Latin America." *Time & Society* 7, 1 (March 1998): 25–54.

Schmill, Ulises. *Las revoluciones. Teoría jurídica y consideraciones sociológicas*. Madrid: Trotta, 2009.

Shnookal, Deborah. *Operation Pedro Pan and the Exodus of Cuba's Children*. Gainesville: University of Florida Press, 2020.

Shorten, Richard. "Conceptions of 'The Political': A Note on Contrasting Motifs in Hannah Arendt's Treatment of Totalitarianism." *Journal for Political Thinking* 2, 1 (Septembers 2006): 1–13.

Shklar, Judith. "The Political Theory of Utopia: From Melancholy to Nostalgia," *Daedalus* 94, 2 (1965): 367–81.

Sierra Madero, Abel. *El cuerpo nunca olvida: Trabajo forzado, hombre nuevo y memoria en Cuba (1959-1980)*. Ciudad de México: Rialta Ediciones, 2022.

Smith Chowers, Gary, (ed.) *Benjamin: Philosophy, Aesthetics, History*. Chicago: University of Chicago Press, 1989.

Sorensen, Diana. *A Turbulent Decade Remembered: Scenes from the Latin American Sixties*. Palo Alto: Stanford University Press, 2007.

St. Augustine. *City of God*, Book 11. Hyde Park, New York: New City Press, 2013.

Suárez, Lucía. "Ruin Memory: Havana Beyond the Revolution." *Canadian Journal of Latin American and Caribbean Studies* 39, 1 (2014): 38–55.

Suárez, Virgil. *Spared Angola: Memories from a Cuban-American Childhood*. Houston: Arte Público Press, 1997.

Sweig, Julia. *Inside the Revolution: Fidel Castro and the Urban Underground*. Cambridge: Harvard University Press, 2002.

Tassone, Giuseppe. *A Study on the Idea of Progress in Nietzsche, Heidegger, and Critical Theory*. New York: E. Mellen Press, 2002.

Torres, María de los Ángeles. *In the Land of Mirrors: Cuban Exile Politics*. Ann Arbor: University of Michigan Press, 1999.

———. *The Lost Apple: Operation Pedro Pan, Cuban Children in the US and the Promise of a Better Future*. Boston: Beacon Press, 2001.

———. "Donde los fantasmas bailan el guaguancó: Where Ghosts Dance el Guaguancó." In *By Heart/De memoria: Cuban Women's Journeys In and Out of Exile*, edited by Maria de los Ángeles Torres, 23–57. Philadelphia: Temple University Press, 2003.

———, ed. *By Heart/De Memoria: Cuban Women's Journeys in and out of Exile*. Philadelphia: Temple University Press, 2003.

———. "Multiculturalism and Democracy: Expanding Notions of Citizenship." In *Our Diverse Society: Race and Ethnicity—Implications for 21st Century American Society*, edited by David. W. Engstrom and Lisette M. Piedra, 161-182. Washington, D.C.: NASW Press, 2007.

———. "History Will Absolve Me," in Alan West-Durán, ed., *Cuba* (New York: Charles Scribner's Son, 2012).

———. "Operation Pedro Pan: the 1960s transport of unaccompanied children to the United States." In *Research Handbook in Child Migration*, edited by Jacqueline Bhabha, Jyothi Kanics, and Daniel Senovilla Hernández, 37–43. Cheltenham: Edward Elgar Publishing, 2018.

Torres, María de los Ángeles, Irene Rizzini, and Norma Del Río (eds.) *Citizens in the Present/Youth Civic Engagement in the Americas*. Urbana: University of Illinois Press, 2013.

Triay, Víctor Andrés. *Fleeing Castro: Operation Pedro Pan and the Cuban Children's Program*. Gainesville: University Press of Florida, 1999.

Trouillot, Michel-Rolph. *Silencing the Past: Power and Production of History*. Boston: Beacon Press, 1995.

Trumbull, Charles. "Prostitution and Sex Tourism in Cuba." November 2001, https://www.ascecuba.org/asce_proceedings/prostitution-and-sex-tourism-in-cuba/, accessed February 20, 2023.

U.S. Congress. Senate. Committee on the Judiciary. *Cuban Refugee Problems: Hearings before the Subcommittee to Investigate Problems Connected with Refugees and Escapees*. Testimony of Rev. Bryan Walsh, National Conference of Catholic Charities. 87th Cong., 1st sess., 1961. Washington, D.C.: Government Printing Office, 1962.

Valdés, Zoé. *La nada cotidiana*. Barcelona: Editorial Planeta, 1996.

Varela, Félix. *Escritos políticos*. La Habana: Editorial Ciencias Sociales, 1977.

Vasconcelos, José. *La Raza Cósmica*. Translated by Didier Jaen. Baltimore: Johns Hopkins University Press, 1997.

Veciana, Antonio, and Carlos Harrison. *Trained to Kill: The Inside Story of CIA Plots against Castro, Kennedy, and Che*. New York: Skyhorse, 2017.

Veiga, Marisella. *We Carry Our Homes with Us: A Cuban American Memoir*. St. Paul: Minnesota Historical Society Press, 2016.

VerbiClara. "La Operación Peter Pan y los niños cubanos." June 2, 2009, https://verbiclara.wordpress.com/2009/06/02/la-operacion-peter-pan-y-los-ninos-cubanos/, accessed February 21, 2023.

Viso, Olga. 2015. *Tania Bruguera: Artivism and Repression in Cuba,* https://walkerart.org/magazine/tania-bruguera-artivism-gerardo-mosquera-cuba, accessed February 20, 2023.

Viveros-Faune, Christina. "How Tania Bruguera's 'Whisper' Became the Performance heard Around the World." *Artnet News*, January 8, 2015, https://news.artnet.com/art-world/how-tania-brugueras-whisper-became-the-performance-heard-round-the-world-213637/amp-page, accessed February 21, 2023.

Ware, Owen. "Dialectic of the Past/Disjuncture of the Future: Derrida and Benjamin on the Concept of Messianism." *Journal for Cultural and Religious Theory* 5, 2 (2004): 99–114.

Waterlow, Sarah. "Aristotle's Now." *The Philosophical Quarterly*, 135 (1984): 104–128.

Watts, Jonathan. "Cuban dissident Oswalda Payá's death 'no accident' claims daughter." *The Guardian,* July 23, 2012.

Weeks, Kathi. *The Problem with Work: Feminisms, Marxism, Anti-Work Politics and Postwork Imaginaries*. Durham: Duke University Press, 2001.

192 · Bibliography

Wegner, Phillip E. *Imaginary Communities: Utopia, the Nation, and the Spatial Histories of Modernity.* Los Angeles: University of California Press, 2002.

Weiss, Mark (ed.) *The Whole Island: Six Decades of Cuban Poetry, A Bilingual Anthology.* Translated by Mark Weiss. Oakland: University of California Press, 2009.

West-Pavlov, Russell. *Temporalities.* New York: Routledge, 2013.

Whitfield, Esther. "The Body Impolitic of *Trilogía Sucia de La Habana.*" *Revista de Estudios Hispánicos* 36, 2 (May 2002): 329–351.

Whitney, Robert. "The Architect of the Cuban State: Fulgencio Batista and Populism in Cuba, 1937–1940." *Journal of Latin American Studies* 32, 2 (May 2000): 435–59.

Widder, Nathan. *Reflections on Time and Politics.* University Park: Pennsylvania State University Press, 2008.

Zalloua, Zahi. "The Ethics of Trauma/The Trauma of Ethics." In *Terror, Theory and the Humanities,* edited by Jeffrey R. Di Leo and Uppinder Mehan, 223–243. Ann Arbor: Open Society Press, 2012.

Žižek, Slavoj. "Neighbors and Other Monsters: A Plea for Ethical Violence." In *The Neighbor: Three Inquiries in Political Theology,* edited by Slavoj Žižek, Eric L. Santner, and Kenneth Reinhard, 134–90. Chicago: The University of Chicago Press, 2005.

Zweig, Stefan. *The World of Yesterday.* Lincoln: University of Nebraska Press, 2013.

Zygmunt, Bauman. "Time and Space Reunited." *Time & Society* 9, 2/3 (June 2000): 171–85.

Interviews

Interview with María Martínez-Cañas, March 2017.
Interview with Nereida García Ferraz, March 2017.
Interview with Jorge Olivera, April 18, 2022.

Index

ABC uprising, 34

Acción Católica (Catholic Action), 35

Adaptation (Martínez-Cañas), 125

Adios, Mi Pequeña Habana (Fernández), 116

Adorno, Theodor, 18, 135

Afro-Cubans. *See* Black Cubans

Agamben, Giorgio, 82–83, 155

Aguirre, Eduardo, 44

Alfaya, Nancy, 6

Al partir (On leaving) (Gómez de Avellaneda), 155

Angola, xiii–xiv, 3

anti-racism, 95

Antonio Maceo Brigade (Brigada Antonio Maceo), xiii, 42–43, 111–112, 121

Appadurai, Arjun, 135–136

Approaching Freedom: An Exile's Quest for a New Self (Nodarse), 117

Arendt, Hannah, xx, 1

    Bruguera and, xx, 141

    conception of history, 25, 31, 33, 37–38, 54, 62–63, 84, 132

    poetic present and, 84–85

    on temporality, 14–17

    utopianism and, 76

Argentina, 16, 64

Aristotle, 13, 81

Arrufat, Antón, 47, 131

El arte de la espera (The art of the waiting) (Rojas), 90

authoritarianism. *See also* totalitarianism

    anti-communism and, 2

    artistic protests against, 119

    of Castro, 30, 38–40, 85

    in Cuba, 2, 18–19, 20, 36, 73, 153

future temporalities and, 75–76, 83, 133

history and, 33, 51

the *masses* and, 69

philosophical underpinnings of, 36–40

present temporality and, 15, 90, 107–108

sameness and, 152

silence and, 107

utopianism and, 75–76, 79, 84

Badiou, Alain, 150

Baquero, Gastón, 96

Barr, Alfred H., Jr., 124

Batista, Fulgencio, 27–30, 34–37, 64, 145

Bauman, Zygmunt, 26

Bay of Pigs invasion, 3, 39, 45

Behar, Ruth, 80, 111, 117

Benjamin, Walter, 9, 19, 54, 82, 90, 107, 134

Berlin Wall, 154

Bermúdez, Cundo, 124, 128

Biografía (Diego), 100–102

Birkenmaier, Anke, 80

Bishop, Elizabeth, 94

Black Cubans, 2, 34, 37, 146, 149–151

    Afro-Cuban culture, 95–96

    Cuban independence movement and, 28, 37, 150–151

    Cuban Revolution of 1959 and, 151

black markets, 89–90

Blanco, Richard, 113

Bloch, Ernst, 135, 137

Bofill, Ricardo, 4

Bolívar, Simón, 57–58, 60

Braun, Kathrin, 16–17

Bravo, Estela, 113

Brazil, 64, 79

194 · Index

Bridges to Cuba project, 111–112
Brigada Antonio Maceo. *See* Antonio Maceo
   Brigade
Bruguera, Tania, xvi, xx, 22, 138–141
By Heart/De Memoria: Cuban Women's Jour-
   neys in and out of Exile (Torres, ed.), 112

La Cabaña fortress, 66, 140
Cabrera, Lydia, 124
Cabrera Infante, Sabá, 39–40
Cámara, Madeline, 5
Campanería, Albertico, 45
Campanería, Virgilio, 45
capitalism, 78, 82
   end of Cold War and, 154
   post-authoritarian capitalism, 91
   in post-Soviet Cuba, 90
Cardona, José Miró, 3
Carpentier, Alejo, 9, 52
La Carta de los Diez (The Letter from the
   Ten), 5
Casal, Lourdes, 111
Castañeda, Jorge, 79
Castro, Fidel, 20–21, 41, 65
   1953 trial of, 27–30, 39
   artistic representations of, 118, 132, 140
   authoritarianism of, 2, 30, 38–40, 85
   as author of *History Will Absolve Me*, 20, 23,
      27, 30, 33, 39–40, 66
   CIA and, 114–115
   conception of history, 30–32
   contemporary political conflict and, xiv
   Cuban sex workers and, 89
   death of, xvi, 8, 155
   Guevara and, 68
   Marxism and, 37
   nostalgia and, 7
   Operation Pedro Pan and, 44
   propaganda and, 86
   PSP and, 4
   uprising of 1953 and, 27–29
   use of slogans, xvi, 143
Castro, Raúl, 4, 65–66, 90
   contemporary political conflict and, xiv–xv
   resignation of, xv, 142
Catholic Welfare Bureau, 49
Centeno, Guillermo, 113

Central Intelligence Agency (CIA), 114–115
   Operation Pedro Pan and, 45
Cepero, Harold, 6
Cerejido, Elizabeth, 119
Céspedes Barracks, 9, 27, 64
Chávez, Hugo, 79
Chibás, Eduardo, 35
children, xvi–xvii, 21, 58–62. *See also* Opera-
   tion Pedro Pan
   Eliseo Diego on, 98
   future temporalities and, xviii, 58–60, 72–73
   Guevara and, 72–73
   pedagogical projects, 64, 74, 98
   present temporalities and, xviii, 98
Chirino, Willy, 44
Chovel, Elly, 45–46
Cienfuegos, Camilo, 34
Cold War, 64, 77, 85
   effects of end of, 154–155
collective memory, 25, 43, 122–123
communism, 16–17, 63–64, 154. *See also*
   Marxism; Partido Socialista Popular;
   socialism
   anti-communism, 2, 74, 125
   anti-racism and, 95–96
   Communist Party of Cuba, xiv–xv, 4–5, 88
   Cuban emigration and, 44, 48–49, 112, 125
   democracy and, 39
   following collapse of Soviet Union, 5, 90,
      155
   future temporalities and, xviii, 154
   Guevara and, 66–69
   history and, 17, 36–38, 54, 63, 155
   market-Leninism, 88, 154
   New Man ideology and, 74
   socialism and, 70
   temporality and, 14
Communist Party of Cuba, xiv–xv, 4–5, 38, 88.
   See also Partido Socialista Popular
   spring 2020 Party Congress of, 7
compañero, 149–150
Con permiso de la historia (With history's
   permission) (Toirac), 118
Constitution of 1940, 2, 21, 27, 35
   anti-discrimination and, 151
   Article 40 of, 28, 39
   Batista and, 64

Castro's trial and, 29–30
conception of history in, 32
Cuban Revolution of 1959 and, xi, 2, 38–39
education of children and, 60
freedom of expression and, 39
nationalism and, 2, 29, 35, 64
Right of Rebellion against Tyranny, 28, 39
Constitution of 1976, 6
Constitution of 2019, xv, 143–144
Contra viento y marea, 43
Cooper, Peter, 59
Coplas del Tiempo (Diego), 99–100
Corrales, Raúl, 118
COVID-19 pandemic, xiv–xv, 155
Cruz, Nilo, 112–113
Cruz Varela, María Elena, 5
Cuban Adjustment Act, 49
Cuban Committee for Human Rights, 4
Cuban exiles. *See* emigration from Cuba
Cuban independence movement, 33, 145
  Black Cubans and, 28, 37, 150–151
  future temporalities and, 52
  Martí and, 62, 150, 154
  slavery and, 150
  War of Independence, xii, 27, 62, 145
A Cuban Refugee's Journey to the American Dream: The Power of Education (González), 115
Cuban Revolution of 1959, 2–3, 9, 64–67, 153–154
  art and, 118, 140
  author's experience of, xi–xii
  Black Cubans and, 151
  children and, xviii
  concept of "past" and, 20–21, 65
  Constitution of 1940 and, xi, 2, 38–39, 151
  cultural repression following, 39–40, 85, 151
  decline of socialism following, 79–80
  democracy and, xix, 65, 145
  democratic opposition to, 2–3
  Directorio Revolucionario Estudiantil and, 35–36
  education of youth and, xviii, 72–73
  emigration following, 40–44
  exile memoirs and, 110–111, 113–114
  future temporalities and, 52, 65–66, 73, 85
  Guevara and, 65–70

history and, 34, 36–37, 40, 68, 110, 130–131
  Man and Socialism in Cuba and, 67–70
  nationalism and, 40–41, 64, 92
  "New Man" and, xviii
  nostalgia and, 7, 86
  novels about, 91–92
  photography and, 85–86
  political repression following, xii, 36, 38–40, 67–68, 130–131, 145–146
  pre-revolutionary struggles and, 34–35
  present temporalities and, 85–86
  social control and, 3–4
  socialism and, 67–68, 86, 153–154
  temporality and, 7, 9, 37, 142, 153–154
  whiteness of leadership, 3
Cuba on My Mind: Journeys to a Severed Nation (De la Campa), 112
Cuevas de Jaruco, 138
cultural repression, 39–40, 85, 143–144, 151

Daedalus, 76
Dancing with Dictators: A Family's Journey from Pre-Castro Cuba to Exile in the Turbulent Sixties (Santeiro), 115–116
de Castro Tagle, Augusto, 128–129
de Certeau, Michel, 132
Declaration of Independence (USA), 28–29
Declaration of the Rights of Man (France), 28–29
Decree 349, xvi, 143
De Ferrari, Guillermina, 119
de Laboulaye, Édouard René, 61
De la Campa, Román, 112
de la Nuez, Iván, 5, 80, 155
De Lasa, José Maria, 114, 117
De las Casas, Bartolomé, 60–61
Del otro lado del cristal (Centeno), 113
democracy, 10–11, 148
  art and, 141
  Cuban Revolution of 1959 and, xix, 2, 65, 145
  defined, 10–11
  democratic deliberation, 148
  Diego's poetry and, 106, 109
  education of children and, 59
  equality and, 150
  future temporalities and, xviii, 133–137

Index

democracy—*continued*
  history and, 131
  hope and, 135
  inclusivity and, xviii–xix
  poetic present and, 148, 156
  political culture and, 11, 22, 87 109, 155
  political disengagement and, 91
  post-Revolution Cuba and, 38–39
  repression of democracy rights advocates, 5–6
  structural democracy, 10
  temporality and, 18–19
Derrida, Jacques, 13, 82, 134
de San Martín, José, 60
DeSantis, Ron, 47–48
El deseo de morir por otros (The desire to die for others) (Leyva Novo), 119
Desnoes, Edmundo, 42
Dewey, John, 148–149
Díaz, Jesús, 36
Díaz-Canel, Miguel, xv–xvi, 142
Díaz Lanz, Pedro Luis, 3
Díaz Martínez, Manuel, 5
Diego, Eliseo, xx–xxi, 21, 81, 92–94, 97–98, 155
  photo of, 108
  on poetry, 104–107
  temporality in poetry of, xxi, 98–104, 107, 108–109, 110
Dienstag, Joshua Foa, 137
difference/sameness, 151–152
Directorio Revolucionario Estudiantil (Student Revolutionary Directorate), 2, 35–36
Dirty Havana Trilogy (Gutiérrez), 88–89
dynamic present, 81

Echeverría, José Antonio, 35–36
La Edad de Oro (The Golden Age) (Martí, 1889), 60–62
Einstein, Albert, 12
Eisenhower, Dwight, 85
emigration from Cuba, xix, 40–44, 80. *See also* Antonio Maceo Brigade (Brigada Antonio Maceo); Operation Pedro Pan
  deaths during, 139
  exile artists, 118–130, 139
  exile history and, 119
  exile memoirs, 110–118

  experiences of emigres in USA, xii, 110–111, 115–117, 120
  foreign education and, 60
  Mariel Boatlift, 80, 113
  nostalgia in exile communities, 51, 53, 111, 112, 119, 121
  origin myth of, 47–48
  remittances from emigres, xiv
  return of emigres, xiii, 111–113, 117, 121
Engels, Friedrich, 63
Enlightenment, 78–79
Erie, Carlos, 112
Escalante, Aníbal, 4
La Espera (The wait) (Estévez), 92–93, 155
Estévez, Abilio, 8, 80
Estévez Jordan, Rolando, 8, 92–93
eugenics, 64
exile artists, xx, 118–130. *See also* García Ferraz, Nereida; Martínez-Cañas, María
Exiled Memories: A Cuban Childhood (Medina), 113
exile memoirs, 110–118, 131

fascism, 64. *See also* authoritarianism; totalitarianism
  future temporalities and, xviii
Fass, Paula, 111
Federación de Estudiantes Universitarios (Federation of University Students), 35
Fernández, Cecilia M., 116
55 Hermanos (Díaz), 43
Figueroa, Sylvia, 49–50
Finding Mañana: A Memoir of a Cuban Exodus (Ojito), 113
Five Nights (Leyva Novo), 119
Foucault, Michel, 55–56
Frankfurt School, 18, 135
Fuentes, Carlos, 79
future imaginary, 135–137
future temporalities, xviii, 52–53
  authoritarianism and, 75–76, 83, 133
  children and, xviii, 58–60, 72–73
  collapse of futuristic projects, 78–79
  collapse of socialism and, 80
  communism and, xviii, 154
  contemporary Cuba and, 142
  Cuban Revolution of 1959 and, 52, 65–66, 73, 85

democracy and, xviii, 133–137
end of Cold War and, 154
future imaginaries, 135–136
Guevara and, 8, 65–67, 73–75
modernity and, 52–54, 75–76
nation-building and, 57
nostalgia and, 65
relationship with the present, 134
as secularized Christian thought, 73–74
utopianism and, 52, 63, 135–136

La Gaceta del Caribe, 95–96
García, Yunior, xvi
García Ferraz, Nereida, xx, 21, 119–123, 130, 132
García Marruz, Fina, 94, 99
generational conflict, 149
Gómez de Avellaneda, Gertrudis, 155
Gómez-Sicre, Horacio, 124
Gómez-Sicre, José, 124–125, 127–128, 132
González, Elián, 46–47
González, Flora, 112
González, Gerardo M., 115
Griesse, James M., 92
Griffet, Henri, 30
Grundberg, Andy, 123
Guerra, Lillian, 35
Guevara, Ernesto "Che," 21, 34, 52, 65–71, 86
future orientation and, 8, 65–67, 73–75
Man and Socialism and, 66–70, 74
Sarol's painting of, 31–32
youth and, 72–74
Guillén, Nicolás, 95–96
Gutiérrez, Pedro, 88
Gutiérrez Alea, Tomás, 42

Haiti, 47
Hatuey, 56–57
Havana and Other Missing Fathers (Leonin), 116
Havana/Miami (García Ferraz), 121–123
Havel, Václav, 79, 155
Hegel, Georg Friedrich, 24, 30–31, 77
conception of history, 31, 36–37, 53–54, 56
Heidegger, Martin, 13
Heroes, Martyrs, and Political Messiahs in Revolutionary Cuba, 1946–1958 (Guerra), 35

Hidalgo, Miguel, 60
history, 24–25, 30–33, 50–51, 130–132
1990s as end of history, 78
Arendt's conception of, 25, 31, 33, 37–38, 54, 62–63, 84, 132
Castro's conception of, 30–32, 40
communism and, 17, 36–38, 54, 63, 155
Cuban exile community and, 119
Cuban Revolution of 1959 and, 34, 50–51
democracy and, 131
exiled artists and, 118–123, 130–132
in García Ferraz's art, 120
Hegel's conception of, 31, 36–37, 53–54, 56
inclusivity and, 110, 130, 132
La Edad de Oro and, 60–61
as legitimizing force, 33–36
Marxist conception of, 24, 37
modernity and, 37–38, 54
nation-building and, 26, 33–34
Operation Pedro Pan and, 50
past as history, 26
poetic present and, 83–84
pre-revolutionary struggles and, 34–35
progress and, 54–55
repression and, 131
totalitarianism and, 33, 54, 130
trial of Castro and, 28–31
as unitary process, 33–34
History Will Absolve Me (Castro, 1954), 20, 23, 27, 30, 33, 39–40, 66
Constitution of 1940 and, 29–30
understanding of past in, 30–31
homogeneous time, 9
homosexuality, 3–4, 137
Horkheimer, Max, 135
Hortensia and the Museum of Dreams (Cruz), 112–113
Hoy, David Couzens, 11–12
human rights, xv, 18, 91
Cuban human rights organizations, 4–5
International Bill of Human Rights, 143–144

idle present, 90, 108, 155
indigenous population of Cuba, 56–57, 60–61, 63–64
Iniciales sobre la Tierra (Initials over the Earth) (Díaz), 36

198 · Index

Instituto de Artivismo Hannah Arendt (Hannah Arendt Artivism Institute), xx, 141
Instituto de Historia (History Institute), 36
International Bill of Human Rights, 143–144

James, William, 81
Jameson, Fredric, 76
jineterismo (jockeying), 89
Johnson, Samuel, 104
journalists, 143
  repression against, 5–6
July 26th Movement, 2–3, 9, 27, 64, 141

Kant, Immanuel, 13
Klee, Paul, 9–10
Korda, Alberto, 118

Lam, Wilfredo, 123
Latin American unity, 57–58
Lauten, Flora, 43
Leal, Francisco, 89
Leal, Orlando Jiménez, 39–40
Lechner, Norbert, 79
Lefebvre, Henri, 137
Leonin, Mia, 116
Levinas, Emmanuel, 151
Levitas, Ruth, 135
Leyva Novo, Reynier, 118–119, 132
Lezama Lima, José, 9, 94–96, 107
liberalism, 77, 152–153
  neoliberalism, 87
Lone Star conspiracy, 150
López, Iraida, 112
López, Melinda, 113
López Berenstein, Julio, 128–129
Lula, Luiz Inácio, 70
Lunes de Revolución, 40
Luque Escalona, Roberto, 5

Maceo, Antonio, 28, 34, 85, 150
  Antonio Maceo Brigade (Brigada Antonio Maceo), xiii, 42–43, 111–112, 121
Machado, Gerardo, xi, 27, 34, 115
Man and Socialism (Guevara), 21, 66–70, 74
Mantilla, María, 62
Marcuse, Herbert, 136
Mariátegui, José Carlos, 63–64

Mariel Boatlift, 80, 113
market-Leninism, 88, 154
Martí, José, xii, 7–8, 21, 27–29, 57–60, 78, 85, 98, 149–150, 156
  Castro trial and, 28–29
  children and, 58–62
  Cuban independence movement and, 150
  La Edad de Oro and, 60–62
  future orientation and, 8
  Latin American unity and, 57–58
  uprising of 1953 and, 27
Martínez, Mel, 44
Martínez-Cañas, María, 21, 119–120, 123–130, 132
Marx, Karl, 15–17
  conception of history, 24, 37
  utopianism and, 63, 75
Marxism, 54, 152–153. *See also* communism; socialism
  Cuban government and, 37, 72, 92
  future temporality and, 54
masses, 68–69, 74, 79
  consciousness of, 69–70
  race and, 151
  temporality and, 149
Matos, Huber, 3, 36
Mead, George, 82, 149
Medina, Pablo, 113
Mella, Julio Antonio, 37
Memorias de la posguerra (Bruguera), 139
Memories of Underdevelopment (Alea, 1968), 42
Mendieta, Ana, 44, 138–139
Mendieta, Raquel, 87–88, 92, 138
Mexican revolution, 63
Miller, Margaret, 124
Mills, Charles, 152–153
Mistral, Gabriela, 64
modernity, 15, 53–54, 78
  children and, 58–59
  end of, 78
  exceptionalism and, 38
  future temporalities and, 52–54, 75–76
  history and, 37–38, 54
  nationalism and, 75
  nation-building and, 57
  poetic present and, 83, 148

postmodernity, 19
temporality and, xviii, 14–19, 25–26, 55, 75, 94, 98–99, 109–110, 148, 153
totalitarianism and, 14, 18, 153
utopianism and, xvii, 15, 17–19, 55–56, 75
Moncada barracks, 64, 66, 141
Montesquieu, 39
Moore, Carlos, 3
Mouffe, Chantal, 151
Movimiento Cristiano de Liberación (Christian Liberation Movement), 6
Movimiento San Isidro (San Isidro Movement, MSI), 143
Mumford, Lewis, 55
Muñiz, Carlos, 42–43
Muñoz, José Esteban, 136–137
My Story: Family, Cuba & Living the American Dream (de Lasa), 114

La nada cotidiana (Valdés), 91–92
Nasca, Dania Rosa, 114, 117
nationalism, 26, 35
  of Castro, 37
  of Constitution of 1940, 2, 29, 35, 64
  Cuban Revolution and, 40–41, 64, 92
  modernity and, 75
  socialism and, 75
nation-building, 16, 20, 25, 53, 57, 153
  future temporality and, 57
  history and, 26, 33
  modernity and, 57
  utopianism and, 18, 54, 56
  youth and, 58, 65
Nazism, 15–16, 21, 75
neoliberalism, 87
Nettie Lee Benson Latin American Collection, 124
"New Man," creation of, xviii, 18, 21, 66, 69–70, 72, 74–76
  totalitarianism and, 17
Newton, Isaac, 12
Next Year in Cuba: A Cubano's Coming-of-Age in America (Pérez Firmat), 113
Nietzsche, Friedrich, 54, 82
No, no memoria (García Marruz), 94
Nodarse, Maria, 117
nostalgia, 7, 26

Cuban Revolution and, 86
  exile communities and, 51, 53, 111, 112, 119, 121
  future temporality and, 65
  present temporality and, 19
  socialism and, 79, 83
  tourism and, 7, 53
Nuestra America (Martí, 1891), 57–58, 60
"Nuestro Che" (Sarol), 31–32

Obama, Barack, xiv–xv, 6
Obejas, Achy, 80
Ochoa, Arnaldo T., xiii
Ojito, Mirta, 113
Olivera, Jorge, 6
Olivia, Pedro Pablo, 53
Omega 7, 42
Opción Cero, 86
Operación Carlota, xiii–xiv
Operation Pedro Pan, xvii, 21, 24, 43–51
  author's experience of, xii, xvii
  education of youth and, 74
  Elián González and, 46–47
  exile narratives and, 112–113
  mythmaking and, 50, 131
  U.S. government involvement in, 44–45
Operation Peter Pan: Flying Back to Cuba (Bravo), 113
Operation Pierre Pan, 47
Orígenes (literary group), 21, 94–97
orphan train project, 16

Padrón, Claudia, 133, 144–145
Padura, Leonardo, 23, 118
País, Frank, 2, 34
paladares, 144
Pan-Americanism, 57–58
Partido Auténtico (Authentic Party), 35
Partido Ortodoxo (Orthodox Party), 2, 35
Partido Socialista Popular (Popular Socialist Party, PSP), 3–4, 35, 37. *See also* Communist Party of Cuba
  cultural projects of, 95–96
  in post-Soviet Cuba, 88
  as "vanguard," 69
Party Congress of 2021, xv–xvi
past temporality. *See* history

200 · Index

"Patria y vida" (song), xvi, 142–143
Patterson, Enrique, 4–5, 147, 151
Payá, Oswaldo, 6
Payá, Rosa María, 6
Paz, Octavio, 20–21, 78, 81, 109, 155
    poetic present and, 21, 83–85, 93–94
pedagogical projects, 64, 74, 98
Peláez, Amelia, 124
People's Movement for the Liberation of
    Angola, 3
Pérez, Jorge, 119
Pérez, Louis A., Jr., 6–7, 26, 56–57
Pérez Firmat, Gustavo, 113
El periodo especial en tiempos de paz (Special
    Period in Times of Peace), 87–88, 92
    present temporality and, 108
Perón, Evita, 68
Perón, Juan Domingo, 64, 68
Peronismo, 64
Peru, 63–64
Phillips, Anne, 150–151
Piano y tambor (Baquero), 96
PM (documentary, Leal and Infante), 39–40
poetic present, 21, 83–85, 87, 93–94, 109, 148–
    149, 155–156
    democracy and, 148, 156
    temporality and, 149, 153
political culture, xx, 11, 35, 155
    democracy and, 11, 21–22, 87 109, 155
    temporality and, 11, 85, 87, 109, 156
political repression
    cultural repression, 39–40, 85, 143–144, 151
    following Cuban Revolution, xii, 36, 38–40,
        67–68, 145–146
    Obama's Cuba visit and, xv
    in post-Soviet Cuba, 91
Popper, Karl, 54, 76
postmodernity, 19, 152
present temporality, 108–109, 149
    authoritarianism and, 15, 90, 107–108
    change and, 156
    children and, xviii, 98
    in Cuba, 85–87
    definitions of, 81–83
    Diego and, 148
    Eliseo Diego and, 97–98, 108–109, 110
    idle present and, 90, 108, 155
    poetic present, 21, 83–85, 87, 93–94, 109

in post-Soviet Cuba, 87–90
    relationship with future, 134
    relationship with past, 154
    during Special Period, 108
The Prince of los Cocuyos: A Miami Childhood
    (Blanco), 113
Principito (Lauten), 43
Prío Socarrás, Carlos, 27–28
progress, 54–55
Proust, Marcel, 82, 84–85
Proyecto Varela, 6
psychology, xix–xx

queerness, 137
Quién sabe (Diego), 102–103
Quijano, Carlos, 66

*Radical Convention: Cuban American Art
    from the 1980s*, 119
rap music, xvi, 142–143
Rawls, John, 18, 136
la raza cosmica (the cosmic race), 64
Rebus + Diversions (Martínez-Cañas), 128–
    129
Reed, John, 63
Remembrances of Things Past (Proust), 84–85
remittances, xiv
Renan, Ernest, 56
Revolutionary Council, 3
Ricoeur, Paul, 111
Right of Rebellion against Tyranny, 28, 39
Rodríguez, Pepe, 94
Rojas, Fernando, xvi
Rojas, Rafael, 5, 90–91
Roosevelt, Teddy, 33
Rostow, W. W., 17
Rough Riders, 33
Rousseau, Jean-Jacques, 59
Russian Revolution, 63

sameness/difference, 151–152
Sánchez, Elizardo, 4
Sánchez, Osvaldo, 5
Sanders, Bernie, 79
Santamaría, Abel, 27
Santiero, Luis, 115–116
Santiso, Javier, 80–81
Sarmiento, Domingo, 59

Sarol, José A., 31–32
Sartre, Jean-Paul, 94
Savimbi, Jonas, 3
sex work, xiv, 89
slavery, 145
 Cuban independence movement and, 150
 legacy of, 2, 150–151
socialism, 8, 70, 153–154. *See also* communism; Marxism; Partido Socialista Popular
 collapse of, 77, 79, 153–154
 in Cuba, 3, 7–8, 66–69, 72, 79–80, 85–86,
  89–90, 142, 153–154
 democracy and, 147
 nationalism and, 75
 New Man ideology and, 70, 76
 nostalgia and, 79, 83
 in post-Soviet Cuba, 87–90
 Stalin and, 52
 temporality and, 142
 totalitarianism and, 153–154
 utopianism and, 21, 75–77, 79
social protests of 2021, xvi, 143–147
social re-engineering, 21
Solis, Denis, 143
Sonia Flew (López), 113
Son music, 95
Soviet Union, 67
 collapse of, 78, 86–87, 155
 PSP and, 4
 relationship with Cuba, 85–87, 155
 Russian Revolution, 63
 Stalinism, 15, 75
Spanish Empire, 9, 57
Spanish war of 1898, 33
*Spared Angola: Memories from a Cuban-
 American Childhood* (Suárez), 114
Special Period. *See El periodo especial en
 tiempos de paz*
Stalinism, 15, 75
state building. *See* nation-building
St. Augustine, 13, 81
Stevens, Wallace, 94
structural democracy, 10
Suárez, Virgil, 114

La tabla de salvación (Lifeline, 1994) (Bruguera), 139
Taitlin's Whisper (Bruguera), 140

temporalities, xix, 6–10. *See also* future
 temporalities; history; present temporality
 communism and, 14
 COVID-19 pandemic and, 155
 Cuban democracy and, 18–19
 Cuban Revolution and, 142, 153
 Cuban Revolution of 1959 and, 37
 Diego and, 98–104
 in Diego's poetry, xxi, 98–104, 107, 108–
  109, 110
 future (*see* future temporalities)
 modernity and, xviii, 14–19, 25–26, 55,
  75, 94, 98–99, 109–110, 148, 153
 multidimensionality of time, 149
 past (*see* history)
 poetic present (*see* poetic present)
 political culture and, 11, 85, 87, 109, 156
 politics and, 11, 14–20
 postmodernity and, 19
 present (*see* present temporality)
 rap music and, 142–143
 as social constructions, 12
 ways of thinking about time, 11–13
Testamento (Diego), xxi
*The Lost Apple: Operation Pedro Pan,
 Children in the U.S., and the Promise of
 a Better Future*, 44–45
Time of Photography (Diego), 103–104
Tocqueville, Alexis de, 81
Toirac, José Angel, 118, 132
Torres Domínguez, Alberto, xii
totalitarianism, 14–17. *See also* authoritarianism
 artistic protests against, 140–141
 history and, 33, 37–38, 54, 130–131
 modernity and, 14, 18
 political disengagement and, 91
tourism, 86
 COVID-19 pandemic and, xv
 nostalgia and, 7, 53
 present temporality and, 89
 sex work and, 89
 temporality and, 7, 9
Tracings (Martínez-Cañas), 125–126
*Trained to Kill: The Inside Story of CIA
 Plots Against Castro, Kennedy, and Che*
 (Veciana), 114–115

202 · Index

Traveling Heavy: A Memoir in between Journeys (Behar), 117
Trouillot, Michel-Rolph, 14, 24
Tu te inclinas despacio a la tristeza (You bow slowly to sadness) (Diego), 100–101
26th of July Movement, 2, 5, 23, 40
    revolutionary history and, 36

Unidades Militares de Ayuda de Producción (Military Units to Aid Labor, UMAP), 4
union movement, 4
United States of America (USA)
    Cuban emigration to (*see* Mariel Boatlift; Operation Pedro Pan)
    Cuban independence movement and, 150
    experiences of Cuban exiles in, xii, 110–111, 115–117, 120
    independence movement of, 57, 78–79
    Latino population of, 58
    presidential visits to Cuba, xiv–xv, 6
    relocation of Cubans within, 116
    USA-Cuba relations, 85, 114–115, 121
unity, 150–151
Uprising of 1953, 26–30
Urrutia, Manuel, 3, 67
utopianism, 7–8, 17–18, 53, 55–56, 62–64, 75–77
    authoritarianism and, 75–76, 79, 84
    collapse of socialism and, 79–80
    demise of, 78
    failure of in Cuba, 85–87
    future temporalities and, 52, 63, 135–136
    Left criticism of, 76–77
    Marxism and, 63
    modernity and, xvii, 15, 17–19, 55–56, 75
    in *La nada cotidiana*, 91
    pessimistic realism and, 137

poetic present and, 83–84
possibility and, 135–136
socialism and, 21, 75–77, 79
Utopito, 53

Valdés, Concepción, 156
Valdés, Zoé, 91–92
Valdivia, Carmen, 48–50
Varela, Félix, 6
Vasconcelos, José, 64
Veciana, Antonio, 114–115
Velázquez Medina, Fernando, 5
Velvet Revolution, 5
Venezuela, xv, 79
Vestigios (Martínez-Cañas), 125–127
Viega, Marisella, 116
Vigil, Aurelio, xi, 33
Vigil Delgado, María Isabel, xi–xii
Vitier, Cintio, 46, 97, 107

Waiting for Snow in Havana: Confessions of a Cuban Boy (Erie), 112
Walsh, Monsignor Bryan, 45–47, 50
Weber, Max, 134
We Carry Our Homes with Us: A Cuban American Memoir (Viega), 116
Weight of History (Leyva Novo), 119
Wenski, Thomas, 48
Wheeler, Monroe, 124
Whitfield, Esther, 80, 88

Yeats, William Butler, 100

Zambrano, María, 97
Los zapaticos de rosa (Martí), 61–62
Žižek, Slavoj, 150

María de los Ángeles Torres is distinguished university professor of Latin American and Latino Studies at the University of Illinois in Chicago. She has written extensively on Latinos, Cuba, and Cuban exiles' politics and identity, immigration, and culture, and has authored *In the Land of Mirrors: Cuban Exile Politics in the United States* (1999) and *The Lost Apple: Operation Pedro Pan, Cuban Children in the U.S., and the Promise of a Better Future* (2003). She has coauthored *Citizens in the Present: Youth Civic Engagement in the Americas* (2013); edited *By Heart/De Memoria: Cuban Women's Journeys In and Out of Exile* (2003); and coedited *Borderless Borders: Latinos, Latin Americans, and the Paradoxes of Interdependence* (1998) and *Global Cities and Immigrants: A Comparative Study of Chicago and Madrid* (2015).